DIGITAL INNOVATIONS FOR MASS COMMUNICATIONS

In every field of mass communications—advertising, entertainment studies, journalism, public relations, radio-television-film, tourism, and visual reporting—professionals understand the importance of storytelling. Regardless of whether the finished product is a commercial, an in-depth investigative piece, a public service campaign, an independent documentary, a travelogue, or a collection of photographs, effective storytelling requires a combination of creativity, empathy, and expertise. Through the innovative technologies and techniques described in this textbook, students will learn how to turn passive readers and viewers into engaged and regular users.

The sixteen chapters each include a brief introduction, assignments, simple-to-follow step-by-step exercises, and sources for additional information in which users will learn to produce apps, informational graphics, quick response codes, quizzes, simulations, smartphone and tablet icons, social media campaigns, three-dimensional pictures, and video. Students will work with the following programs: Blogger, Dreamweaver, Excel, Facebook, GeoCommons, Google Maps, Illustrator, Imgur, iMovie, Infogram, iShowU, JavaScript, JustGive, Kaywa, Kickstarter, LinkedIn, Onvert, Photoshop, Pixel Resort, QuickTime, Reddit, Second Life, SurveyMonkey, TheAppBuilder, Twitter, Vizualize, Wikipedia, Word, WordPress, and YouTube.

When digital innovations are added to traditional print and screen presentations, a media user is not only allowed to interact with the information but can also physically engage with the story displayed. Giving students the tools they need to transform their storytelling in this manner is the ultimate goal of this textbook.

Paul Martin Lester is Professor of Communications at California State University, Fullerton. He is the author of *Visual Communication: Images with Messages*, *Visual Journalism: A Guide for New Media Professionals*, *The Ethics of Photojournalism*, and, with xtine burre *Visual Communication on the Web*.

DIGITAL INNOVATIONS FOR MASS COMMUNICATIONS

COMMUNICATIONS

ENGAGING THE USER

Paul Martin Lester

Routledge
Taylor & Francis Group

NEW YORK AND LONDON

First published 2014
by Routledge
711 Third Avenue, New York, NY 10017

and by Routledge
2 Park Square, Milton Park, Abingdon, Oxon OX14 4RN

Routledge is an imprint of the Taylor & Francis Group, an informa business

Library of Congress Cataloging-in-Publication Data

Digital innovations for mass communications : engaging the user /
   by Paul Martin Lester.
      pages cm
  1. Mass media—Technological innovations.   2. Communication—
Technological innovations.   3. Mass media and technology.
I. Lester, Paul Martin.
   P96.T42D53 2013
   302.23'1—dc23
   2013022060

ISBN: 978-0-415-66293-2 (hbk)
ISBN: 978-0-415-66294-9 (pbk)
ISBN: 978-0-203-07181-6 (ebk)

Typeset in Garamond
by Apex CoVantage, LLC

SFI® Certified Sourcing
www.sfiprogram.org
SFI-00453

Printed and bound in the United States of America
by Edwards Brothers Malloy

for xtine, allison, parker, and martin

CONTENTS

AUTHOR BIOGRAPHY

Paul Martin Lester is a tenured, full professor of communications at California State University, Fullerton.

After an undergraduate degree in journalism from the University of Texas at Austin and employment as a photojournalist for *The Times-Picayune* in New Orleans, Lester received a Master's from the University of Minnesota and a PhD from Indiana University in mass communications.

He is the author or editor of several books, which include: *Visual Communication Images with Messages Sixth Edition (2014)*, *Visual Communication on the Web Principles & Practices* with xtine burrough (2013), *Images that Injure Pictorial Stereotypes in the Media Third Edition* with Susan Ross (2011), *On Floods and Photo Ops: How Herbert Hoover and George W. Bush Exploited Catastrophes* (2010), *Visual Journalism: A Guide for New Media Professionals* with Chris Harris (2002), *Desktop Computing Workbook: A Guide for Using 15 Programs in Macintosh and Windows Formats* (1996), and *Photojournalism: An Ethical Approach* (1991).

In 2011, Lester was named editor of the AEJMC publication *Journalism & Communication Monographs* published by Sage. From 2006 until 2011, he was editor of the *Visual Communication Quarterly,* a publication of the Visual Communication Division of the AEJMC published by Taylor & Francis.

For several years, he cowrote the monthly column "Ethics Matters" for *News Photographer* magazine for the National Press Photographers Association (NPPA).

Lester has given speeches, presentations, and workshops throughout the United States and in Australia, Canada, Finland, the Netherlands, Northern Ireland, Spain, Sweden, and Turkey.

His research interests include mass media ethics, new communications technologies, and visual communications.

Lester lives in Southern California with his wife xtine, their two sons Parker and Martin, their dog Nietzsche, and is occasionally visited by his daughter Allison.

PREFACE

Digital Innovations for Mass Communications

"You can't hide. Get ready to run!"

As one of the taglines used to market the 2002 summer blockbuster hit *Minority Report* directed by Steven Spielberg, with a cast that was headed by the action star Thomas Cruise Mapother IV, it was meant to refer to the exceedingly advanced investigative resources available in the year 2054 (Figure 0.1). It could also stand for a vision of interactive, in-your-face augmented advertising that might be thought of as equally intrusive.

As Cruise's character tries to elude police officials by walking briskly through a shopping mall, he cannot hide from iris recognition scanners located near each digital wall poster for products such as Lexus and American Express. As he walks past an ad, a flash registers a scan of his eyes. Suddenly, a friendly man's voice calls out, "John Anderton. You can use a Guinness right about now."

Not exactly.

If you saw the movie, the last thing Anderton wants or needs at that point in the film is to stop off at a pub and have a pint of the slow-pouring, dark Irish brew.

If you think such technology used for advertisements that identify you by your eyes and recommends products based on your known preferences is four decades away, you may be surprised to learn that from 2008, digital storefronts and mall displays in Japan have used facial recognition technology to identify the ages and genders of passersby. Today, along the Grand Canal and Palazzo shops within the Venetian resort in Las Vegas, entertainment ideas are projected at you through similar technology. Such diverse companies as Adidas and Kraft Foods have used this technology at other venues.

Some Chicago bar owners have signed up with a company named SceneTap (Figure 0.2). Cameras installed with face recognition software determine the age and gender of those in their clubs. With the SceneTap app, users can discover that Timothy O'Toole's pub on a Tuesday evening is less than 33 percent full, with 19 patrons. Thirty-eight percent of them are women and their average age is 26.

Why would bar owners pay for such an elaborate set-up of cameras and software? Simple. Imagine you are out with your friends and want to find a bar that is packed with others your own age. As noted on the SceneTap app, the technology allows you to "view how full a venue is, the male to female ratio, and the average age of the patrons, all in REAL TIME! [sic]" You no longer have to guess where a hot spot is—your smartphone tells you where to go.

As is the usual case, creative advertising uses were some of the first examples to exploit the attention-grabbing graphics inherent within digital innovations. In 2006, magazines as diverse as *Popular Science* and *Esquire* wowed readers with 3D images that jumped out of their covers after users pointed their passive 2D print versions that included a QR code

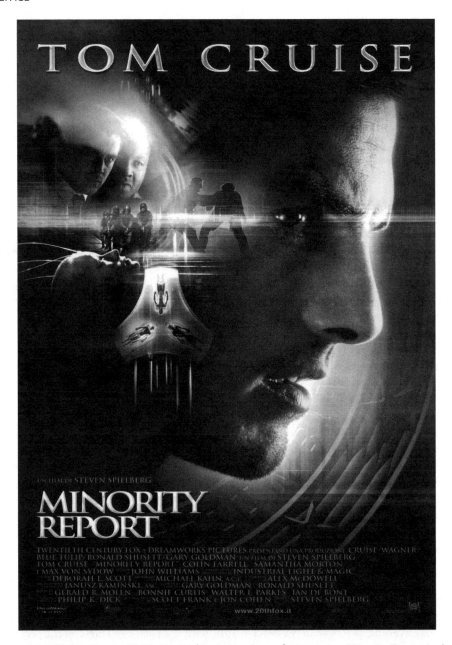

Figure 0.1 The last line in Philip K. Dick's short science fiction story, *Minority Report,* includes "Better keep your eyes open." A poster for the hit movie directed by Steven Spielberg emphasizes the sense of sight through Tom Cruise's pose. As computer scientist Jaron Lanier was one of the advisors for the motion picture, retina scanner technology was employed in scenes that featured its marketing capabilities. *Courtesy of Mary Evans/ DreamWorks SKG/Amblin/20TH Century Fox/Ronald Grant/Everett Collection*

toward their computer's built-in cameras. For the effect, only a free software download was required. For *Esquire,* the always ironically enthusiastic actor Robert Downey, Jr. suddenly appeared to alert readers of 3D content available on other pages. He also plugged his Sherlock Holmes motion picture.

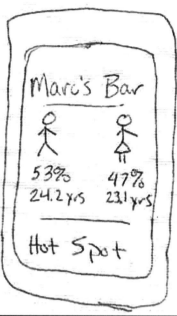

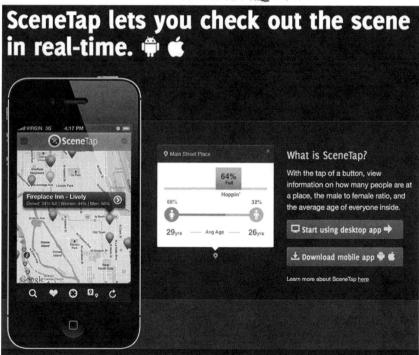

Figure 0.2 From a quick sketch on a napkin, Chicago friends Cole Harper and Marc Doering outlined the features that eventually became their successful facial recognition bar app and website, SceneTap. *Courtesy of SceneTap*

The advertising and public relations professions have embraced digital innovations because those skilled in the art of persuasion know that tools can establish a personalized connection between the consumer and the product or service. Todd Wasserman, for example, of the online publication *Mashable Tech* notes the top innovations for advertising—personalized response videos, Quick Response (QR) codes, smartphone and tablet ads, and specialized Twitter tweets—while Leyl Master Black, managing director of the PR firm Sparkpr, writes that technical innovations for the profession include the use of social media to share news; corporate blogging; the need for longer, in-depth stories; the deployment of multimedia for a variety of digital displays; and an increased reliance on data, illustrations, and apps.

One of the most talked-about digital innovations is augmented reality (AR). It has its roots in the computer-mediated technology known as virtual reality (VR), its once exalted cousin. VR was coined by the dreadlocked futurist Jaron Lanier and used to describe the technology that allowed users to wear everything from goggles to full body suits in order to interact with computer video displays. Practical for medical and military uses, the consumer market was slow to develop. VR failed for the average person because the technology needed to make it happen was too expensive for home use, few developers created programs with compelling content, and the fickleness of savvy consumers who wanted real-time virtual experiences. An amusement park ride that combined elements of a VR movie with a roller coaster was fun for a few minutes, but couldn't compete with a viewer's imagination after she had seen Paul Reiser's character on *Mad About You* interact fully with a digitized Christie Brinkley, members of *Star Trek: The Next Generation* time travel with the aid of a holodeck, and a yard care worker have sex with a partner, both beautifully rendered as flying insects in *The Lawnmower Man*. The virtual never matched the reality.

Augmented reality, however, never claimed to be anything more than a way for users to become more engaged with the actual world. It has developed into a simple, practical, and largely commercial form of interactive multimedia in which users control portable devices to enhance the connection between the worlds of nondigital and digital. AR amplifies experience through the traditional tools of mass communications—audio, images, words, and design—by engaging a user with the content. But whether store locations automatically appear on the screen of a smartphone pointed at an unfamiliar urban environment or a user actively decides to snap a picture of a QR code on a billboard in order to receive a discount offer or to see content not appropriate for public viewing, companies around the world have largely concentrated their efforts on commercial and entertainment uses, rather than for instructional or informational purposes.

Although a bit late to the game, the journalism profession has experimented with innovations with a proverbial toe in the digital pool. For example, to help understand how an American Civil War submarine, the H. L. Hunley operated, the *Florida Sun-Sentinel* newspaper produced a simulation in which users could drive the vessel and try not to drown in the process as unfortunately happened to the inventor of the actual ship. The newspaper's multimedia gallery named "The Edge" is a showcase for games, informational graphic videos, interactive infographics, illustrated news stories, and other examples that help readers understand complex stories and have some fun as well.

Many journalists have discovered how new technologies can enhance storytelling. With circulation figures at historic lows, the death of many renowned publications, and many predicting the end of printed newspapers, the traditional methods of presenting stories in print do not produce new customers that care much about what they read or see. In the usual way words and pictures are presented, a story may be noticed, but the page is turned before the hard work of the various journalists involved—reporters, researchers, editors, designers, and so on—can make much of an impact. A push to online publication with interactive technologies and links to social networks helped somewhat, but did not produce additional readers in large numbers. With digital innovations added to traditional print and screen presentations, a media user is not only allowed to interact with the information but can also physically engage with the story displayed. Such is the ultimate goal of mass communications:

> Through digitally innovative, value added, interactive
> techniques and technologies, passive readers and
> viewers become engaged and regular users.

Features of the Book

Digital Innovations for Mass Communications: Engaging the User stresses the need to teach, learn, experiment, and create ideas and techniques for all students within areas of a mass communications program—advertising, entertainment, journalism, public relations, RTVF (radio, television, and film), and visual reporting. After a brief introduction, each chapter has a section called "Challenges, Critiques, and Amusements" in which the assignments might invoke discussions, creative presentations and writings, and formal papers. Then, exercises in the form of step-by-step guides put the concepts into practice. Finally, the sources used for each chapter are listed, and readers are encouraged to follow up on the links provided to obtain more specific information.

Section One: Essential Knowledge comprises four chapters:

- **Chapter 1: A Historical Perspective** details the rise of communications technologies from cave paintings to smartphones.
- **Chapter 2: Digital Media Consumer Types** explains why different people are attracted or repelled by innovative technologies within a social constructivism theoretical context.
- **Chapter 3: Ethical and Legal Considerations** gives the current cautions in creating, distributing, and using digital innovations within value-driven and regulatory constraints.
- **Chapter 4: Visual Aesthetics** teaches typographical and design choices that enhance a message rather than distract from it.

Section Two: User-Generated Content has three chapters:

- **Chapter 5: Social Networks** shows how various consumer-driven websites contribute to message proliferation and meaning.
- **Chapter 6: Virtual Communities** explains the popularity of several avatar-based online programs in which users engage in simulated social settings.
- **Chapter 7: Virtual Reality** details why the creation of three-dimensional, manipulative space and objects has been important for interactive storytelling.

Section Three: Database-Generated Content contains three chapters:

- **Chapter 8: Suggestive Innovations** advocates the need to make content based on a user's past and presumed preferences.
- **Chapter 9: Personalization** explains how stories can be more effective if they are compared with a viewer's life and experiences.
- **Chapter 10: Mapping** details databases that contextualize complex stories.

Section Four: Software-Driven Content has five chapters:

- **Chapter 11: Games** provides a background in the production of programs that are fun to play and help users remember story details.
- **Chapter 12: Simulations** gives details on the production of complex role-playing scenarios.
- **Chapter 13: QR Codes** details the ubiquitous graphic tags and the complex and creative ways they can be used effectively.
- **Chapter 14: 3D Displays** shows how pop-out illustrations and videos can be added to a story to add interest and information.
- **Chapter 15: Apps** explains the most prolific use of augmented reality for smartphones and tablets and how they can be created to engage users.

Section Five: Immersive Experiences has one chapter:

- **Chapter 16: Transmedia Storytelling** details examples with a complex multimedia lesson that encourages the use of all of the programs and digital innovations discussed in the previous chapters.

Finally, **Conclusion: Tell Stories That Engage** reinforces the theme of this textbook—we are all made better by producing content that matters.

Sources

Black, Leyl Master. (2010). "5 Predictions for the Public Relations Industry in 2011." Accessed January 11, 2013. http://mashable.com/2010/12/23/predictions-pr-industry/.

Cawood, Stephen, and Mark Fiala. (2008). *Augmented Reality: A Practical Guide.* New York: Pragmatic Bookshelf.

Carnegie-Knight Initiative on the Future of Journalism Education. (2011). Boston: Harvard Kennedy School.

Dick, Philip K. (1987). *The Minority Report and Other Classic Stories.* New York: Citadel Press.

"Edge, The." *Florida Sun-Sentinel.* Accessed January 11, 2013. http://www.sun-sentinel.com/broadband/theedge/.

Lanier, Jaron. "Homepage." Accessed January 11, 2013. http://www.jaronlanier.com/.

Lawnmower Man, The. Internet Movie Database. Accessed January 11, 2013. http://www.imdb.com/title/tt0104692/.

Li, Shan, and David Sarno. (2011, August 24). "Facial Recognition In Digital Displays Tailor Ads To You." *Los Angeles Times.* Accessed January 11, 2013. http://printmediacentr.com/2011/08/facial-recognition-in-digital-displays-tailor-ads-to-you/.

Mad About You. Internet Movie Database. Accessed January 11, 2013. http://www.imdb.com/title/tt0638993/.

Mahoney, John. (July 2009). "The future of energy, machines that heal, firefighting tech and the world's first augmented reality magazine cover." *Popular Science.* Accessed January 11, 2013. http://www.popsci.com/scitech/article/2009–06/july-2009-issue.

Minority Report. Internet Movie Database. Accessed January 11, 2013. http://www.imdb.com/title/tt0181689/minority.

"*Minority Report* Mall Scene." YouTube. Accessed January 11, 2013. http://www.youtube.com/watch?v =oBaiKsYUdvg mall scene.

Nieman Reports. "Digital Landscape What's Next for News?" Accessed January 11, 2013. http://www.nieman.harvard.edu/Microsites/NiemanReportsTheDigitalLandscape/AugmentedReality.aspx.

OWNI. (2011). "Manifesto for 'Augmented Journalism, A.'" Accessed January 11, 2013. http://owni.eu/2011/05/22/manifesto-for-augmented-journalism/.

Rowinski, Dan. (June 10, 2011). "Coming to a Bar Near You: Facial Recognition & Real-Time Data." *The New York Times*. Accessed January 17, 2013. http://www.nytimes.com/external/read writeweb/2011/06/10/10readwriteweb-coming-to-a-bar-near-you-facial-recognition-50989 .html.

SceneTap. "Homepage." Accessed January 11, 2013. http://www.scenetap.com/r/Chicago.

"Star Trek Holodeck." Accessed January 11, 2013. http://en.memory-alpha.org/wiki/Holodeck.

Wasserman, Todd. (2010). "Top 10 Digital Advertising Innovations of 2010." Accessed January 11, 2013. http://mashable.com/2010/12/23/tech-advertising-innovations/.

"Welcome to the Esquire Augmented Reality Issue." *Esquire*. Accessed January 11, 2013. http://www.esquire.com/the-side/augmented-reality.

Section I

ESSENTIAL KNOWLEDGE

The four chapters in this section are designed to provide a fundamental understanding of digital innovations related to mass media productions.

A Historical Perspective

Storytelling is the essential role of human interactions. Over time, the tales told have been enhanced through various methods to help illustrate and explain. Cave drawings of animals with colored stone and dyes, songs and dances with poems, descriptive writing with news accounts, illustrations, and photographs with printed stories, voice and music with radio, moving pictures with television, interactive formats with informational graphics, hand gesture controllers for virtual reality devices, and smartphone interfaces with locator apps all demonstrate the steady progression of ways to engage others through various media.

Digital Media Consumer Types

Social constructivism helps explain that in order for someone to learn from a media presentation, a person must engage with the content within a context that she can apply to her view of the world. For those in which this activity is not familiar, encouragement is necessary and can be provided through interactive formats; otherwise, the stories communicated are not remembered. Broadly speaking, there are four types of consumers: the disenfranchised, the randomizers, the crowd surfers, and the engagers. A goal for content producers is to make all users part of the engager class so that they may experience, as philosopher Albert Borgmann notes, the "good life."

Ethical and Legal Considerations

Although what is considered ethical and legal has yet to be fully decided with the relatively new digital applications in use for mass communications, one credo remains true—ethics will always trump the law. For example, facial recognition software connected with cameras discretely placed within a bar that records the number of patrons, their gender, and approximate ages seems marginally ethical and legal. Privacy is probably the most important issue when a company not only knows a user's interests and buying habits, but also where she relaxes. However, there are many other ethical and legal issues you should be aware of in order to avoid questions about your behavior and potential lawsuits.

Visual Aesthetics

The four visual cues that the human brain most notices are color, form, depth, and movement. Having knowledge of how these cues interact with each other to attract attention in print and screen designs as well as a basic understanding of typography and graphic design are vital components in the creation of pleasing and professional digital inventions for mass communications.

1 A HISTORICAL PERSPECTIVE

News of Venice in the Year 1609

May 5: Earthquake in Rhodes, Greece. Half the city is destroyed. The waves have killed ten thousand people. **The sea took the color of blood.**

September 4: Our government has honored Mr. Galileo of Florence, professor of mathematics at Padua because he invented by his diligent study a telescope, with which one can see a place at a distance of thirty miles **as if it were in the neighborhood,** an art he offered the public.

September 11: On August 13 a great fire ravaged Constantinople. Three mosques were engulfed in flames. There was great damage. **The public cries and laments.**

If you were lucky enough to be born in the sleepy German (now French) village of Muhlbach-sur-Munster toward the end of the 16th century, you had two main choices: Make cheese or move.

At the time it was honorable and understandable to do either. After all, the soft Muenster cheese that made the region famous had been first produced within monasteries 200 years earlier. The craft was later adopted by farmers who opened their homes to paying travelers and offered a freshly cut cheese plate usually enjoyed with local beers and wines.

However, for many, the pungent aroma of cheese couldn't compete with the tart odors emitted from a vibrant urban environment. So whether during the 16th or 21st centuries, it's about a two-day's walk from the small, quiet village of Munster to Strasbourg, one of the most cosmopolitan cities in Europe. Ever since Johannes Gutenberg worked on his bibles in the capital around 1456, it has been known as the birthplace of printing.

In his twenties, Johann Carolus made the trek along the Fecht River in the Munster Valley, but probably didn't tarry too long along the route from his hometown to sample the many cheeses and Vosgien wines. As with any young person, he was anxious to leave behind his small-town roots for the opportunities and experiences that a large city offered.

From all accounts, the decision to move was a good one for Carolus.

At the age of 30, he became known to history after he successfully convinced the city elders of Strasbourg in 1605 to produce a weekly news account of local and regional events. His *Relation aller Fürnemmen und Gedenckwürdigen Historien* (*Account of All Distinguished and Commendable News*) is considered by the World Association of Newspapers to be the first printed newspaper with regularly scheduled issues in the world (Figure 1.1). As the beginning quotations for this chapter indicate, his hired writers with news tidbits from Lyon, Cologne, Rome, Venice, and Alsace often used a version of augmented reality in the form of highly descriptive writing.

Figure 1.1 With its visual references to the biblical tale of David and Goliath and three cherubs that symbolize emotion, intelligence, and bravery (does *The Wizard of Oz* ring a bell?), the cover page for a collection of issues for a 1609 edition of the Strasburg *Relation,* is a lively combination of words and images. *Courtesy of the University Library of Heidelberg, Germany*

Carolus's printed weekly reports—bound into a quarto-sized booklet, about 9.5 by 12 inches in size—and encouraged similar publications throughout Europe and the birth of the newspaper. Interestingly, Apple's iPad and similar tablets have been seen as another nail in the newspaper's coffin as users turn from print to screen media for their news and entertainment source (Figure 1.2). Ironically, the original iPad is just a little smaller than Carolus's product—7.5 by 9.5 inches.

If you agree that digital innovations for mass communications refer to enhancements of news and information that add interest and emotion to stories, examples from throughout history abound.

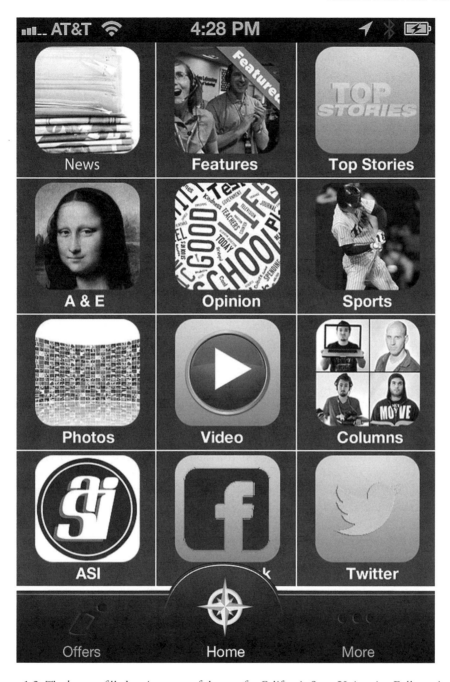

Figure 1.2 The button-filled main screen of the app for California State University, Fullerton's student newspaper, *The Daily Titan,* contains links to all the main sections of a print newspaper plus video, social networks, and special discount offers. *Courtesy of Paul Martin Lester*

As far back as 100,000 years ago, spoken languages probably developed as imitations of the sounds made by birds and other animals and then by humans spontaneously grunting and then controlling noises by their lips and tongues through repetitious rudimentary voice communications. Over time, shamans and other tribal leaders refined and reinforced their oral messages through the innovation of songs and dances.

Writing occurred to humans much later than speech, perhaps inspired by the random marks left by insects on tree stumps that were missing their barks. Eventually, we learned to scrape and paint drawings of animals on cave walls. In 1994, while exploring a cave on his family's land in southern France, Jean-Marie Chauvet discovered the oldest known cave with etchings and paintings. *Le Grotte Chauvet* contains 416 cave paintings of extraordinary detail and cultural significance dating from approximately 30,000 years ago. One of the drawings shows an otherwise accurate painting of a bison running, but it is clearly shown having additional legs. With so many other animals truthfully displayed, archeologists puzzled why this one was not anatomically correct. Speculation about the artist's intent ended after someone brought in a flaming torch to see the drawing as the cave dwellers themselves would have seen it. With the aid of a flickering fire's light, it could easily be seen that the extra legs gave the viewer the illusion that the animal was actually galloping across the cave—an early form of motion pictures and an important communications innovation was first discovered.

Writing evolved from pictographic displays that resembled the objects they were meant to represent to highly symbolic line drawings written on walls, clay, papyrus, and eventually paper. Although the earliest known book is the *Diamond Sutra,* a Chinese Buddhist work from about 868, the German Johannes Gutenberg was the first to develop a commercially successful printing press, although he never profited from his invention after a court's decision awarded his work to a creditor. Nevertheless, others, including the Venetian Aldus Manutius and the British William Caxton, were quite successful using Gutenberg's methods. From these earliest times, words and pictures were displayed on pages to tell stories through their combinations. Innovations eventually followed. With the inventions of lithography in 1796, photography in 1839, and the halftone printing process in 1873, illustrations and photographs could be reproduced within the pages of daily newspapers to attract customers with their large pictorial displays and act as advertisements for themselves against traditional and stuffy word-only typeset pages.

Although invented by the American Thomas Edison, two French entrepreneurs, Auguste and Louis Lumière debuted in 1895 the first public demonstration of motion pictures in a converted Paris café with 10 short documentary films that included *Sortie des Ursines Lumière* (*Workers Leaving the Lumière Factory*). Although talking pictures would take another 30 years, filmed newsreels of important and frivolous world events had their start in 1908 by another French company, Pathé Frères. Still and static pictures were magically transformed into moving and dynamic displays through the innovation of movies.

Five years after the Lumière introduction of motion pictures, radio was invented. This innovation converted words emoted by actors and anchors into emotional presentations with the addition of music, sound effects, and live broadcasts. Audio became as important as pictures to tell stories.

Although first proposed by the German Paul Nipkow in 1884, the American Philo Farnsworth invented the first practical television system in 1927 that combined all the best technological features of radio with moving pictures. The "Golden Years" of the 1950s found viewers at home hearing and watching programs previously available only in movie theaters or on stages. By the 2000s, television stations around the world had converted their analog, electronic system to high definition digital transmissions that offered the innovation of high quality sound and pictures.

The television medium's initial use of a cathode ray tube to provide pictures on the screen led to innovative computer displays in which users could see the work they were manipulating with their mouse devices. Computer video games soon followed, starting with MIT student Steve Russell's Spacewar! in 1962 and progressed to complex online multiuser worlds such as Philip Rosedale's Second Life in 1999.

But the one digital innovation that many think will replace all others was introduced in 1990. While working for a Geneva-based laboratory known as CERN, Tim Berners-Lee, along with collaborator Robert Cailliau, developed a way to transfer large files between researchers using a communication technology invented in the 1970s commonly referred to as the Internet. Originally named the Enquire Project, the result was a program named the WorldWideWeb (without spaces). Three years later, Marc Andreessen and Eric Bina with the University of Illinois introduced the first practical browser, Mosaic. From their invention and the browsers that came afterward, it is predicted that within 50 years there will be no difference between print publications, radios, and televisions—all the content once accessed through those separate media will be combined into one entity—the web. During the 2012 London Olympic Games' opening ceremony, Berners-Lee was honored for his achievement as he tweeted the message, "This is for everyone."

In 2009, augmented reality (AR) products were introduced from such companies as Acrossair, Junaio, Layar, and Wikitude. Commercial and storytelling information could link users with their immediate environments through GPS data available from smartphones and tablets. In that same year, a Technology Entertainment and Design (TED) conference showcased researchers at MIT who presented their technological achievement, SixthSense, "a wearable gestural interface that augments the physical world around us with digital information and lets us use natural hand gestures to interact with that information." With parts that could be purchased for about $350, the nondigital and digital worlds could work in tandem (see Chapter 16).

For many, the ultimate in wearable computers is the technology promised by the search engine giant Google, named Glass. In 2013, if you were lucky enough to be a beta tester (and pay $1,500 for the privilege), you could record still and moving images hands free, get directions before your eyes, easily communicate with friends, listen to music, and engage with other innovations simply by wearing what appears to be highly fashionable glasses.

The idea of innovations for communications is as old as human social interaction and as recent as the latest app for sale on iTunes. A complete history of mass communications can fill a library in its depth and breadth. You are strongly advised to seek other sources to learn more. As the web grows and technologies improve, the seemingly ubiquitous computer may be as outdated as drawings on cave walls. A historical appreciation of the digital innovations that have come before will help prepare you to create and use futuristic modes of mass communications.

■ CHALLENGES, CRITIQUES, AND AMUSEMENTS

- Why is it important to know a bit about the historical developments that have lead to a medium's current use?
- If you were only able to walk within a 15-mile diameter from where you live as the reporters for the Strasbourg *Relation* did, what news would you report to others?
- Johannes Gutenberg created the first printed book with interchangeable metal letters using the Latin language. What was its impact and how long did his printing process remain the norm throughout the world?
- Visit a print shop in your town or area where metal typefaces are used for printed pieces. What do you see, feel, and smell? What is missed when printing became digital? What is gained?

- Use a non-web source and find a recipe for Muenster cheese, make it, and treat your classmates and instructor.
- Translate a news story, television show, movie, commercial, public service announcement, or multimedia slideshow into crude drawings suitable for a cave, or a poem, song, or dance. If the latter choice is made, perform your creation for the class without irony or self-consciousness.
- Watch a silent movie made during the early era of motion picture history and a current film with the sound off. Are there differences in the acting and the way the plot is communicated?
- Spend a day avoiding all media (or maybe just your smartphone). What was that like? Could you go a week? A month? Longer?
- Fifty years from now, what do you think will be the most advanced communications technology?

■ EXERCISES

By now, you should have accounts with some of the major social media. Through familiarity with them you learn what others—friends and organizations—emphasize, the manner in which words and images contribute to messages, and how best to organize and present your work. If you don't already have free accounts with Facebook, LinkedIn, Twitter, YouTube, and Wikipedia, let's make that happen. Plus, you should have access to a smartphone and/or tablet to display their corresponding apps.

Also, it is vital you have your own website. If you don't have one through your school or place of employment, the last exercise in this chapter will give you information on how to obtain one.

1. Facebook: Go to <https://www.facebook.com/> and sign up (Figure 1.3). Make sure you read and understand the privacy options.

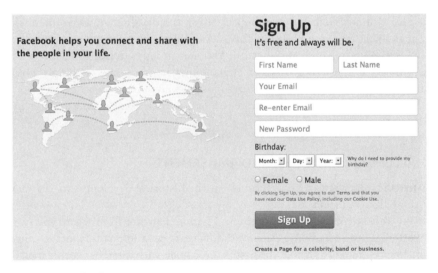

Figure 1.3 The Facebook sign-up page.

2. LinkedIn: Go to <https://www.linkedin.com/> and get started (Figure 1.4). Try to be as professional as you can when creating your profile.

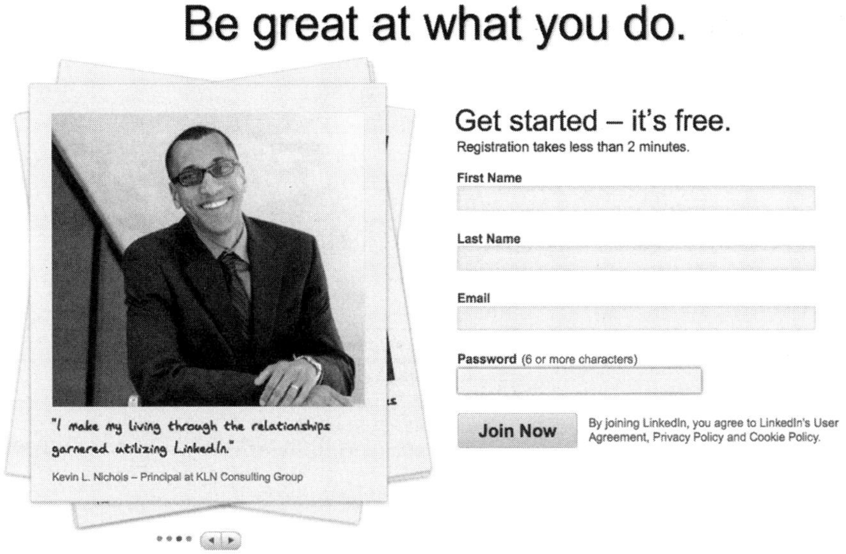

Be great at what you do.
"I make my living through the relationships garnered utilizing LinkedIn."
Kevin L. Nichols – Principal at KLN Consulting Group
Get started – it's free.
Registration takes less than 2 minutes.
First Name
Last Name
Email
Password (6 or more characters)
Join Now
By joining LinkedIn, you agree to LinkedIn's User Agreement, Privacy Policy and Cookie Policy.

Figure 1.4 The LinkedIn start-up page.

3. Twitter: Go to <https://twitter.com/> and sign up (Figure 1.5). Find persons to follow who relate to your mass communications professional area.

Welcome to Twitter.
Find out what's happening, right now, with the people and organizations you care about.
Username or email
Sign in
New to Twitter? Sign up
Full name
Email
Password
Sign up for Twitter

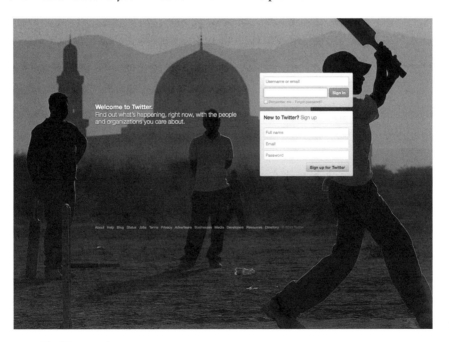

Figure 1.5 The Twitter sign-up page.

4. YouTube: Go to <https://www.youtube.com/t/about_getting_started> and get started (Figure 1.6). If you don't have one already, you will first need to create a free Gmail account from Google. Collect videos that help in your professional development. You will also need a YouTube account for the short movies you make in Chapters 3, 7, and 16.

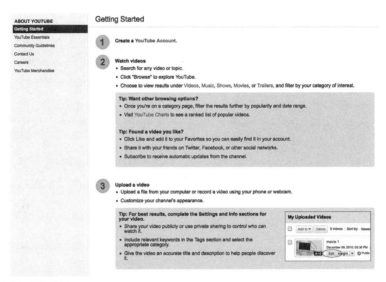

Figure 1.6 The YouTube start-up page.

5. Wikipedia: Go to <http://en.wikipedia.org/w/index.php?title=Special:UserLogin &returnto=Breaking+Bad&type=signup> and create an account (Figure 1.7). Find topics that you are familiar with and add information. Make sure you include credible sources.

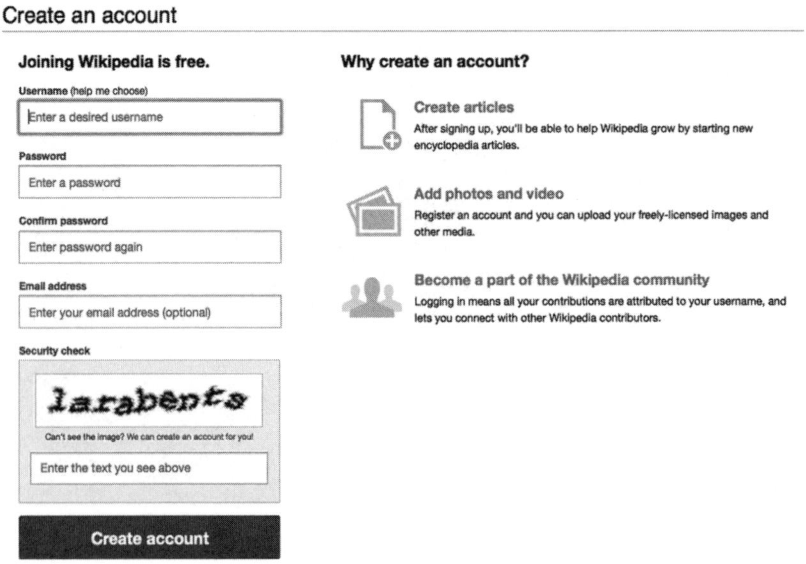

Create an account

Joining Wikipedia is free.

Username (help me choose)

    Enter a desired username

Password

    Enter a password

Confirm password

    Enter password again

Email address

    Enter your email address (optional)

Security check

    larabents

Can't see the image? We can create an account for you!

    Enter the text you see above

Create account

Why create an account?

Create articles
After signing up, you'll be able to help Wikipedia grow by starting new encyclopedia articles.

Add photos and video
Register an account and you can upload your freely-licensed images and other media.

Become a part of the Wikipedia community
Logging in means all your contributions are attributed to your username, and lets you connect with other Wikipedia contributors.

Figure 1.7 The Wikipedia account creation page.

6. Each of the social media above has app versions for smartphones and tablets. From Apple's App Store and other sources, download the free apps to your portable devices so you can make convenient updates and check content from others (Figure 1.8).

Figure 1.8 The logos for Facebook, LinkedIn, Twitter, YouTube, and Wikipedia free smartphone and tablet apps.

A website consists of two main components—a unique domain name and an account so you can store, add, delete, and edit files. Both usually require a small financial commitment from you.

There are several companies willing to provide you with both services—Media-Temple <mediatemple.net>, 1&1 <1and1.com>, DreamHost <dreamhost.com>, and if you're a fan of racer Danica Patrick, Go Daddy <godaddy.com>. Each one of these sites has simple instructions to acquire a domain name and a website. Go Daddy has a good deal if you obtain an .INFO domain suffix and one, three, or twelve month offers at reasonable prices (Figure 1.9). A three-month website is usually all you need for a course, but chances are, you will get more serious and want a long-time commitment. One important aspect to keep in mind—just as with an email address, chose the name of your domain wisely (perhaps just your name). You want to appear professional to those who don't know you.

Figure 1.9 How could you deny the smiling face of Danica Patrick? But what does she really know about website production? At any rate, you will need a unique domain name (left) and a hosting plan for your website.

Sources

"100 Photographs That Changed the World." *LIFE.* (August 25, 2003). New York, NY: Time, Inc.

"About Adobe." Accessed January 11, 2013. http://www.adobe.com/aboutadobe/.

About.com. "Reginald Fessenden (1866–1931)." Accessed January 11, 2013. http://inventors. about.com/library/inventors/blfessenden.htm.

Association Frères Lumière. "The First Public Pay." Accessed January 11, 2013. http://www.institut-lumiere.org/francais/films/1seance/accueil.html.

Bolman, Katherine. "Chauvet Cave." Applied History of Art and Architecture Educational Foundation. Accessed January 11, 2013. http://www.ahaafoundation.org/Chauvet_France/02Chauvet_Cave.html.

Burns, R. W. (1998). *Television: An international history of the formative years.* London: IEE History of Technology Series, 22.

Carolus, Johann. (2005). *Relation et Strasbourg inventa la presse.* Strasbourg, France: Ville de Strasbourg.

International Center for the History of Electronic Games. "Video Game History Timeline." Accessed April 24, 2013. http://www.icheg.org/icheg-game-history/timeline/.

Lanier, Jaron. "Homepage." Accessed January 11, 2013. http://www.jaronlanier.com/.

Mistry, Pranav. "SixthSense integrating information with the real world." Accessed January 11, 2013. http://www.pranavmistry.com/projects/sixthsense/.

Morison, Stanley. (1980). "The Origins of the Newspaper." In *Selected Essays on the History of Letter-Forms in Manuscript and Print,* edited by David McKitterick. Cambridge, England: Cambridge University Press.

The Quotation Page. "Frank Lloyd Wright." Accessed April 24, 2013. http://www.quotationspage.com/quote/506.html.

Stephens, Michael. (2007). *A History of News.* 3rd Edition. New York, NY: Oxford University Press.

2 DIGITAL MEDIA CONSUMER TYPES

Before this chapter begins, please take this simple personality test. Answer yes or no:

1. As a general rule, I make up my own mind on which media I use. ____
2. For the most part, I make media content choices based on convenience. ____
3. I am a regular user of social media websites. ____
4. I am most interested in media that challenges me intellectually. ____
5. I am happy to work with others on a task. ____
6. I value the opinions of my friends when it comes to what's available in the media. ____
7. It usually makes no difference to me whether I access print or screen media. ____
8. I really don't get online all that much. ____
9. I know that if news happens, I will learn about it eventually. ____
10. I usually read online stories that are highly rated by others. ____
11. I tend to believe "opinion leaders" that I respect. ____
12. I usually don't care about the daily news. ____
13. My friends would classify me as a "digital media junkie." ____
14. My media choices mostly have to do with what is available at the time. ____
15. My primary concern is finding (or keeping) a job and not what media I use. ____
16. I really don't care much about the media. ____

We'll come back to your responses at the end of this discussion section.

It was 1896—a leap year.

After outlawing polygamy, Mormon-centric Utah became the 45th US state, the world was able to study Anna Röntgen's rings and the bones in her hand, the modern Olympic Games opened in Athens, the US Supreme Court shamefully upheld the "separate but equal" doctrine that legalized segregation, William McKinley became the 25th US president and the third to be assassinated, and psychologists Jean Piaget and Lev Vygotsky were born (Figure 2.1).

At the age of 11, the Swiss-born Jean William Fritz Piaget wrote a paper on the albino sparrow that won him considerable attention. From his interest in botany, he became an expert on mollusks and received a PhD in the natural sciences. Later in Paris, he worked with Alfred Binet and his famous IQ tests. After he noticed that children scored differently than adults, he devoted his life to learning about the psychology of children. He no doubt profited from his family experience as he and his wife, Valentine Châtenay,

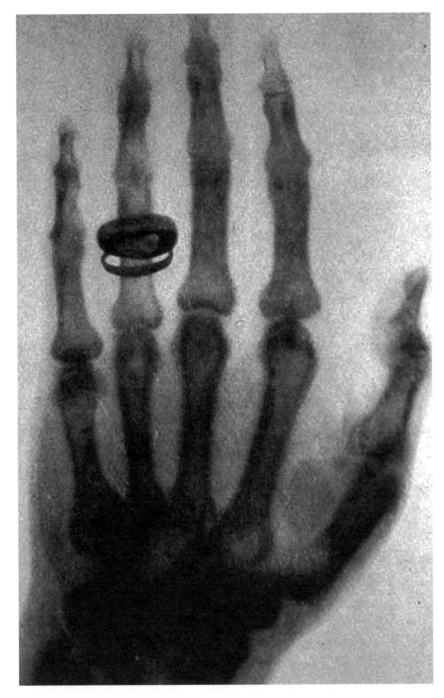

Figure 2.1 "Hand with Rings" was one of the first examples of the revealing power of X-rays. Taken by Wilhelm Röntgen, it shows the 27 bones that comprise the left hand of his wife Anna. Upon seeing the picture she reportedly exclaimed, "I have seen my death." *Courtesy of NASA*

Figure 2.2 The ever joyous Jean Piaget and the ever serious Lev Vygotsky. *Courtesy of Paul Martin Lester*

had three children that he used for his many developmental experiments. His two most famous books are *The Moral Judgment of the Child* and *The Origins of Intelligence in Children*. Testifying to his influence, he was awarded honorary doctorates from such diverse educational institutions as the University of Brazil, Harvard, the Sorbonne, and Yale. Piaget died in Geneva in 1980 at the age of 84. In *Origins* he wrote, "The principal goal of education in the schools should be creating men and women who are capable of doing new things, not simply repeating what other generations have done." Such a sentiment could be the theme of this textbook.

Born in what today is Belarus, Lev Semyonovich Vygotsky was able to attend Moscow State University, the oldest in Russia, after he was selected by a so-called "Jewish Lottery" that required a three percent quota for Jewish students. He wanted to be a literary critic. Since he was also interested in the human mind, his dissertation combined the two, which he converted to a book published in 1925, *The Psychology of Art*. Later, he was less interested in art and became more concerned about the basic functions of the mind—from children to adults. This focus led to another classic work, *Thought and Language* published in 1934, the year he died of tuberculosis in Moscow at the age of 37. In a testament for taking chances in life and with digital innovations he famously wrote, "People with great passions, people who accomplish great deeds, people who possess strong feelings, even people with great minds and a strong personality, rarely come out of good little boys and girls."

Piaget and Vygotsky, through different routes, understood that it is possible for someone to learn a new task if she is introduced to it at the appropriate developmental time and is encouraged to advance to a more complex level (Figure 2.2). However, the two famous developmental psychologists believed that the process came about through different means. Piaget thought that learning came from an individual's motivation, while Vygotsky's social constructivism model theorized that education should take place within the context that it is to be applied.

Knowing about the work from Piaget and Vygotsky, believe or not, can help you understand how to design presentations that engage the maximum number of participants.

Piaget is most known for formulating four stages of development in children:

Stage One: Skills,
Stage Two: Preferences,
Stage Three: Rules, and
Stage Four: Flexibility.

For example, before the age of two, a Stage One child learns to control her hand movements. From three to seven-years-old, a child in Stage Two knows what activities provide satisfaction. A seven- to eight-year-old in Stage Three demonstrates a strict adherence to known rules. Finally, a Stage Four child beginning about the age of 11 understands that exact instructions are guidelines that can be altered.

These stages can be applied to adults working with digital innovations. Someone stuck in Stage One may be afraid to learn how to use a computer or apps on a smartphone. A person attached to Stage Two finds a product or activity and sticks with it perhaps for a lifetime. A Stage Three person might become frustrated when explanations do not exactly match the performance of a software product. However, someone who has progressed to Stage Four realizes that learning how to use a program is an enjoyable game.

Piaget's stages stress the importance of individuals being responsible for their own development. Contrastingly, Vygotsky's social constructivism theory emphasizes that learning is a result of interactions with others. He understood that mastering an activity is achieved if someone helps along the way. The "More Knowledgeable Other," as Vygotsky described, might be any person or entity that is respected. Traditionally, a teacher, mentor, coach, or elder come to mind, but learning can also come from friends, someone younger, and even a well-designed computer program.

Contemporary researcher Mongolian Borchuluun Yadamsuren, a post-doctoral fellow at the University of Missouri's Reynolds Journalism Institute put the work of Piaget and Vygotsky into practice when she surveyed 148 adults in 2009 to find out how they obtained information from the media and how they felt about it. Yadamsuren concluded that her subjects could be divided into four user types: avid news readers or news junkies that visit several online sites a day, news avoiders who resist the news because it might be filled with unpleasant or negative stories, news encounterers who are passive consumers as they know that they will learn about important stories in a variety of ways, and crowd surfers who rely on recommendations from friends and online web communities for important information. Yadamsuren concluded that any user type could be motivated to learn about the news if an engaging connection is made with the material (See Chapter 11 for information about her news game for college students that puts her ideas into practice: "MU Tiger Challenge").

Consequently, for the digital innovations detailed in this textbook, four groups of users were formulated based on the previous research and ideas from Piaget, Vygotsky, and Yadamsuren.

Four Groups of Digital Media Users

Disenfranchised Their only concern is that basic needs are met. These potential users have more important worries than being online, such as making sure they have a job, housing, their bills are paid, and they have adequate resources to feed themselves and others. Consequently, their media interests are necessarily limited. These consumers are not innovative and are mostly digitally uninformed. They are passive consumers. They prefer their information to be obtained, if at all, through the easiest means possible. In fact, "news" to them might be what they read in a supermarket tabloid or any viewing of an afternoon confessional talk show. They are not likely to reach a higher level of news consumption without educational, economic, and social incentives. Television is the model for this group. Presentations aimed at disenfranchised users should be simple, quick, informative, and perhaps contain incentives in the form of special deals and sales.

Randomizers Once a person feels secure, she can decide what media content is of interest. In this group, initial positive experiences with a media entity can brand a user for a lifetime. And yet, for the most part, these users are ambivalent as to which choice is made. However, when a surprising story or app is discovered serendipitously, the "WOW" factor makes a strong connection for this user. Their level of involvement with the media is haphazard and coincidental because their interest in the media is generally low. If they do learn of stories (usually because of proximity or direct experience), they are not motivated to think of societal implications. They do not care much beyond their immediate self-interests. Their desires are fragmented, even parochial in nature and revolve around single or localized issues like sports or an approaching storm. Their main motivation is entertainment or sensationalism. Worked aimed at these users should sometimes be surprising in order to capture and sustain their interest. For example, while a randomizer watches a video, a scroll along the bottom might provide additional quirky facts.

Crowd Surfers After some interest in digital innovations is noted, opinion-setters, celebrities, mentors, peers, and various respected others can influence user choices in specific products or content. A friend-to-friend recommendation, for example, is the core feature of most social media. Members of this level of news consumers stick with familiar websites and are highly informed. When they like something, they are known to eagerly pass along preferences and information to others. However, sometimes their passion for a topic leads to unethical practices. For example, Reddit, a news and entertainment website dependent on crowd surfing, was criticized after users during the hunt for the Boston Marathon bombers in 2013 wrongly identified several innocent individuals as suspects. An executive of Reddit apologized for the "dangerous speculation which spiraled into very negative consequences." Nevertheless, crowd surfers are generally useful in discovering and establishing innovative trends. They tend to enjoy all types of media presentations— from the traditional to the most innovative—as long as they come recommended. Since most crowd surfers rely on friends for their endorsements, a producer of work aimed at this media type should use as many social media websites as possible to publicize a story. Getting as many "Likes" as possible on Facebook, for example, is often a successful strategy.

Engagers Eventually, a user reaches this group in which the confidence level in choosing and operating digital innovations is high. Correspondingly, collaboration among others is encouraged. This group of digital media consumers is highly creative, intellectual, and informed. As such, they benefit themselves and society. They enjoy personalized, connected, interactive, knowledgeable, and contextual presentations. It is this reason that members of this level are the ideal group for innovative presentations and why efforts should be made to promote all of the other types to this level.

Creators of innovative digital content would prefer that most users are interested, proactive, opinionated, and motivated. In fact, it should be the job of media producers to teach users to be engagers as much as possible. Thinking of digital consumers as learners helps explain why we have a need to engage with others. As we live our lives, social constructivism, the theory from Vygotsky that we learn by actively participating during an activity with the help from others, helps explain the interplay between our own experiences and understandings from others. Through interest and collaboration, we build knowledge about our world and ourselves. As such, knowledge building is not a passive activity. As a consequence, learners are encouraged to work in groups to understand real life challenges and to receive rewards for the associations and the conclusions they make.

Creating a Culture of Engagers

Without massive governmental aid in the form of educational and economic incentives, the disenfranchised will probably not proceed to higher levels. Nevertheless, through a concerted effort of educational innovations with encouragement from peers and mentors, they can learn to use the media in less passive and more informed ways. However, many of the digital innovations described in this textbook should be immediately appealing to randomizers, crowd surfers, and engagers.

Ideally, the content and experience of digital innovations for mass communications should be of maximum benefit to individuals and to society. It should therefore be the goal of creators to elevate consumers to be engagers. They are the ones who are most able through their personality, inclination, and intellect not only to consume media in innovative ways, but also to engage others to join them in their creative pursuit of information that is relevant and useful for all.

Social constructivism helps explain that, in order for someone to learn from a media presentation, a person must engage with the content within a context that she can apply to her view of the world. For those in which this activity is not familiar, encouragement and feedback are necessary and can be provided through interactive formats. Otherwise, the stories communicated are not remembered.

Find Your Digital Media Consumer Group

Score three points for each Yes response and one point for each No answer.

Disenfranchised

8. I really don't get online all that much. ____
12. I usually don't care about the daily news. ____
15. My primary concern is finding (or keeping) a job and not what media I use.
____
16. I really don't care much about the media. ____

Total _____

Randomizers

2. For the most part, I make media content choices based on convenience. ____
7. It usually makes no difference to me whether I access print or screen media.
____

9. I know if news happens, I will learn about it eventually. ___

14. My media choices mostly have to do with what is available at the time. ___

Total _____

Crowd Surfers

3. I am a regular user of social media websites. ___

10. I usually read online stories that are highly rated by others. ___

11. I tend to believe "opinion leaders" that I respect. ___

6. I value the opinions of my friends when it comes to what's available in the media. ___

Total ____

Engagers

1. As a general rule, I make up my own mind on which media I use. ___

4. I am most interested in media that challenges me intellectually. ___

5. I am happy to work with others on a task. ___

13. My friends would classify me as a "digital media junkie." ___

Total _____

If your highest score is Disenfranchised, you probably should change your major. However, high scores (eight points or more) for Randomizers, Crowd Surfers, and Engagers indicates that you are attuned to the content of this textbook and should find the lessons learned helpful in your mass media professional career.

■ CHALLENGES, CRITIQUES, AND AMUSEMENTS

- Make copies of the survey included in this chapter. Give it to as many friends as you want. (If you are in a class, your instructor might have to get approval from the Institutional Review Board at the school). Calculate their scores. From what you know about each person, do the digital media consumer groups make sense? Why or why not? How would you refine the questions or categories?

- How do X-rays compare with other forms of electromagnetic energy?

- Using only information from a library's printed sources, find out all you can about the albino sparrow. Why do you think a young Piaget was so intrigued by the bird?

- Take an IQ test. How did you do?

- In 1934, the number one cause of death around the world was typhoid fever (btw, "air transportation accidents" was last place). Find out how tuberculosis was ranked through the publication, Mortality Statistics 1934 US Department of Commerce, Bureau of the Census. Also, notice the wonderful old-fashioned typography.

- What strategies would you employ to create more engagers of digital media?

■ EXERCISES

It is estimated that there are more than one billion blogs worldwide. Because of their popularity, they are rapidly overtaking web homepages as the platform for content-driven information you create for others. If you don't already have a blog, there are several free blog publishing websites that are easy to use. The two most popular are Blogger and WordPress. WordPress gives you the option to pay for premium features that gives you customized options that you might want to use as you become more practiced and experienced with blogging. Otherwise, its free blog works for now. Either one is fine.

1a. Blogger: Go to <http://www.blogger.com/> to create a blog. With your Gmail address created for the YouTube account from the previous exercise, you can sign into Blogger and create a new blog (Figure 2.3). You should also select other blogs to follow to get useful ideas.

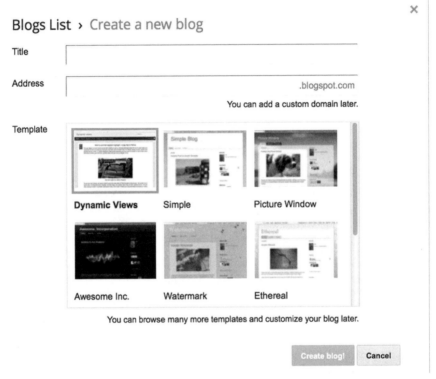

Figure 2.3 After you click on the "New Blog" button, you can type in a title, write the prefix for your blog's URL address, and select a template for the graphic design. Remember to be professional with your entries. A blog's template should be easy to use and read. You can always change your mind later.

1b. WordPress: Go to <https://signup.wordpress.com/signup/> and sign up for a free, basic blog. If at some point you want to create customized templates and include videos, you can pay for a premium service (Figure 2.4).

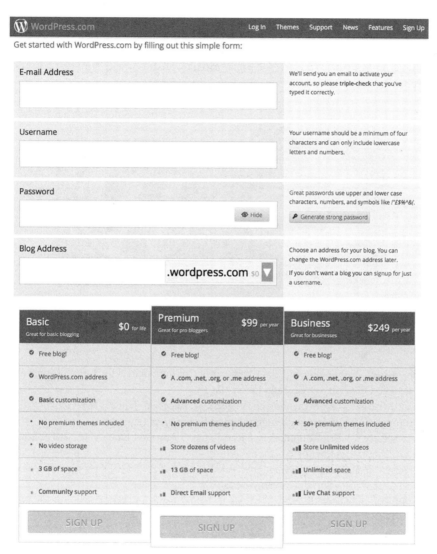

Figure 2.4 The "Get started" page for WordPress requires you to include basic information and to choose either a free blog or a premium or business service. How large is your budget?

2. After your email address and password are approved, look in your email account and click the button "Activate Blog." You will be sent back to WordPress where you can choose topics you find interesting, find out if any of your Facebook friends have a blog, write your title and optional tagline, choose a graphic look for your blog (Note: Some have price tags), and start adding content.

With both blog services listed here, there are plenty of helpful links to answer any question you might have. As with the social media websites, make sure you add the Blogger or WordPress app to your smartphone or tablet (Figure 2.5).

Figure 2.5 The Blogger and WordPress smartphone and tablet app logos.

Sources

Borgmann, Albert. Technology and the Character of Contemporary Life A Philosophical Inquiry. Chicago: The University of Chicago Press, 1984.

Gallagher, Christina. "Lev Semyonovich Vygotsky." Accessed January 11, 2013. http://www.muskingum.edu/~psych/psycweb/history/vygotsky.htm.

Jean Piaget Society. "A Brief Biography of Jean Piaget." Accessed January 11, 2013. http://www.piaget.org/aboutPiaget.html.

Kim, Beaumie. "Social Constructivism." Accessed January 11, 2013. http://projects.coe.uga.edu/epltt/index.php?title=Social_Constructivism.

Patterson, Philip, and Lee Wilkins. (2014). Media Ethics Issues and Cases. 8th Edition. New York: McGraw-Hill.

Phelps, Andrew. "Surprise! The news shows up in the least expected places." Nieman Journalism Lab. Accessed January 11, 2013. http://www.niemanlab.org/2012/01/surprise-the-news-shows-up-in-the-least-expected-places/.

Pickert, Kate, and Adam Sorensen. "Inside Reddit's Hunt for the Boston Bombers." Time US, April 23, 2013. Accessed April 25, 2013. http://nation.time.com/2013/04/23/inside-reddits-hunt-for-the-boston-bombers/.

"So How Many Blogs Are There, Anyway?" Accessed April 25, 2013. http://www.hattrickassociates.com/2010/02/how_many_blogs_2011_web_content/.

Wikipedia contributors. "1896." Wikipedia, The Free Encyclopedia Accessed January 11, 2013. http://en.wikipedia.org/wiki/1896.

Yadamsuren, Borchuluun, and Jannica Heinström. "Emotional reactions to incidental exposure to online news." Information Research 16, no. 3. Accessed January 11, 2013. http://informationr.net/ir/16–3/paper486.html.

3   ETHICAL AND LEGAL CONSIDERATIONS

Which would disturb you more?

You're in an unfamiliar part of town and want to find a nice place to eat. Just before the locator app on your smartphone points you to a possibility, an avatar of a person pops on the screen and urges you to go to a particular restaurant and try one of its lunch specials.

OR

You're in an unfamiliar part of town and want to find a nice place to eat. Just before the locator app on your smartphone points you to a possibility, a man comes up to you and says, "I understand you're looking for a restaurant. Here's a coupon for a lunch special at the place around the corner."

Because the various digital innovations featured in this textbook are relatively new, issues that arise about their appropriateness and permissible functions often infringe upon our actual and virtual worlds. Nevertheless, if you know the difference between right and wrong in the real world, you should be able to make the same determination for a simulated one. The tricky part, however, is that the cleverness of some technological innovations have surpassed our ability to quickly formulate adequate responses.

The brief scenarios above are matters related to the ethics of privacy, but are not illegal. However, if you are equally upset about a software program that recommends an eatery and an actual person able to discover what you are looking for on your smartphone and then make a suggestion, you probably have a strong need for privacy. Perhaps you refuse to tell a store clerk during checkout your zip code or telephone number or don't want to revel to a faceless speaker in a drive-thru burger joint that you will or will not eat your meal in the car. More seriously, you might decline to join many social media websites because of your privacy concerns. But then again, you might not worry about confidentiality and let your smartphone report your location so you don't miss out on important features of many software programs such as special deals and friend meet-ups. Still, a 2013 Pew Internet poll reported that out of the 88 percent of all Americans who use smartphones, 54 percent decided not to install an app "once they discovered how much personal information they would need to share in order to use it."

Never installing or removing an app out of privacy concerns may feel empowering, but what if you're not aware of any data collection about yourself? As mentioned in the preface, SceneTap is a smartphone app that allows you to know the number of patrons, their gender, and their approximate ages without having to visit a bar. It does this by taking a picture of everyone that enters the establishment and with facial recognition software, makes those determinations. Perhaps a first step toward an Orwellian "Big Brother" *1984* future, the software could also allow the scanned faces from the bar to be entered into a database to recognize *who* you are (Figure 3.1). Does anyone ever go for a drink with someone they don't want anyone else to know about? That contingency may or may not concern you; it does, however, concern the Federal Trade Commission (FTC) and other civil liberty groups.

Figure 3.1 Children play in front of a billboard advertisement for the 1949 motion picture, *1984. Courtesy of ©Topham/The Image Works*

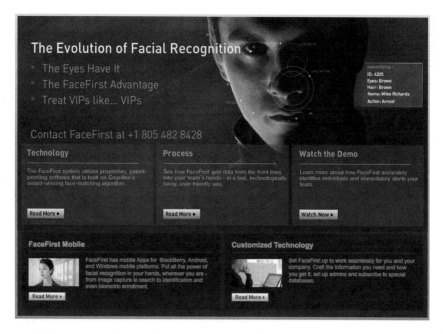

Figure 3.2 The webpage for the facial recognition technology company FaceFirst gives a hint how the software can recognize a human face and match it with a database—in this case, a collection of wanted criminals. *Courtesy of FaceFirst*

In a 2012 report, the FTC concluded that businesses that use facial recognition technology do so with customers' privacy in mind, delete the data when not needed, have strong security measures, and get the informed consent of any potential consumers. Also, in sensitive areas such as hospitals where a patient's privacy is often an ethical and legal mandate, the technology should not be used at all, according to the FTC document. The Electronic Privacy Information Center noted that the FTC's recommendations were similar to what "is found in the Madrid Privacy Declaration, which is endorsed by more than 100 civil society organizations worldwide. Facebook has ceased the use of facial recognition in the European Union and suspended it in the United States. However, companies such as FaceFirst offer facial recognition software for use in airports, casinos, and retail stores that can quickly scan a face from a security camera and display information about the person (Figure 3.2). Jennifer Lynch of the Electronic Frontier Foundation argues, "People who show their face in public aren't thinking about how their image is being stored or connected with other data."

Ethics and law are both generally concerned with the way persons act toward each other. It is usually considered to be ethical behavior if a person performs her role-related responsibilities, whether in personal or professional realms, without causing unjustified harm. Law is a set of rules devised by various governments and organizations that regulates behavior if persons cannot act ethically on their own. As such, ethics and law are similar in that they are both based largely on social constructs developed over centuries that incorporate customs, rules of etiquette, moral philosophies, and regrettably, the fear of punishment. Although what is considered ethical and legal has yet to be fully decided with the relatively new application of some of the programs discussed in this textbook, one credo remains:

Ethical behavior should always be more important than legal considerations.
Privacy is a topic worth studying in-depth because it overlaps ethical and legal

considerations and is often a criticism of many innovative programs. Ethics addresses a need for privacy while the law considers a right to it. Over time and through many court cases, privacy law has been divided into four areas:

- **Unreasonable intrusion into the seclusion of another.** Showing a video of a celebrity in an embarrassing situation on "TMZ" may be harmful to that person's reputation, but as long as reasonable, objective persons deem the airing acceptable, the harm can probably be justified and considered ethical. However, if hidden microphones and cameras were used on private property, a legal unreasonable intrusion case could be made.
- **Public disclosure of private facts.** Any information about another person not contained within public records that is disclosed is subject to legal repercussions. Lindsay Lohan's much publicized troubles with the legal system are fair game for reporters because the details are contained within public records. However, somehow revealing her exact location 24/7 with a fictitious app for your smartphone named "Where's Lindsay?" is unethical and illegal.
- **Placing a person in a false light in the public eye.** Probably the most complicated area of privacy, false light laws are intended to guard a person's well-being by preventing untrue information from being printed, aired, or disseminated online. Of course, mistakes happen, which is why media entities have a corrections page (one of my favorite sections to read in a newspaper). Most of these errors are forgiven because of deadline pressures, wrong information, or carelessness. But if false information was published that is proved to be done with intentional malice *and* a reasonable person is offended by the action, the unethical behavior crossed over to the realm of illegality. Naming a woman walking on a sidewalk as a sex worker in a voice-over for a video when she is not demonstrates reckless behavior and a classic false light example.
- **Misappropriation of a name or likeness for commercial gain.** After the social media website known as Instagram (owned by Facebook that has weathered many criticisms of its changing privacy conditions) announced in 2012 that a user's private pictures could be subjects for advertising purposes, the firestorm that resulted caused the company to back off that position. Using a photograph without permission or the creator's full knowledge is unethical and in most cases illegal.

As noted, privacy is an important ethical and legal consideration not only for producers of programs intended for mass communications but for all citizens. And yet, in this era of reality stars who get their "Fifteen Weeks of Fame," supermarket club cards that track every purchase, still and video cameras in the hands of almost everyone and installed on street corners and businesses by governmental and corporate entities, and GPS-based apps that know where your smartphone is located every minute of the day, privacy may be a quaint, anachronistic relic of a bygone era.

Digital innovations for mass communications offer many opportunities for ethicists and legal experts to debate. Here are some other present and future considerations that have been brought up by various writers. You should decide if they are primarily ethical or legal, or if, in truth, there is little difference between the two:

Abuse: More opportunities for negative confrontations, offensive images, and hate speech.

Access: Making sure that all those who want and need access to online programs are granted such opportunities.

Awkwardness: With augmented eyewear, it could be possible to obtain real-time information during a first date, which may lead to a sooner-than-expected exit.

Advertising: Unwanted, unwarranted, and unlimited commercials vying for your attention, disposal income, and memory space.

COPPA (Children's Online Privacy Protection Act): Sensitivity to a child's exposure to inappropriate age-related content and marketing come-ons. Most would agree that children are a special case and need protection. That is why the FTC has investigated complaints from parents about smartphone apps that collect their children's personal information without permission.

Copyright: The protection of a creative's intellectual property whether a small one-person shop or a multifaceted entertainment corporation.

Detachment: With so many opportunities to stay in your room to interact with programs and persons online, isolation might be the norm.

Digital Labor: Adequate credit and compensation for those who contribute to user-generated content.

File Sharing: Providing access to and the downloading of digital material without permission.

Flaws: Protection from errors in a program's design and/or execution when a product causes a malfunction with a device.

Graffiti: The ability to project visual messages for economic, political, or other reasons over billboards, walls, or previously produced virtual signs.

Hacking: The penetration of a computer program by an unauthorized party regardless of whether for entertainment, economic, or political reasons.

Injuries. With more reasons to use speech or text messaging or opportunities to see information on the screens of your smartphones, tablets, eyewear, and your car's windshield, the chance for accidents grows.

Manipulation: Image alterations that mislead.

Misinformation: The need to make sure that what you see on a screen is accurate and legitimate is greater than ever.

National Security: A government's continued need to keep certain matters private despite media technologies that are able to bring secrets out of formerly locked closets.

Network Neutrality: Government policies that make sure Internet providers give all users access to online networks regardless of their content.

Patents: Successful claims of infringement must be made from obvious determinations of significant differences between products.

Pornography: The proliferation of interactive virtual reality presentations with explicit sexual subject matter.

Profiling: Marketing based on such factors as your use of the media, your interests, your physical location, your travels, and even your face.

Security: The protection of your private information including medical history, passwords, bank accounts, travel plans, and so on.

Stereotyping: The proliferation of text and images that shows bias.

Trademark: The acknowledgment and possible compensation for a product's use within a digital display.

Violence: The making and marketing of shooter and other similarly themed apps.

Whenever ethics and law are brought up, the conversation inevitably leads to a discussion of values—general concepts (truthfulness, fairness, diversity, and so on) that correspond with a particular job or role-related responsibility. An advertiser, a travel website writer, a journalist, a public relations specialist, an employee for a motion picture company, and a visual reporter—the target audience for this textbook—all have different job requirements and thus, a slightly different set of values. Since most disagreements between what is ethical and legal involve conflicts in values, the concept is important to consider. Batya Friedman and Peter H. Kahn, Jr. of the University of Washington, Seattle, and others have written about value-sensitive design (VSD) related to digital innovations. VSD is primarily concerned with practices that "center on human well-being, human dignity, justice, welfare, and human rights." If you keep in mind larger social and educational purposes for the work you produce and try to avoid the creation of a one-time, market-driven, flashy, trinkets for someone who can afford an iPhone and needs to be relieved of her boredom, you are probably safe to assume that your ethical and legal values are highly evolved.

■ CHALLENGES, CRITIQUES, AND AMUSEMENTS

- Make a quick sketch with a pencil of an informational graphic that charts the many times during the day you think your privacy has been violated. Consider how many times you didn't know you were being watched.
- Apply to be a contestant on "Survivor" or "The Bachelor/Bachelorette" (or imagine you did). What do you think you would be willing to reveal to a large television audience?
- Do you have any creepy violations of privacy stories you want to share?
- Read George Orwell's book, *1984*. Would you rebel against the system or go along?
- Do facial recognition scanners make you a little afraid to show your face in public?
- What's the difference between ethical and legal issues? Can you think of an example that blurs the two?
- The social media sites Instagram and Facebook have both been criticized from their record on user privacy that is not totally surprising since they are part of the same company. What are the issues for both, and what is your reaction?
- What do you think is the difference between etiquette and ethics? Are some issues better controlled by proper manners or a systematic ethical analysis?
- Choose one of the ethical and legal considerations mentioned at the end of the chapter and that calls to you and find out more about it. Are there missing topics that should be on the list?
- Value-sensitive design. Is that a concept that would really catch on or merely an academic ideal?

■ EXERCISES

Although there are several free virtual community choices (see Chapter 6) such as Active Worlds, Smeet, and Twinity, for the purposes of this book you should obtain a free account to Second Life and download the program to your computer. Unfortunately, Second Life (SL) does not offer an app for smartphones and tablets and no third-party vendors can be recommended at this time.

1. Go to <https://join.secondlife.com/?lang=en-US> and click the "Join Now for Free" button on the Second Life webpage. Your first task is to choose your avatar (Figure 3.3).

Figure 3.3 The Second Life avatar selection page.

2. Create a unique username; enter an email, birthdate, password, and security question; and answer. Click the "Create Account" button. If you don't want to pay for a house and other extras, click on the "Free Account" select button.

3. However, you will need to have some funds in your account to create a group for the exercise in Chapter 6. It costs about 100 Linden dollars (the currency of Second Life) to start a group. The equivalent in US dollars is about 40 cents. Click on the "Account" link at the top left of your Dashboard to open a menu and then select "Billing Information." Add a PayPal or credit card payment method and fill out the forms.

4. Once your account is activated, the next step is to download and install the free program (Figure 3.4).

Figure 3.4 The Second Life download page.

5. After you double-click the downloaded Second Life program, you will be asked to agree to the "Terms of Service." Once you click the check box, you are transported to Destination Island where you can find out how to make SL work for you and visit other areas of interest (Figure 3.5).

Figure 3.5 Every new avatar arrives on Destination Island and stands around in awe for a while. Explore other areas.

Sources

"5 Real Problems in an Augmented World." Accessed January 11, 2013. http://digitallynumb. com/post/399172973/augmented-reality.

"AVN Augmented Reality Virtual Sex from Pink Visual." Accessed January 11, 2013. http://www. youtube.com/watch?v=fBYbKPhxuxQ.

Bilton, Nick. (2012, February 22). "Behind the Google Glasses, Virtual Reality." *The New York Times.* Accessed January 11, 2013. http://www.nytimes.com/2012/02/23/technology/google-glasses-will-be-powered-by-android.html?_r=2&.

Bilton, Nick. (December 12, 2012). "Facebook Changes Privacy Settings, Again." *The New York Times.* Accessed January 11, 2013. http://bits.blogs.nytimes.com/2012/12/12/facebook-changes-privacy-settings-again/.

Boyles, Jan Lauren, Aaron Smith, and Mary Madden. (September 5, 2012). "Privacy and Data Management on Mobile Devices." Pew Internet Report. Accessed April 25, 2013. http:// pewinternet.org/Reports/2012/Mobile-Privacy/Main-Findings/Section-1.aspx.

Broadcast Law Blog. Accessed January 11, 2013. http://www.broadcastlawblog.com.

Burgess, Anthony. (1978). *1985.* London: Hutchinson & Co.

Electronic Privacy Information Center. Accessed January 11, 2013. http://epic.org/.

Federal Trade Commission. "FTC Recommends Best Practices for Companies that use Facial Recognition Technologies. Accessed January 11, 2013. http://www.ftc.gov/opa/2012/10/facial recognition.shtm FTC report.

Friedman, Batya, and Peter H. Kahn, Jr. "New Directions: Value-Sensitive Design Approach to Augmented Reality." Accessed January 11, 2013. https://docs.google.com/viewer?a=v&q =cache:_VXynnFrYQQJ:www.vsdesign.org/publications/pdf/friedman00newdirections.

pdf+&hl=en&gl=us&pid=bl&srcid=ADGEEShh5NOeM5e8jXsIqen2g3UgUYwyXX
4J716sCMqhk3FoWsURkn6fgOuPYasPmc6b9dzmxmv6n0WX15sizfHU317sCeonl
aXm_sWRMNZZNARHM2io07IIK-Pfs0tVzFtoOjGhEtus&sig=AHIEtbTu_VbJOuaB_
yrVhZbhOOtlLl_1IA.

Future Conscience. "Augmented Reality: The Good, the Bad, and the Ugly (Part Two: The Bad)."
Accessed January 11, 2013. http://www.futureconscience.com/augmented-reality-good-bad-
ugly-part-two-the-bad/.

"Futuristic View of the Ethical Issues of Augmented Reality." (July 30, 2012). Accessed January
14, 2013. http://www.tagroom.com/futuristic-view-ethical-issues-augmented-reality/.

Guynn, Jessica. "Kids' Apps Targeted in Privacy Inquiry." *Los Angeles Times,* December 11, 2012,
B1.

Havens, John C. "Augmented Reality and Ethical Futurism." Institute for Ethics & Emerging
Technologies. Accessed January 11, 2013. http://ieet.org/index.php/IEET/more/3247.

Nelson, Laura J. (November 14, 2012). "Matching Faces Instantly." *Los Angeles Times.* B1.

Orwell, George. (1949). *1984.* London: Secker and Warburg.

Pomfret, Kevin D. "Augmented Reality: Legal and Policy Considerations." Accessed January 11,
2013. http://www.technollama.co.uk/augmented-reality-law.

Ross, Susan Dente, and Paul Martin Lester (Eds.). (2011). *Images that Injure Pictorial Stereotypes in
the Media.* Third Edition. Santa Barbara, CA: Praeger Publishers.

Wassom, Brian D. "First They Came for the Doritos: AR Campaign Spurs Legal Complaint, With
More to Come." Accessed January 11, 2013. http://www.wassom.com/doritos01.html.

4   VISUAL AESTHETICS

Put your computer to sleep and go outside until you find a one-cent US coin on the sidewalk. Go ahead. The walk will do you good. I'll wait.

You've got your penny (or are at least pretending you have one)? Okay. Take a close look at the "heads" side with its profile of the 16th president, Abraham Lincoln. The coin was introduced in 1909 on the 100th anniversary of the great leader's birthday. As with many illustrations, the image is the result of collaboration between artists. In this case, it is the work of a photographer and a sculptor separated by two score and five years.

Anthony Berger, a staff photographer working for the more famous Mathew Brady, took the wet collodion portrait of Lincoln at Brady's Washington, DC, studio on February 9, 1864, less than three months after the Gettysburg Address and about a year before his assassination (Figure 4.1). Incidentally, a daguerreotype made the same day by Brady is the basis for Lincoln's portrait on the five-dollar bill. Perhaps if they had taken more pictures that day, Lincoln would have been on all the US coins and paper money.

When the 10th president after Lincoln, Theodore Roosevelt wanted to honor his fellow Republican by placing his likeness on a coin, he chose the Lithuania-born engraver Victor David Brenner to do the work. He proceeded to create the bas-relief image based on Berger's photograph. If you look closely at the bottom of Lincoln's shoulder, you can see the sculptor's initials. If not, perhaps you should buy a magnifying glass.

So what, you may ask? (Tough crowd).

If you measure only the little Lincoln head, it is about a 1/4-inch square, or about 16x16 pixels. That size is the smallest display a graphic designer has to fill.

Nevertheless, whether you create digital media designs for tiny browser and favicon icons (tiny illustrations that front a URL in a web browser) or increasingly larger graphics for augmented reality eyewear, smartphones, MP3 players, tablets, laptops, monitors or classrooms, theaters, or outdoor screens, designers should keep in mind the four visual cues that our brains notice—color, form, depth, and movement; the concepts of contrast, balance, rhythm, and unity; practical considerations such as resolution, size, and software coding; and perhaps most importantly, the needs and wants of the audience.

Brenner's profile of Lincoln exhibits the four visual cues: the color of copper, the easily recognizable shape of the president's face, the raised impression of the engraving because of the bas-relief technique, and the way it moves from your hand into a child's piggybank. The coin also presents the design suggestions of contrast, by the difference between the words and picture, balance, by the placement of the profile in the middle of the coin's circle, rhythm, by the quiet dignity of its uncluttered design, and unity, by the similarity in style to the other coins in the US collection. Practical considerations are also invoked. Although the image's sharpness is good, with side lighting you can discern marks for his cheekbone and beard—because of its small size, the resolution doesn't have to be high.

Figure 4.1 The well-known profile of President Abraham Lincoln is an albumen print on a cartes-de-visite mount taken by Anthony Berger within Mathew Brady's Washington, DC, studio in 1864. It was later used as the reference work for the image on the one cent US coin. *Courtesy of the Library of Congress*

For a comparison, look at Lincoln's portrait on a five-dollar bill for an example of a high-resolution engraving. Also, for this example the equivalent to software coding is knowledge of the photographic and bas-relief arts. Finally, the audience is accounted for by its unchanging color, feel, and size that can be easily identified whether one is sighted or not as well as its utilitarian purpose as the humble leftover at the end of a day. Spare change? A penny qualifies. Likewise, an icon for a smartphone or tablet app should be as carefully considered as the design of the modest penny.

The graphic elements required for most digital innovations involve more than simple icons. They may include:

- Linking, information, search, and specialty buttons;
- Background images; and
- Titles, headings, descriptions, informational balloons, and other text features.

More specifically, there are two types of graphic components that are employed for almost any mass communications presentation—art and copy. Art comes in the form of icons, photographs, and illustrations while copy includes various typographical choices.

Buttons

Color	No More than Three
Form	Simple
Depth	Two-Dimensional
Movement	Centered
Contrast	High
Balance	Symmetrical
Rhythm	Uncluttered
Unity	Consistent Style
Resolution	72dpi
Size	16x16 Pixels
Coding	Linking
Audience	Noticeable and Memorable

Think of buttons the same as logos for companies. With automobile logos, for example, the best have a simple, easily recognizable design that draws attention to itself regardless of the size. The four rings of Audi, the tri-pointed shape of Mercedes-Benz, the circular blue and white pattern of BMW, and the script typographical treatment of Ford are good examples (Figure 4.2). Avoid colors that clash such as red and cyan, green and magenta, and blue and yellow; complex figures, 3D effects; and off-centered displays. Your buttons should probably show extreme differences in tones, be centered in the frame, have only one main element, and have a similar look. With online presentations, a low resolution is fine for a button's small size. The software coding used for specific projects is discussed in the exercises. Finally, users of digital innovations often enjoy symbolism that corresponds with a presentation's theme. For example, if a smartphone app gives details about fuel-efficient cars, the buttons should reflect that theme with illustrations of smiling hoods, pumps, or dollar signs. You can think up better examples, I'm sure.

Images

Color	Full, Tinted, or Black and White
Form	Horizontal or Vertical
Depth	Two-Dimensional
Movement	Internal to the Piece
Contrast	Normal
Balance	Asymmetrical or Symmetrical
Rhythm	Busy or Uncluttered
Unity	Consistent Style
Resolution	72dpi or Higher
Size	Depends on the Use
Coding	From None to Extensive
Audience	Informative

Images can be in the form of graphic illustrations, photographs, or video. Each requires their own set of skills; hand or computer-based drawings, if artistically rendered, can result in visual messages that accurately reflect their intended purpose without being misunderstood. Photographs and video, either taken or found, often create more user interest because of their real-world quality. In either case, it is vital to remember that if

Figure 4.2 The familiar four-ringed logo of the German automobile manufacturer Audi, part of the Volkswagen Group, symbolizes the merger in 1932 of four distinct car companies with four distinct logos—Audiwerke GmbH, Dampf Kraft Wagen, August Horch & Cie, and Wanderer. Lucky for Audi owners, the four typographically awkward brand symbols were replaced with an elegant ring design—it looks so much better on an R8. *Courtesy of Carlogos.org and Paul Martin Lester*

you use work from another source, you will need to seek and possibly pay for permission. Most images will be in color (using a medium tone level), with a vertical or horizontal orientation. They will be flat, but will have the effect of moving a viewer's eyes around it with their internal elements. With online presentations, a medium resolution is fine for the size required for a smartphone and high for tablet apps. Software commands specific to images are usually simple. Images should also present useful information and not simply be displayed as window-dressing.

Typography

Color	Foreground and Background
Form	Horizontal
Depth	Two-Dimensional
Movement	Left-to-Right
Contrast	High
Balance	Symmetrical
Rhythm	Uncluttered
Unity	Consistent Style
Resolution	Highest Possible
Size	Depends on the Use
Coding	Depends on the Use
Audience	Legible and Readable

With more than 50,000 typefaces (sometimes called "fonts") to choose from, the field of typography divides them into six families: blackletter, roman, script, square serif, sans

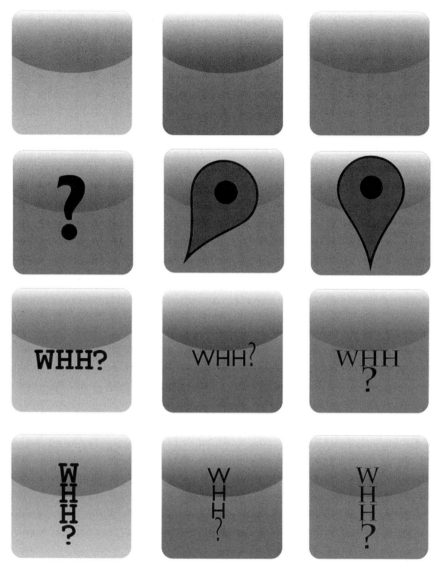

Figure 4.3 This series of proposed buttons for the locative app, "What Happened Here?" (see Chapter 15) are combinations of colors, images, and typography with varying degrees of acceptability. Used as the first graphic in the interface design for the app, a simple, easily recognizable and remembered logo within an often-crowded smartphone or tablet display were the primary motivations for the visual message. In order to be easily noticed with a pleasant aesthetic, it was decided that the button would have a gradient off-white reversed arcing shape in contrast with a common color. However, the yellow buttons looked too much like a glass of beer and blue reminded some of water. Green served best for a land-based product. The three different fonts in two orientations were rejected because the initials for the app were considered unattractive. Finally, the tilted map marker image was selected for its familiar and recognizable features. *Courtesy of Paul Martin Lester*

serif, and miscellaneous. The histories, nuances, and uses for members within each family fill books that can be purchased in art museum stores. Fortunately, only one family is almost universally accepted for online presentations—sans serif. Introduced in 1832 by William Caslon IV, the typestyle without serifs was originally intended to help printers save money. Over the years, artists and online creators alike have praised the clean look of the family.

Seldom is more than one typeface family used. Exceptions might include a title or section heading using a sans serif typeface versus body copy in a roman font (as with many textbooks) as well as with headlines and captions that might use sans serif versus stories printed in a roman family. Almost always, the best color choices come from reading books—black for typefaces while the background color is white. Other colors are of course used, but make sure that they are not similar tones or the words will be hard to read. Although it looks cool, avoid long passages of text in white over a black background. If text overlays an image, the contrast of the illustration or photograph should be slightly lowered. Titles should only run one line with attention to kerning (the space between the letters). Copy should be short, to the point, justified on both sides, and with ample leading (the space between the lines) for maximum legibility (the ability to distinguish individual letters) and readability (the ease with which the words can be understood).

One of the major goals of graphic design for digital innovations should be to create work in which buttons, images, and copy have stylistic consistency—in other words, they are integrated into a cohesive whole, they compliment the content, and they are appropriate for the intended audience. When the elements work together, all of the multivariate decisions used to create them become practically invisible to the user, who intuitively knows their meaning and purpose (Figure 4.3).

■ CHALLENGES, CRITIQUES, AND AMUSEMENTS

- The US one-cent piece, or penny, has an interesting history other than the facts detailed in this chapter. Share an intriguing detail about the lowly coin with others. Explain why you think that in some states it is rare to receive one as change.

- Mathew Brady is one of the most respected names in the history of American photography. However, he often took credit for the work made by others. What is your view on appropriation and Brady's actions?

- Find out about albumen prints and cartes-de-visite mounts and their importance during the American Civil War.

- Give examples of the smallest and largest visual messages you can find. Take pictures of each one. Discuss any similarities between the two.

- The four visual cues that the visual cortex in the brain notices before our minds recognize what the image is are color, form, depth, and movement. Which is your favorite and why?

- Maintain a collection of buttons—for software programs and political causes. What are their common characteristics? Which ones catch your eyes more than the others? Why do you think that is?

- Study automobile company logos. Which ones do you like and why? Which ones are overly busy and distracting and why?

- Imagine you are creating an app that gives details about one block within the town you live. Take at least 30 photographs and shoot three short videos. Make at least 10 rough pencil sketches that would show how you would use the videos in an app.

- Create quick sketch button designs for an imaginary app that emphasizes color more than the other three visual cues. Then, do the same for form, depth, and movement.
- Walk around your town and take 12 photographs—two each—of the six typeface families you find on printed signs.
- Why do you think the sans serif typography family is preferred for stop and exit signs as well as digital presentations?

■ EXERCISES

For this exercise, you will use Photoshop and Pixel Resort to create a mock-up of an app icon for an iPhone home screen.

1. Go to Michael Flarup's free app icon maker Pixel Resort at <http://appicontemplate.com/> and click on the "App Icon Template" to download the files you need (Figure 4.4).

Figure 4.4 After you click on the "App Icon Template" within the blue box at the right, the files should download on your computer.

2. Start up Photoshop. If Layers is not opened already, from the Windows menu select Layers. From the File menu select Open. . . and double-click on the App Icon Template.psd file from the "App Icon Template" folder you downloaded (Figure 4.5).

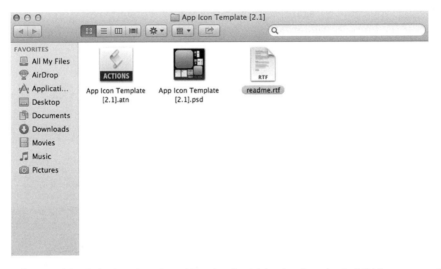

Figure 4.5 Double-click the "App Icon Template" within the downloaded folder to open it in Photoshop.

3. Press the Control key or the right mouse button and click to the right of the eye icon next to "Edit This Smart Object" within the Layers window. An options menu will open (Figure 4.6).

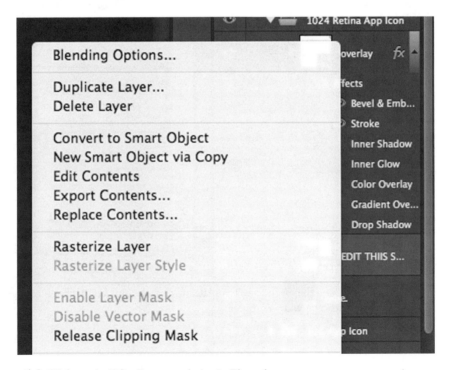

Figure 4.6 Click on the Edit Contents choice in Photoshop.

4. Select "Edit Contents." An Adobe Photoshop message should appear within a box. Click OK and the file Icon.psb appears—a blue square (Figure 4.7).

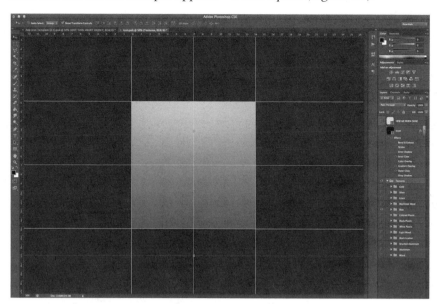

Figure 4.7 Within Photoshop, the blue square, where you want to place your icon, appears in the center of the desktop.

5. From the File menu, select Place. . . and from your computer, find your icon and double-click it. The image will appear within the blue square. Make the image larger or smaller and move it as you wish. Double-click the picture to securely place it. If you change your mind about the image, click its name in Layers and drag it to the Trashcan icon at the bottom. Start again. If you're happy with it, from the File menu select Save (Figure 4.8).

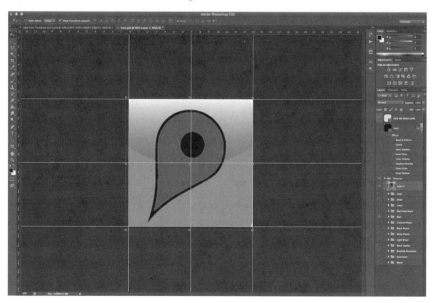

Figure 4.8 The favorite icon for the app "What Happened Here?" is placed over the blue square in Photoshop.

6. Click on the App Icon Template file and you will notice that your icon is now included within all the possible choices. Press the Command and the "+" key until the view is at 200%. Move the slide bars until the "Home Screen" display fills the frame. Take a screen save so you have a copy of it to show (Figure 4.9).

Figure 4.9 The "Home Screen" for a mock iPhone includes the icon created earlier.

Sources

burrough, xtine, and Michael Mandiberg. (2008). *Digital Foundations: Intro to Media Design with the Adobe Creative Suite.* San Francisco: Peachpit Press.

——, and Paul Martin Lester. (2013). *Visual Communication on the Web Principles & Practices.* New York: Routledge.

Car Logos. Accessed January 11, 2013. http://www.carlogos.org/.

Lester, Paul Martin. (2014). *Visual Communication Images with Messages.* 6th Edition. Boston: Cengage Learning.

National Portrait Gallery. "The Penny Image." Accessed January 11, 2013. http://www.npg.si.edu/exhibit/lincoln/pop-ups/02–09.html.

Norton, Roger J. "The Controversy Over the Lincoln Penny." Accessed January 11, 2013. http://rogerjnorton.com/Lincoln14.html.

Wroblewski, Luke. "Visual Communication & Web Application Design." Accessed January 11, 2013. http://www.lukew.com/ff/entry.asp?174.

——. "VizThink 99: Visual Communication for the Web." Accessed January 11, 2013. http://www.lukew.com/ff/entry.asp?174.

Section II

USER-GENERATED CONTENT

The three chapters in this section should inspire a traditional, passive, and unassuming consumer of print, screen, and online media to become a modern, proactive, and engaged user who contributes to the content.

Social Media

Newspapers were the first to allow readers to add story comments and details on their online versions. More sophisticated weblink systems such as Delicious, Digg, and Reddit were introduced later. Today, most forms of social media—blogs, crowdsourcing, and other friend and interest-based communities such as Facebook, Foursquare, Instagram, Twitter, Wikipedia, and YouTube—rely on users to create work that others enhance with their own factual additions, ratings, opinions, and audio and visual responses.

Virtual Communities

ActiveWorlds, Second Life, SmallWorlds, Smeet, and Twinity are avatar-based virtual social communities filled with residents who can walk, fly, drive, and teleport to rural and urban simulated environments that they either visit or create themselves. Although essentially elaborate chatrooms, these online worlds combine the visual cues found in the real, nondigital world (color, form, depth, and movement) with interactive communicative experiences.

Virtual Reality

The concept of artists escaping from their flat boards or canvases can be traced to three-dimensional *trompe l'oeil* (trick of the eye) paintings of the 16th century. Since then, viewers with digital media can now interact with images seen in their actual environments that do not exist in the world.

5 SOCIAL NETWORKS

The practice of working a net to catch fish is older than recorded history.

In 1913, a farmer from what was then Antrea, Finland, found remnants of an intricate willow-stick net that was dated to 8300 BCE. About 10,000 years later, you might have referred to *net-work* as an occupation that fabricated thread, rope, or wire mesh. By 1839, *network* was commonly used to describe any complicated system of interrelated fabric-like entities such as roads, rivers, canals, sewers, railways, and similar configurations found in plants and animals. With the invention of various technologies—telegraph, radio, television, and computers—the term became a common addition to the modern vernacular (Figure 5.1). However, none of these uses can be thought of as particularly social.

What made networks social was the connections that can be established through the digital innovations that have been created by web developers. With user-generated presentations, users are allowed by the software to input personal information, interests, and opinions in order to modify what they see on the screen.

Newspapers were some of the first websites to display input from readers—from letters to the editor and guest columns in print to detailed comments added to online blogs. Ken Sands, an "interactive editor" with *The Spokesman-Review* in Washington State was one of the first reporters to use the blog concept when reporting on a high school basketball championship. Sands brought a laptop with a wireless connection to basketball games and filed his observations, images, and audio clips that readers could access on the newspaper's blog site. Through email and instant messaging, readers added their comments or asked questions that then became part of the sports story. Imagine somewhat dull city council meetings enlivened with online users offering real-time opinions while discussions take place or an already compelling investigative piece made more engaging through user input.

Just as you might trust a close and credible friend telling you of a product you should buy, a news event you should know about, an organization that deserves a donation, a television show you should watch, or a picture story that might change your perspective, well-designed, easy-to-use, and popular social media can have the same effect.

Researchers danah boyd (she prefers her name in lowercase) and Nicole Ellison define social media as:

> Services that allow individuals to (1) construct a public or semi-public profile within a bounded system, (2) articulate a list of other users with whom they share a connection, and (3) view and traverse their list of connections and those made by others within the system. The nature and nomenclature of these connections may vary from site to site.

From the early 1990s, innovative dating, community, classmate, and chat websites exhibited elements of the three conditions, but were not as inclusive as what is considered the first

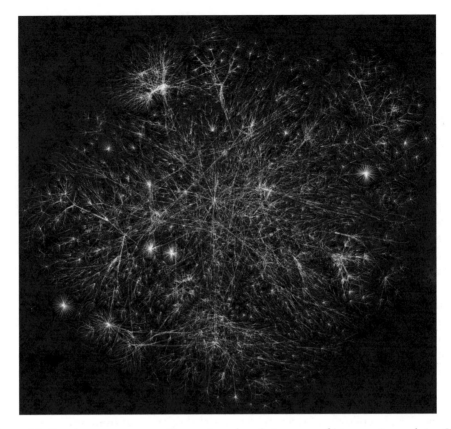

Figure 5.1 Computer programmer Barrett Lyon based the name of his mapping website Opte after the Latin word for optical, *opti*. This data visualization program charts the world-wide network known as the Internet. *Courtesy of Opte.org*

social network site in 1997—SixDegrees.com. Based on the concept that we are all within six personal connections of each other (including the actor Kevin Bacon), the site allowed users to connect to each other whether acquaintances or not and became the inspiration of later friend circles such as Myspace, LinkedIn, Twitter, and Facebook.

Introduced in 2003, Myspace became known as a site where indie rock bands could connect with their fans, mostly teenaged users. In 2005, Rupert Murdoch's News Corporation bought the site for $580 million hoping to use it to promote its Fox Broadcasting content. Instead, the sale led to a downturn of Myspace. Fox was not good at producing innovations fast enough for impatient young users. Plans are set to upgrade the website. Stay tuned.

Launched in 2003 by former Yahoo! executive Jeff Weiner, LinkedIn is a popular social network used to foster professional contacts. In 2011, its shares began to be traded on the New York Stock Exchange. It now boasts almost 200 million members.

With Twitter, who ever thought 140 characters would be so powerful? Well, web developer Jack Dorsey did in 2006 when he started the microblogging website. Today, there are more than 500 million active users producing more than 340 million tweets *a day*.

Still, Facebook is considered the gorilla in the cyberzoo.

The social media website Facebook started as a program called Facemash by Harvard computer science major Mark Zuckerberg in 2003 when he was 19. The site was simply a game in which side-by-side portraits of fellow Harvard students were compared—a kind of "who is hot and not" sarcastic game. In order to populate his site with pictures, Zuckerberg copied images from university records. This invasion of privacy almost got him kicked out of school, but the charges were dropped. The next year, he created a website called "thefacebook" which had the social networking aspects common to Facebook today. Initially limited to Harvard students, it soon became popular with other Ivy League students at Columbia, Yale, and Stanford, and then with students at other universities in the United States and Canada. In 2005, the "the" was dropped from the name.

The success of the social network, the same name as the movie about it released in 2010, made Zuckerberg rich. Facebook expanded its Internet presence and member options by teaming with the music-sharing service Spotify, the video services Hulu and Netflix, the image producer Instagram, the video chat service Skype, and the location sharing site Gowalla.

In 2012, the company made headlines around the world when it offered its stock for public purchase. Its IPO (Initial Public Offering) had an initial market value of about $100 billion and made 1,000 employees instant millionaires. The 28-year-old Zuckerberg's personal wealth was raised to about $20 billion. The day after the IPO, he married his college sweetheart, Priscilla Chan, days after she graduated from medical school. However, his good times didn't last long. There were lawsuits from potential investors left out of the deal and talk of possible Congressional and Justice Department investigations. The price of the stock plummeted, but recovered somewhat.

In 2012, Facebook had 900 million registered users, with more than 80 percent of its members living outside the United States. In a 2013 survey, the number of "friends" one has on a Facebook page appears to be generational. The overall average number of friends reported by users 12 to more than 65-years-old is 282; but if you are older than 65, you might have 115 friends; if between the ages of 45 and 64, you probably have 148 friends (I maintain a strict rule of only 100 friends—people I actually know well); if you are 35 to 44-years-old, 209 friends; 25 to 34, you might have 328 Facebook friends; while those between the ages of 12 and 24 have 508 friends. My daughter, who is 24-years-old, lists 1,459 friends. That number makes me question her definition of *friend*. Nevertheless, these findings suggest the perhaps sad conclusion that the older you get the fewer friends you have.

Facebook has the same status as the web had when it was first introduced—it is almost more important for individual users, organizations, and companies to have a presence on the social media network than the quality of the content that is available (Figure 5.2).

Regardless of whether you become an advertising, entertainment, journalism, public relations, RTVF, or visual reporting professional, maintaining user-generated social media networks will be a major responsibility. Likewise, all forms of social media—the ones detailed above and also blogs, crowdsourcing, and other friend and interest-based communities such as Foursquare, Instagram, Pinterest, Reddit, Wikipedia, and YouTube—rely on users to create work that others enhance with their own comments, performances, and visual materials.

Pepsi soft drink officials know the social power of crowdsourcing. For the 2013 Super Bowl halftime show, viewers of Pepsi's website were asked to submit photographs to earn a chance to have the picture seen during the broadcast and to win a trip to the show

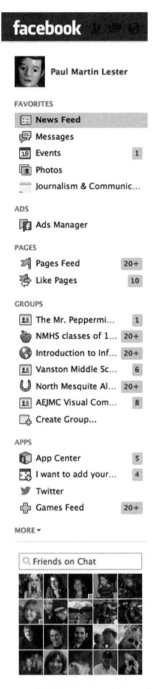

Figure 5.2 A sliver of the author's Facebook page reveals professional and personal interests.

headlined by Beyoncé. Pepsi also used crowdsourcing to change the way it contributes money to worthy causes. Users were asked to submit recommendations from "health, environment, culture, and education-related organizations" and then voted on the winners of grants from $25,000 to $250,000. Mass communicators need to possess the same level of creativity and take advantage of a user's desire to include information so that stories and other presentations can feel more personal.

■ CHALLENGES, CRITIQUES, AND AMUSEMENTS

- If you can't remember a time in which you didn't have the web, interview someone about first hearing and using it. What was the first networked interactive program used?
- Which social media do you regularly use and why? Are any out of the mainstream that we should know about? If so, why do you like them?
- Who is danah boyd and why should you know about her work?
- Produce at least five different drawings (quick sketches are fine) that graphically represent the Internet.
- Do you think a friend on Facebook is different than a face-to-face friend? How so?
- What is the subject of the most popular tweets on Twitter? Why do you think that is?
- Seek out videos on YouTube that have to do with the contents of this book. Write serious comments about the work you find. Did you get any responses to your comments?
- How much dedication do you think it would take to add content to a blog every day?
- Do you think it would be easy to simply make up facts in Wikipedia about a fictional topic? What are the safeguards now in place to prevent such a happening?
- Do you have any international friends on Facebook? Do you use the language translation feature to chat with them or add to their walls?
- How difficult do you think it would be to get 100 Likes for a group on Facebook? What strategies do you think would be best to get that many?
- How important will social media be for your chosen mass communications profession?
- Can you think of any other uses for social media other than the usual ways?

■ EXERCISES

These exercises encourage you to contribute a little more to various social media.

1. Complete your LinkedIn profile as much as possible. Try to obtain 30 contacts within your chosen communications area. Get at least three contacts to recommend you (Figure 5.3).

Figure 5.3 The LinkedIn profile page.

2. From your Twitter account, try to send a new Tweet every day for two weeks. Write a comment that gets retweeted five times. Try to get at least 50 followers. Always aim for more followers than tweets as you run the risk of appearing desperate for attention if your inputs are more numerous than your audience (Figure 5.4). Link your Twitter and Facebook accounts. Go to <https://support.twitter.com/articles/31113-how-to-use-twitter-with-facebook#> to find out how your tweets can show up on your Facebook wall.

Figure 5.4 The author's Twitter summation page.

3. On your YouTube account, upload a simple, one-take, and one-minute video you made with your digital video camera that has nothing to do with cats. Try to get at least 10 Likes and comments (Figure 5.5).

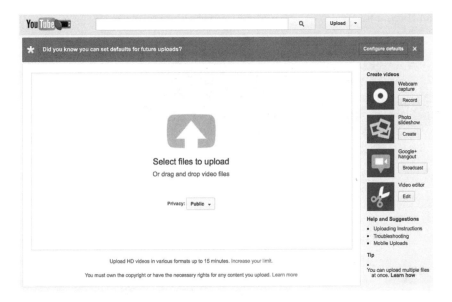

Figure 5.5 The YouTube video upload page.

4. In Wikipedia, create a legitimate topic with factual information and sources that no one else has thought to put on the site. Search Wikipedia first to be sure you have a unique topic. And remember, your article must be approved before it is included. You will first need to go to <http://en.wikipedia.org/wiki/Wikipedia:Your_first_article> to learn about how to create a new article. Then, the Article Wizard at <http://en.wikipedia.org/wiki/Wikipedia:Article_wizard> will help you with uploading the article (Figure 5.6).

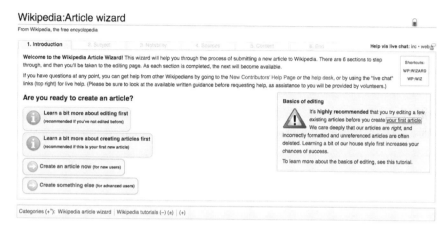

Figure 5.6 The Wikipedia article wizard page.

5. Use Blogger or Wordpress to document a single block in the town where you live. Update your blog with stories, interviews, and images every day for a month. Solicit comments about your blog from your friends and others.

6. Register with Myspace at <http://new.myspace.com> (Figure 5.7). On second thought, never mind.

Figure 5.7 The Myspace welcome page.

Sources

"Average Number of Facebook Friends, by Age Group." Marketing Charts. Accessed April 26, 2013. http://www.marketingcharts.com/wp/direct/18–24-year-olds-on-facebook-boast-an-average-of-510-friends-28353/attachment/arbitronedisonresearch-avg-number-of-facebook-friends-by-age-apr2013/.

BagNewsNotes. Accessed January 11, 2013. http://www.bagnewsnotes.com.

Betancourt, Leah. (September 2, 2009). "The Journalist's Guide to YouTube." Accessed January 11, 2013. http://mashable.com/2009/09/02/journalists-youtube/.

boyd, danah m., and Nicole B. Ellison. "Social Network Sites: Definition, History, and Scholarship." Accessed January 11, 2013. http://jcmc.indiana.edu/vol13/issue1/boyd.ellison.html.

Dictionary.com. Accessed January 11, 2013. http://dictionary.reference.com/browse/network.

Fernandez, Maite. (September 26, 2012). "Social Media Etiquette for Journalists: The Rules Have Changed." Accessed January 11, 2013. http://mashable.com/2012/09/26/social-media-etiquette-journalists/.

Fincham, Kelly. (June 12, 2012). "7 Ways Journalists Can Make Better Ethical Decisions when Using Facebook." Accessed January 11, 2013. http://www.poynter.org/how-tos/digital-strategies/176649/7-ways-journalists-can-make-better-ethical-decisions-when-using-facebook/.

Friedman, Jacob. (August 18, 2010). "Blogging vs. Journalism: The Ongoing Debate." The Next Web. Accessed January 11, 2013. http://thenextweb.com/us/2010/08/18/blogging-vs-journalism-the-ongoing-debate/.

Ingram, Mathew. (October 10, 2012). "Lessons in How to Crowdsource Journalism from ProPublica." Accessed January 11, 2013. http://gigaom.com/2012/10/10/lessons-in-how-to-crowdsource-journalism-from-propublica/.

Johnson, Bobbie. (September 15, 2012). "Why Journalists Love Reddit for Its Brains, Not Just Its Beauty." Accessed January 11, 2013. http://gigaom.com/2012/09/15/why-journalists-love-reddit-for-its-brains-not-just-its-beauty/.

Kanalley, Craig. (February 12, 2011). "10 Tips for Making the Most of Twitter." Accessed January 11, 2013. http://www.twitterjournalism.com/2011/12/02/10-tips-for-making-the-most-of-twitter/.

Kiss, Jemima. (April 5, 2010). "Foursquare and Gowalla: Location Games Are Where It's At." Accessed January 11, 2013. http://www.guardian.co.uk/media/2010/apr/05/gowalla-foursquare-location-jemima.

———. (January 3, 2007). "The Trouble with 'User' Generated Content." Accessed January 11, 2013. http://www.guardian.co.uk/media/pda/2007/jan/03/thetroublewithusergenerate.

Lavrusik, Vadim. (February 27, 2011). "Facebook's Growing Role in Social Journalism." Accessed January 11, 2013. http://mashable.com/2011/02/27/facebooks-growing-role-in-social-journalism/.

Mandiberg, Michael (Ed.). (2012). *The Social Media Reader.* New York: New Yorker University Press.

Naím, Moisés. (December 20, 2006). "YouTube Journalism." *Los Angeles Times.* Accessed January 11, 2013. http://www.latimes.com/news/la-oe-naim20dec20,0,5193084.story.

Ojanperä, Maija. (October 30, 2012). "Use the Power of the Crowd to Get Unique Photos from the Scene." Accessed January 11, 2013. http://www.scoopshot.com/blog/use-the-power-of-the-crowd-to-get-unique-photos-from-the-scene/.

ONA12. "Social Media Debate: Best Practices vs. Bad Habits." Accessed January 11, 2013. http://ona12.journalists.org/sessions/social-media-debate-best-practices-vs-bad-habits/.

Open Education Database. (July 16, 2012). "The 40 Best Blogs for Journalism Students." Accessed January 11, 2013. http://oedb.org/library/beginning-online-learning/the-40-best-blogs-for-journalism-students.

Outing, Steve. (March 13, 2002). "Interactive News is Newspaper-Wide Effort in Spokane," *Editor & Publisher.*

Perez, Sarah. (July 16, 2012). "Pew: YouTube Represents New Kind of 'Visual Journalism.' " Accessed January 11, 2013. http://techcrunch.com/2012/07/16/pew-youtube-represents-new-kind-of-visual-journalism/.

Pew Internet. Accessed January 11, 2013. http://pewresearch.org/pubs/2262/facebook-ipo-friends-profile-social-networking-habits-privacy-online-behavior.

Schwartz, Ariel. (January 4, 2010). "Pepsi Ditches the Super Bowl, Embraces Crowdsourced Philanthropy Instead." Accessed January 11, 2013. http://www.fastcompany.com/1505387/pepsi-ditches-super-bowl-embraces-crowdsourced-philanthropy-instead.

Shorty Awards. Accessed January 11, 2013. http://shortyawards.com/category/JOURNALIST social media awards.

Sonderman, Jeff. (August 31, 2012). "A Journalist's Quick Guide to Reddit, the Next Thing You Have to Learn." Accessed January 11, 2013. http://www.poynter.org/latest-news/top-stories/187078/a-journalists-quick-guide-to-reddit-the-next-thing-you-have-to-learn/.

Ward, Stephen J. A. "Digital Media Ethics." Accessed January 11, 2013. http://ethics.journalism.wisc.edu/resources/digital-media-ethics/.

Wikipedia contributors. "Antrea Net." *Wikipedia, The Free Encyclopedia.* Accessed January 11, 2013. http://en.wikipedia.org/wiki/Net_of_Antrea.

"XLVII Pepsi Halftime Show." Accessed January 11, 2013. http://halftime.pepsi.com/.

Youseph, Ramon. "3 Ways Crowdsourcing is Owning Journalism." Accessed January 11, 2013. http://dailycrowdsource.com/crowdsourcing/articles/opinions-discussion/1052-crowdsourcing-in-journalism.

6   VIRTUAL COMMUNITIES

"No flying during class."

I taught a large-lecture (230 students) visual communication class using the online avatar-based virtual social community known as Second Life (SL). Students sat in "air chairs," sofas, or carpets strewn on the ground and experienced my lectures enhanced with PowerPoint slides and digital movie clips. As with an actual course, questions were asked and answered, flirtations and off-topic conversations happened, and somehow, through it all, learning was achieved. At the end of the appointed time, we all had a bit of fun and flew around the course site that also contained examples of classic visual messages and a student art gallery (Figure 6.1).

Second Life was not the only choice I could have made for my educationally based virtual community. Other virtual worlds include ActiveWorlds, SmallWorlds, Smeet, and Twinity. Just as with SL, these programs allow you to acquire property, shop, and sell products. However, their emphasis is more on online chatting and dating.

One of the most influential thinkers concerned with the social aspects of online communication is Phoenix-born Howard Rheingold. Singly or with a coauthor, he has written 15 books, with his latest published in 2012 titled *Net Smart: How to Thrive Online.* Much of his free thinking attitude was inspired from classes he took at Portland, Oregon's Reed College, the same school Apple cocreator Steve Jobs attended.

In 1985, Stewart Brand and Larry Brilliant created a telephone dial-up discussion-based forum called The WELL, an acronym for Whole Earth 'Lectronic Link. It is considered one of the oldest virtual communities still in existence. After Rheingold's experiences with it, he made up the term *virtual communities* and described their importance in a book he wrote in 1993 with the same name. He described virtual communities as:

> A group of people who may or may not meet one another face to face, who exchange words and ideas through the mediation of . . . digital networks. In cyberspace, we chat and argue, engage in intellectual discourse, perform acts of commerce, exchange knowledge, share emotional support, make plans, brainstorm, gossip, feud, fall in love, find friends and lose them, play games and make games, flirt, create a little high art and a lot of idle talk. We do everything people do when people get together, but we do it with words on computer screens, leaving our bodies behind.

Despite Rheingold's acknowledgment that activities prevalent in simulated and genuine worlds will overlap, he advocates that online social networks should be based on serious topics and inspire serious discussions. In that sense, back in 1993 and before the web, he predicted the ubiquitous presence of blogs from personal to political and the use of virtual communities to initiate and sustain interest in stories produced by mass communicators.

Figure 6.1 The author's avatar in the foreground waits with his students who sit on carpets, couches, and air chairs before an online visual communication class on SL.

Traditionally, the concept of community involves persons in close proximity to each other with usually one primary interest that binds them. Geographically based communities might include neighbors along a common avenue, citizens of a district or town, students taking the same course, workers for the same company, and so on. Interest-based communities could be established through efforts to beautify an area of town, study groups at a university, those with similar hobbies, and so on. For the most part, interest-based groups are often more complex than geographical ones.

Virtual communities emphasize interests between members without the requirement that they share a physical space. The concept is hundreds of years old. Before there were international conferences devoted to the sharing of scientific knowledge, as far back as the 16th century, scientists exchanged letters to seek information on particular topics. With the invention of radio in the 1900s, amateur operators either through Samuel Morse's Code or by voice communications shared news, stories, and information with each other. With the public popularity of computers, user groups or bulletin boards (named for their nondigital, index-card-on-cork precursor) linked telephone lines and later, wireless systems in order to perpetuate virtual communities.

For The WELL, organizers view conferences on innumerable topics where experts and users can "meet" and learn as the main point of the online program. With 10 broad categories of conference topics with some featuring up to 35 subcategories, the sense of an active, interest-based, nonspecific geographical orientation of those serious about thoughtful conversations is clear. Perhaps inevitably, participation comes at a price. For $100 a year you can access the conferences. For a $150 annual fee, you can also dream up your own conference topics, receive an email address, and obtain web publishing space.

The benefit of SL is that it is free to join and download its program to your computer. With credit card information, residents can accessorize their avatars with skin, hair, and clothing. With a premiere account you can buy land and build stores and homes and sell your creations to other users. With a physics degree from UC San Diego, Phillip Rosedale in 1999 established Linden Lab, where he developed SL. Roughly inspired by Neal Stephenson's 1992 science fiction classic *Snow Crash* about a user-dominated virtual reality,

SL was launched in 2003 and currently has more than 20 million registered accounts. During a conference organized by The WELL with W. James Au, the author of *The Making of Second Life,* moderator Jennifer Powell admitted that "I think one thing that might surprise someone who has never been in a virtual world before is how immersive the experience is. . . ."

It was the shiny lure of story immersion that initially interested established journalism organizations such as CNN, Reuters, and Sky News to invest time and funds to experiment with SL. Each had elaborate structures that encouraged the production of stories and the education of journalists to this new medium of presentation. Despite initial attention, interest waned and the news companies no longer maintain a SL presence. Professor Amy Schmitz Weiss of San Diego State University created a "Virtual Journalism Learning Center" (VJLC) with a grant from the Knight Center that funded a reporter teaching center on SL in 2009. It was closed after her experiment was over. Whether it's ahead or behind its time, the perception that SL is the Myspace of virtual communities and on its way out as few who teach mass media courses bother with online versions of their face-to-face classes, it is difficult to find any examples of serious storytelling amid all the places to dance and buy clothes on SL.

There are alternatives to SL that have been used for instruction. Researchers at Duke University with a grant awarded by the Andrew W. Mellon Foundation created a virtual community simulator called Open Cobalt. However, the system is currently not intuitive to use without some computer programming knowledge. Other possibilities are Open Simulator and Open Source, free products if you have the training and know-how to build a virtual world with its tools. Otherwise, a university can rent classroom space from companies such as ReactionGrid for a $150 set-up fee and a $75 monthly charge.

When the word *university* is searched on SL, 795 places are available that include SL-only Caledon Oxbridge University to established institutions such as USC's Marshall School of Business and Indiana University (Figure 6.2). Since the program is free and still available to download, there is no reason to prevent anyone from at least trying to create a virtual community on SL.

Figure 6.2 The author's avatar hovers over the elaborately produced Caledon Oxbridge University on SL. Modeled and named after established English educational institutions Oxford and Cambridge, the site offers numerous classes to help new residents of the virtual community have a more enriching experience.

Given the uncertainties of the world we live in, virtual communities may become a necessity. With worries about the various threats to the environment and the economy caused by global warming, terrorists who get their hands on nuclear weapons, possible wars over water rights, fossil fuels, food supplies, and religions, as well as pandemics from various biological pathogens, in the near future it may be unsafe to venture outside the confines of your home. In this unlikely pessimistic scenario, it may be that the only way we communicate safely with one another is through virtual communities such as SL.

■ CHALLENGES, CRITIQUES, AND AMUSEMENTS

- Transport to the author's class site on SL named "Fullerton Island" located at <http://slurl.com/secondlife/CSU%20Fullerton/146/156/25> and explore the space. Go to other, sometimes crowded and more social locations. What are your impressions?
- Register with other virtual communities such as ActiveWorlds, SmallWorlds, Smeet, or Twinity. How are they similar and different from SL?
- When was the last time you wrote a letter (not a postcard)? You know what's coming. Write a two-page hand-written letter to a friend or family member that lives far from your town. Wait for a return letter and write back. Continue until you run out of stamps.
- Read Howard Rheingold's *Net Smart: How to Thrive Online.* Do you think there is more you could be experiencing that is offered on the web? What prevents you from branching out?
- Would you pay $150 a year (about $2.50 a day) for a premium subscription to The WELL? If not, what keeps you from the purchase? Don't you pay that much a day for a decaf, tall, skinny latte with soy?
- Read Neal Stephenson's *Snow Crash.* How has science fiction works as books and motion pictures inspired actual science?
- How could you use SL in your mass communications professional life?
- Will the future ever be as bleak to require us to live in virtual communities? What can you start doing today to prevent the scenarios mentioned at the end of this chapter?

■ EXERCISES

You will create a group and lead a chat in SL concerned with the unique topic you initiated for the Wikipedia exercise in the previous chapter. At the end, you will save the chat session and share it with your class or work partners.

1. The cost to initiate a group in SL is 100 Linden dollars (the currency of SL) or about 40 US cents. You should have set up a payment method with a balance for your SL account in Chapter 3. The name of your group must not be longer than 39 characters, be unique within all of SL, and cannot be changed once it is accepted. Your group will automatically be disbanded if you do not have at least two members within the first 48 hours. So, once you create a group, get busy asking your fellow classmates, work partners, and friends to join.

2. Since you will want to have a record of your text-based chats, you need to tell SL where you want your chats to be saved. Create a folder somewhere on your computer named "My Chat Logs." In SL, click on the menu item Me, then Preferences, and finally Privacy. Under "Location of logs:" click the Browse button, find your

folder, and select it. The location and name should be seen in the small window. Click the OK button (Figure 6.3).

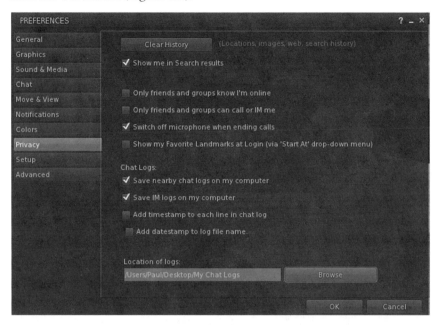

Figure 6.3 The Privacy window within Preferences is where you set the location of your chat logs.

3. To create a group, start by clicking on the Communicate menu item and then Groups (Figure 6.4).

Figure 6.4 Within the Communicate menu item is where you find Groups.

4. Click the "+" button at the bottom of the window and select "New Group . . ." to see your group's data entry screen (Figure 6.5).

Figure 6.5 The "+" button at the bottom of the screen allows you to either join or create a group.

5. Type in your group's name, check the box for "Anyone can join." Unless you want to charge members, do not check the "Cost to join" box. Select "General Content" from the pull-down menu. Click the "Create Group" button to see the group's profile screen (Figure 6.6).

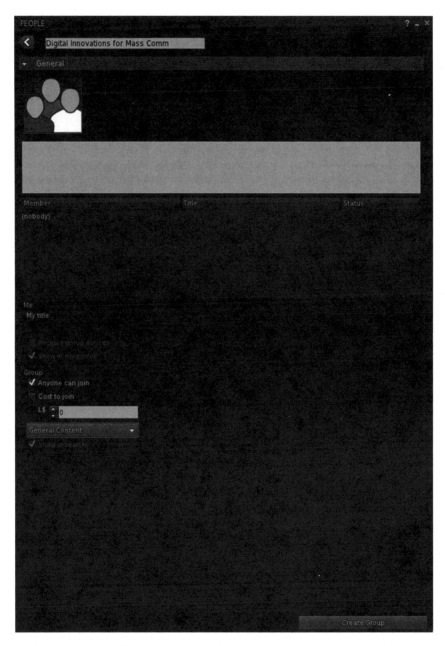

Figure 6.6 After you press the "Create Group" button at the bottom, you can add features to your group's profile.

6. If you want to add a picture, you will need to upload one and pay 10 Linden dollars. From the Build menu, select Upload and then Image to place a picture in your Textures folder. Double click the image area in your group's screen and find the image you uploaded within Textures. Add a description for your group and click the "Save" button. After you press the "Create Group" button at the bottom, you can add features to your group's profile (Figure 6.7).

Figure 6.7 The "People" window shows the profile of a group with a picture, description, and members added.

7. In the "People" window, click on the "My Groups" tab. You will see a check mark at the bottom. Make sure you click it to activate your group. You cannot add members to your group until this is accomplished (Figure 6.8).

Figure 6.8 After your group name has been accepted as unique on SL, click the check button to activate it.

8. Next, you will want SL residents to join your group. Ask those you know for their SL avatar names. Make sure your group name is selected and press the "Group Profile" tab at the bottom. Press "Roles," and with the Members tab selected, click the Invite button. Press the "Open Resident Chooser" button within the "Group Invitation" window. Under the "Choose Resident" section, click Search. Type in the name of a resident's avatar and click Go. After the name appears, press the Select button at the bottom and the name will be included in your "Group Invitation" list. Repeat this process until you have added all the residents you want to invite and then press Close (Figure 6.9).

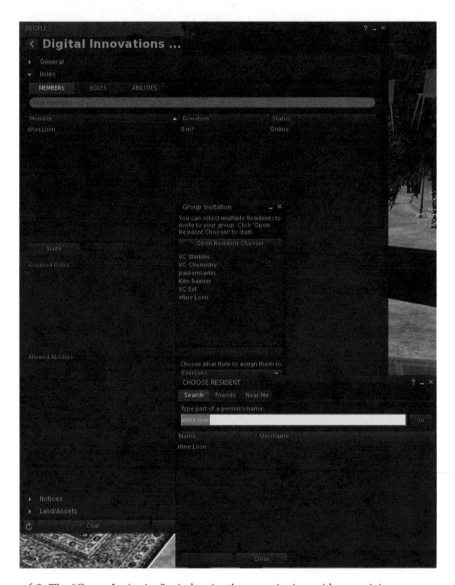

Figure 6.9 The "Group Invitation" window is where you invite residents to join your group.

9. Your invited residents will receive an email informing them of your invitation. Hopefully, they will accept and join your group. Announce a group chat by selecting the "Notices" tab at the bottom of the group's profile window. Click the "+ New Notice" button and add your message for all group members (Figure 6.10).

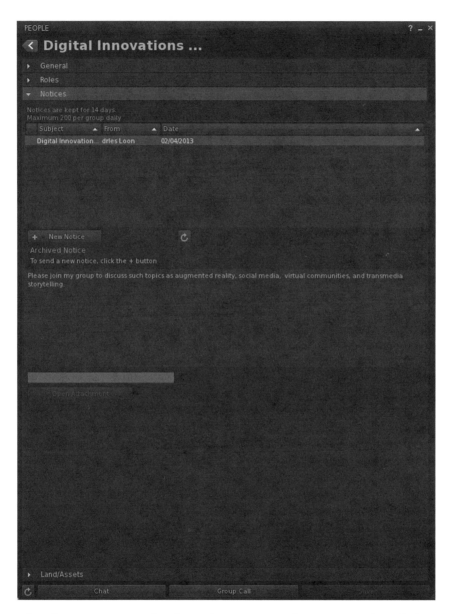

Figure 6.10 Let your group members know that you want to discuss an issue through the Notices window.

10. When you are ready for your discussion, click the "Group Chat" tab at the bottom of your "People" window. Once your group members are aware that a chat is taking place through a notice, each one needs to select the Communication menu and then Groups. Your invited member must double click on the name of the group and join the chat (Figure 6.11).

Figure 6.11 Part of a chat between two members of a group is displayed in a separate window within an SL desktop.

11. Your group's chat will be saved as a simple text file in the location you previously set within a folder with your avatar's name and a file that has the same name as the title for your group (Figure 6.12).

Figure 6.12 Part of a chat between two members of a group is saved in a text file named after your group's name in the location that you specified within the Privacy window in Preferences from the Communicate menu.

A webpage on the SL Knowledge Base explains how to start and maintain a group: <http://community.secondlife.com/t5/English-Knowledge-Base/Creating-managing-moderating-and-disbanding-groups/ta-p/700111>. Plus, you can get help at any time within SL by clicking the question mark icon.

Sources

Active Worlds. Accessed January 12, 2013. http://www.activeworlds.com/.

Apple, Green. (August 25, 2010). "Mitch Wagner: Journalist Turned Second Life Expert." Accessed January 12, 2013. http://www.squaremartinimedia.com/mitch-wagner-journalist-second-life-expert/.

Au, W. James. (March 3, 2008). "The Making of Second Life." The Well. Accessed January 12, 2013. http://www.well.com/conf/inkwell.vue/topics/322/W-James-Au-The-Making-of-Second-page01.html.

Brennen, Bonnie, and Erika dela Cerna. (2010). "Journalism in Second Life." *Journalism Studies* 11, no. 4. Accessed January 12, 2013. http://epublications.marquette.edu/comm_fac/65/.

CNRS. "The Beginning of International Collaboration at the CNRS." Accessed January 12, 2013. http://www2.cnrs.fr/en/169.htm.

Curtis, Anthony. "Second Life News Media." Accessed January 12, 2013. http://www.uncp.edu/home/acurtis/NewMedia/SecondLife/SecondLifeNewsMedia.html.

De Vitis, Tom. *Society of Mass Media/Virtual Communities* (blog). Accessed January 12, 2013. http://sociologymassmedia.blogspot.com/.

"Fullerton Island." Second Life. Accessed January 12, 2013. http://slurl.com/secondlife/CSU%20Fullerton/146/156/25.

Gothly, Darrius. (September 6, 2012). "Today Marks the End of Second Life." Accessed January 12, 2013. http://www.dgp4sl.com/wp/2012/09/today-marks-the-end-of-second-life/.

Harlow, Summer. (October 15, 2010). "Using Second Life to Teach Real-World Journalists in a Virtual World." Accessed January 12, 2013. http://knightcenter.utexas.edu/blog/using-second-life-teach-real-world-journalists-virtual-world.

Knight Center. "Knight Center Tests the Use of Second Life in Journalism Training." Accessed January 12, 2013. http://knightcenter.utexas.edu/knight-center-tests-use-second-life-journalism-training.

Kuhr, Peggy. "Virtual Worlds, Technology and Community." Accessed January 12, 2013. http://www.coveringcommunities.org/training/VirtualCommunities.html.

Laranjeiro, Catarina. "Being Journalist in Second Life." Accessed January 12, 2013. http://vimeo.com/40037514.

Lester, Paul Martin, and Cynthia King. (2009). "Analog vs. Digital Instruction and Learning: Teaching within First and Second Life Environments." *Journal of Computer-Mediated Communication*, 457–483.

Open Cobalt Virtual Workspace. Accessed January 12, 2013. http://www.opencobalt.org/.

Rheingold, Howard. (2012). *Net Smart: How to Thrive Online.* Boston: The MIT Press.

———. (1994). *The Virtual Community Homesteading on the Electronic Frontier.* New York: Harper-Collins.

Small Worlds. Accessed January 12, 2013. http://www.smallworlds.com/login.php?login=true.

Smeet. Accessed January 12, 2013. http://en.smeet.com/virtualworld.

Stephenson, Neal. (2000). *Snow Crash.* New York: Spectra.

Tenore, Mallary Jean. (March 3, 2011). "Virtual Communities Spark Coverage Ideas as Primary Season Ends." Accessed January 12, 2013. http://www.poynter.org/latest-news/top-stories/89264/virtual-communities-spark-coverage-ideas-as-primary-season-ends/.

Twinity. Accessed January 12, 2013. http://www.twinity.com/en/choose-your-free-avatar.

Van Dijk, Jan A. G. M. "The Reality of Virtual Communities." Accessed January 12, 2013. https://
docs.google.com/viewer?a=v&q=cache:c4XMmP37enQJ:www.utwente.nl/gw/vandijk/
publications/the_reality_of_virtual_communi.pdf+&hl=en&gl=us&pid=bl&srcid=ADGEES
gYClkSyRT5CX6lXaEsZmovAH6zAOo7KXMqbCuL2GbTatcv9MfcP07gAzkTM1CcL4CS
DwK3gMZbFJ9ja_3BY4EH40O_J1g8rr3bHmYx6Zxv__rGD1Z_rSL7Wp2qzXswJjSuS7fa
&sig=AHIEtbRwLFxaviMyuQHHTqOWjaUwDGIkOQ.
"Virtual Worlds." Accessed January 12, 2013. http://eme6409.wikispaces.com/Virtual+Worlds.
Young, Jeffrey R. (February 14, 2010). "After Frustrations in Second Life, Colleges Look to New
Virtual Worlds." *The Chronicle of Higher Education.* Accessed January 12, 2013. http://chronicle.
com/article/After-Frustrations-in-Second/64137/.

7 VIRTUAL REALITY

It's thirty minutes before Dr. Mark Premack's advanced visual reporting class. Premack, a tenured professor at a California liberal-arts commuter school with about 45,000 students, walks into the area that contains virtual reality workstations. His students have been waiting for him.

Called a VR-3000 by the manufacturer, virtual reality technology has revolutionized the way students and professionals produce images for advertising and commercial purposes. Funding for this workstation, and the 11 in the multipurpose room shared by advertising, entertainment, journalism, public relations, RTVF, and photography classes, came from lottery money designated for education purposes plus grants from the manufacturer and software producers.

Premack's students can work with others on a newspaper simulation; work in the studio with the VR-3000 to create food, fashion or editorial illustrations; or take the role of a photographer in a number of different situations and assignments. For example, there is a lesson that teaches sports photojournalism based on Super Bowl LXXV, where a dramatic come-from-behind win gave the Dallas Cowboys football team their third Super Bowl win in a row. There is a lesson on shooting a rock concert which most students like because they enjoy the loud music; a lesson that takes students to a remote area of Alaska to complete a picture story on Native American fishing; and the lesson Premack selects for today's class, the R. Budd Dwyer press conference and suicide. Although the event happened several decades ago, Premack thinks it is an excellent example of a general news assignment, a press conference that suddenly turned into a horrifying assignment. It teaches photojournalism students that they must be prepared for any type of eventuality. Since the students are learning about spot news coverage, this is an excellent lesson choice. He takes it off the shelf, locks the cabinet, and downloads the program into his VR-3000 player.

All of his students walk onto the press conference scene as if it were a set in a stage play. Dwyer is in the middle of a long, rambling speech at the front of the room behind a podium with several microphones attached to it. The room is crowded with reporters and photographers so his students, to get any good pictures, must weave their way between the computer-generated figures. All of the students have digital cameras around their necks and shoulder bags that contain an assortment of lenses supplied by the computer program. Any pictures they take are saved by the program for later retrieval.

[To read the full fictional account of virtual reality as a teaching tool, see the Appendix.]

Figure 7.1 This 1905 newsprint copy shows the entrance of the movie theater known as "Hale's Tours" operated by the Hungarian Adolph Zukor in New York City. In 1912, Zukor began his Famous Players Film Company that later became Paramount Pictures. *Courtesy of the Library of Congress*

Artists became inspired to experiment with techniques to create virtual worlds because of an amateur filmmaker and promoter. Since the invention of motion pictures for audience viewing in 1895, the concept of what is considered a "theater" has been stretched, reworked, discarded, and reinvented. In 1905, the fire chief of Kansas City, George Hale, constructed theaters that looked like train cars (Figure 7.1). As a short film of the front of a locomotive was projected on a front screen, as many as 72 "passengers" were jostled, heard the sound of whistles and wheels on tracks, and felt wind on their faces. In two years, this realistic effect named "Hale's Tours" was so popular there were about 500 train car movie houses throughout the world. However, by 1911, the fad had faded.

Years later as military flight simulators were seen as useful training exercisers, immersive effects caught the interest of computer scientists. As mentioned earlier, the American programmer and philosopher Jaron Lanier is credited with creating the phrase "virtual reality" (VR). In 1985, he teamed with Thomas Zimmerman, who had invented the data glove when he worked for the Atari video game company, to start VPL Research, Inc. The two sold goggles and gloves for use with VR systems. In 1987, the popularity of immersive virtual effects was begun with the debut of the "Star Tours" motion simulator ride at Disneyland and the first reference of the "holodeck" in the television pilot episode of "Star Trek: The Next Generation." In 1992, the first motion picture to feature virtual reality as a major plot device was the low-rated *The Lawnmower Man,* in which two characters engaged in virtual reality sex. Two years later, an episode of the popular situation comedy "Mad About You" starring Paul Reiser and Helen Hunt was titled "Virtual Reality." It featured Reiser using an advanced VR system in which he engages romantically with the model/actress Christie Brinkley. Are you cheating on your spouse if your sexual partner isn't real?

The era of the virtual reality experience had begun in which viewers could actively or passively enjoy the effect. The public's interest perhaps culminated with Universal Studios' "King Kong 360 3D" motion ride based on creatures from director Peter Jackson's motion picture. As one rider enthusiastically said, "You're really in it."

Figure 7.2 Users who wear virtual reality headgear witness a man who collapses while waiting for a food handout in Nonny de la Peña's "Hunger in Los Angeles." *Courtesy of Nonny de la Peña*

The key with virtual reality as a digital innovation for mass communications is to make the user feel she is "really in it" no matter what story is being told. For example, Nonny de la Peña, a former reporter for *Newsweek* magazine, created a virtual reality simulation based on actual eyewitness accounts titled "Hunger in Los Angeles." The program re-creates a medical incident in a food bank line at the First Unitarian Church in Los Angeles. Her example of immersive journalism debuted at the prestigious Sundance Film Festival in 2012. The work was praised because a user is made to care more about issues homeless persons experience by the virtual reality quality of the simulation (Figure 7.2).

Imagine this type of display used to sell a client on a new advertising campaign, to entice a donor to contribute to a cause that needs publicity, or to interest a viewer in seeing a movie, and the benefits of VR technologies become clear.

■ CHALLENGES, CRITIQUES, AND AMUSEMENTS

- This chapter begins (and concludes in the Appendix) with a fictional story concerned with virtual reality in the classroom. What is your imagined future of VR for education and your chosen profession?
- Jaron Lanier. You really should explore his mind through his work and interviews. Go to iTunes and find Philip Blackburn's free podcast, "New Music, New Thoughts: Measure for Measure." Download the interview with Lanier titled, "Soulful Music for the Future." What do you think of the discussion related to nondigital versus digital musical instruments? If you have further interest, you can buy his latest book, *You Are Not a Gadget* and his album, "Proof of Consciousness," or a song from the album to get an idea of his interest in music, "The Upper Atmosphere" or "Gallup."
- How practical would it be to create a VR program for a news event or for commercials? Do you think first- and third-person video games offer clues to what is possible?
- Why are VR examples in the media so much more advanced than in real life? Do they help to inspire new technology or make us frustrated?
- Go to an arcade, amusement park, and science museum and ride a VR attraction in each venue. What did you learn from each one? How are they different?

■ EXERCISES

Let's get real.

Even one virtual reality workstation as described in the science fiction story at the start of this chapter would cost tens of thousands of dollars. For example, a good quality head-mounted display with a head tracking system runs at least $2,000, software for 3D/VR presentations is about $5,000, an upright simulator costs $10,500, one data glove is $900 (not to mention a whole body suit), and the salaries for computer programmers, VR experts, filmmakers, actors, animators, caterers, cameras, set and prop rentals, and other charges are at least twice the cost of the technology combined.

Construction of Nonny de la Peña's virtual world project "Hunger in Los Angeles" was a collaboration developed by individuals at MxR Lab, an entity established by the USC's Institute for Creative Technologies and the School of Cinematic Arts with additional support from the deep pockets of the Annenberg School of Communications and Journalism. The headsets included motion tracking technology and software so users could have the illusion of moving through virtual space and interacting with other participants (Figure 7.3). Expensive software came from the game development company Unity 3D.

In other words, unless you have an unlimited budget, enthusiastic and knowledgeable programmers, and at least a year from the initial concept to the finished project, it is difficult to independently construct a virtual reality program.

So, what should you do as a meaningful exercise for this chapter?

If you are particularly ambitious or have already established a base on the popular gaming site Minecraft, introduced as a full release to the public in 2011 by Swedish computer programmer Markus "Notch" Persson, you can use the tools and building blocks to create a world related to your mass communications interest. More than nine million persons have bought the game that can be played on smartphones, tablets, computers, and

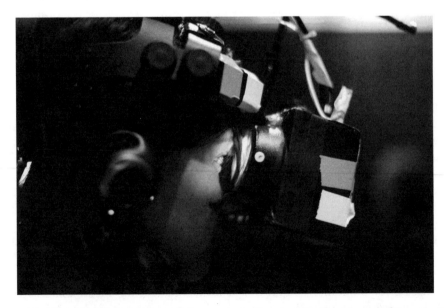

Figure 7.3 With headphones to hear audio, a user during the New Frontiers exhibit at the 2012 Sundance Film Festival stares at the images contained within the dual-screen head mounted display to experience Nonny de la Peña's "Hunger in Los Angeles." *Courtesy of Devaki Ananda Murch*

Figure 7.4 An elaborate, security-minded fortress created by a skilled artist can be found in the Strategic Medieval Minecraft Town, Altsen-Upon-Brine within the virtual reality game of Minecraft. *Courtesy of Jelle Wieggers*

television viewing systems. Of the three game playing options, I would suggest you try the creative mode. In the other two modes—survival and adventure—you may wind up dead. There is an educational version of the game called MinecraftEdu that teachers have used to teach fundamental lessons in anthropology, chemistry, and so on, but its usefulness is limited. The removing of brush and other obstacles and the selection of various building stones can be a bit daunting and time consuming (Figure 7.4). By all means, if you are curious, try it and let me know if it works for you. However, I think we should stick with what we know.

The virtual online community Second Life (SL), that you should be familiar with by now, has a feature that simulates VR. As long as you are not in chat mode, when you press the "M" key (the "M" is for Mouselook), you see the world through your avatar's eyes. To return to the hovering viewpoint and to chat with someone, simply press the Escape key.

Start up Second Life and keep your eyes open as we tour some locations that are particularly known for their realistic settings.

Grove Marketing is a real-life firm located in Concord, Massachusetts <http://maps.secondlife.com/secondlife/Dachstein/29/205/90>. The reason for a Second Life presence is explained on its website: "Grove has been experimenting with SL for a couple of years now, and has found ways to leverage it successfully for some of our clients. For those new to it, SL may seem strange, but we're finding innovative ways to use it to our clients' benefit."

For those interested in advertising, entertainment studies, film, and public relations, the SL cabin-in-the-words location of the Grove has an attractive main building with client work on display and comfortable chairs for meeting and chatting with others (Figure 7.5). Explore the well-manicured grounds, and you will find a stage ready for speakers and singers (Figure 7.6). Walk or fly behind the stage area, and you will discover a Japanese village that might be suitable as a backdrop for a film (Figure 7.7).

The well-rendered cityscape that is a part of SLebrity City <http://maps.secondlife.com/secondlife/North%20Genesis%20County/166/69/173> with its downtown streets,

Figure 7.5 You are always welcome to enter and admire the style of the folks at Grove Marketing on Second Life. *Courtesy of Grove Marketing*

Figure 7.6 Arrange a performance or invite a guest speaker to use this elaborate staging area.

storefronts, and looming skyline is an excellent location for shooting a movie (Figure 7.8). Also, the re-creation of New York's Harlem district with its famous Apollo Theater <http://maps.secondlife.com/secondlife/Virtual%20Harlem/180/163/30> and Cotton Club is a good choice for a film scene (Figure 7.9).

For journalists with or without cameras, there is no better place to people watch and to find interview subjects than a busy international airport. The Bay City Municipal Aeroport <http://maps.secondlife.com/secondlife/Hau%20Koda/80/58/26> is no exception (Figure 7.10).

Figure 7.7 Perhaps you are in the mood for sushi? You might find it in this Japanese village or use this village as a background for a film.

Figure 7.8 This view from the eyes of my flying avatar shows a breathtaking vantage point of a city.

Finally, Vassar College's astounding recreation of the Sistine Chapel should not be missed <http://maps.secondlife.com/secondlife/Vassar/112/113/27>. Seen through the eyes of your Second Life avatar, the 16th-century ceiling painting by Michelangelo is a virtual reality treasure that quite possibly saves you a trip to Vatican City (Figure 7.11).

I bet you thought all of the above was the exercise. Wrong. Were any of the SL links mentioned above part of a numbered list? Here we go.

For this chapter, you will make a short film composed of about 10 shots that runs for less than a minute and is completely shot in Second Life with a subjective point of view (POV).

Figure 7.9 Walk the streets of Harlem and take a seat inside the historic Apollo Theater where you might get your picture taken by the paparazzi, get a glimpse of trumpeter Louis Armstrong, and hear Ella Fitzgerald sing.

Figure 7.10 Don't be shy and hide behind a baggage cart at the Bay City Municipal Aeroport, go over and introduce yourself. Although Second Life avatars look a bit intimidating, they almost always are socially awkward individuals eager to chat. Nevertheless, if dinner is offered, it is best to avoid the fried catfish.

Rick Connors has a brief video you should watch that explains subjective POV <http:// vimeo.com/11206669>. This camera technique is simply the virtual reality simulation technique that has been discussed previously—a film that tells a story from the main character's POV.

Figure 7.11 You might experience dizziness as your avatar looks straight up to see Michelangelo's "The Creation of Adam," the masterpiece in the center.

Another example of a POV film that you absolutely must watch is a 10-episode tale from filmmaker Douglas Gayeton, *Molotov Alva and his Search for the Creator: A Second Life Odyssey* <http://molotovalva.submarinechannel.com/>. At least view the first episode.

This exercise is a bit complicated, so try to be patient. As a disclaimer, you should know that I am a Mac user. Many, but not all of the software products and instructions are necessarily Mac-centric. However, most of the time, you can get PC equivalents, if that is your preference. If you are a student, your computer labs are probably equipped with these basic digital innovative tools in Mac and PC versions.

In addition to a Second Life account, you will need a screen capture program for video, a video presentation program, and movie editing software. You will also need a computer that records audio. These instructions are based on iShowU that costs $20 from Shiny White Box <http://shinywhitebox.com/> and QuickTime<http://www.apple.com/quicktime/> and iMovie that come with Apple computers.

For a set of instructions for PC users, the SL Wiki has a useful how-to: <http://wiki.secondlife.com/wiki/Making_movies>. Admittedly, this exercise could be accomplished with still screen saves that any computer could take.

1. The first step in making a video is to write a script. Since you will use voice-over narration recorded by your computer's microphone, each shot of your film needs to have a sentence or two that corresponds with each image. When combined with other shots and audio, they tell a story. If your interests are in advertising, your film should try to sell a product or service. For entertainment, your film is about the people and sights at some exotic locale—not too difficult to find on SL. For journalism, discover a Second Life area devoted to a serious subject or social problem such as the Breast Cancer Awareness Center <http://maps.secondlife.com/

secondlife/TriBorough%20New%20York/114/68/23> and report on the topic.
For public relations, make a public service announcement related to a good cause,
event, or organization. On the other hand, if you want to make an indie film,
you're welcomed to use "How I Learned to Drive" by Paul Bibbo:
I always felt as if I were the outsider.
Alone among imposing forces.
A higher perspective didn't help.
But getting closer, I sensed direction.
I found myself at the water's edge.
I made some new friends.
They taught me how to drive.

2. You need to set your computer display to approximate the video's resolution.
Within the Apple logo at the top of your desktop, select Systems Preferences,
select Displays, check the Scaled button, and then select "960 x 600." Click OK
(Figure 7.12). Don't worry about the warning message. The work on your screen
will appear much larger.

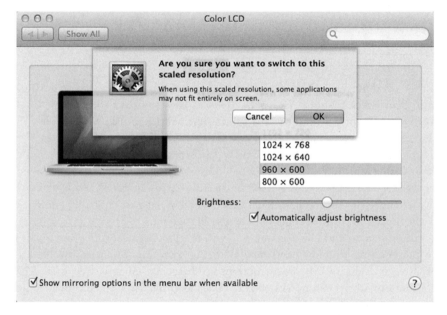

Figure 7.12 The screen resolution on your computer's display must be changed to accurately
render the movie within the frame.

3. For recording video, download a trial or $20 version of iShowU from <http://
shinywhitebox.com/>. Start up the program. You may need to minimize the
window (the green circle at the top) to see all the settings. In the window, select
"YouTube (640x480)" on the left side. On the right side, check the "Record microphone audio" box, select the Audio quality as "AAC 44.1k, 256kbps," select
the Microphone Input as "Built-in Microphone," set the Microphone monitor
as "Off," set the Normal frame rate at "20," set the Scale at "100%," set the
Compression at "H.264," set the Mouse recording at "With each frame as it is
captured," set the Mouse clicks and Rights clicks at "None," set the Countdown

at "0," and check the "Show capture guide when recording" just like the picture below (Figure 7.13).

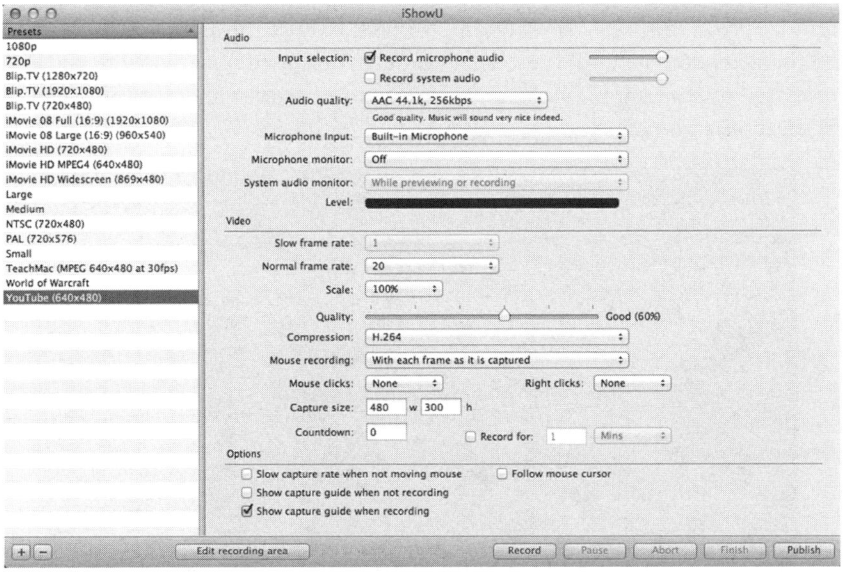

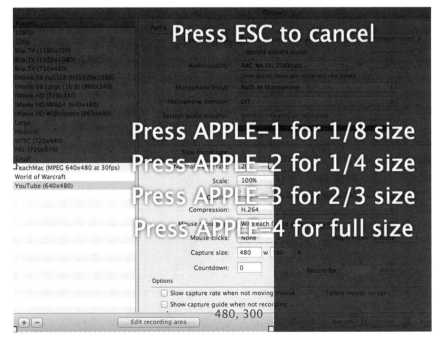

Figure 7.13 The iShowU preference dialog box.

4. Click the "Edit recording area" button at the bottom and the Apple and the number "2" keys together to see the recording area window. Click and drag the window to the lower left corner of your desktop (Figure 7.14). With a pencil, lightly mark the left and top of the sides of your monitor to remember the limits of the frame. Press the Enter key to set the frame's size and location.

Press ESC to cancel

Press APPLE–1 for 1/8 size
Press APPLE–2 for 1/4 size
Press APPLE–3 for 2/3 size
Press APPLE–4 for full size

Figure 7.14 Depending on your choice of frame, a window will reflect its size.

5. Now you need to go to Second Life for your first shot. If you are using your avatar or someone else's, you can zoom in or out if you press the Option key and the up or down arrows on your keyboard. You can also move the viewpoint to the left or right by pressing those corresponding arrows. Adjust the arrows to get the view of the character you want. Then, click and drag the entire SL window to the lower left corner so that the frame is full, inside your pencil marks, and does not show any of the SL tools and menu choices (Figure 7.15).

Figure 7.15 Click and drag the entire Second Life desktop to position the framing of your shot without showing tools or menu choices.

6. Return to the iShowU settings window. Press the Record button and click back onto to Second Life. You are now recording video and audio, but you can edit out the starting and ending portions of the shot. The iShowU software shows a thin line that represents the frame. To be more precise with the shot, move your SL window to fit what you want inside the rectangle (Figure 7.16).

Figure 7.16 Fine tune the frame of your shot within the thin black line.

7. Start the shot. Keep it short—about five seconds or so. Have your character move, zoom in and out if you like, or make a steady, static shot. When you are ready, speak any voice-over copy. When you are done, return to iShowU and click the Finish button. A QuickTime window of your film will pop on the screen (Figure 7.17).

Figure 7.17 In QuickTime you will edit the starting and ending points of your clip.

8. Now you are ready to edit your shot. In QuickTime, press the Apple and T keys or from the Edit menu select Trim. . . . a yellow cropping frame will show. Click and drag the left and right edges of the yellow sliding bars to crop the beginning and ending segments of your clip (Figure 7.18). Press the Space Bar to play and pause the clip and then move the left or right yellow bars to crop the clip precisely. When you have it the way you want, click the Trim button to crop your clip. Click and drag the small diamond icon at the bottom to the left to start your clip from the beginning. If it needs more cropping, simply select Trim again. If you have cropped too much, press the Cancel button and start over.

Figure 7.18 Use the yellow sliding bars to crop your clip.

9. When you are happy with your cropping (or trimming), from the File menu, select Export . . . . Within the Export As: window, type the file name as SL_Part1.mov. The Format should be Movie (Figure 7.19). Press the New Folder button, type "SL Movie," and press the Create button. Then, press the Export button to save your clip within the new folder on your desktop.

Figure 7.19 Export the edited movie clips within your "SL Movie" folder.

10. From the File menu, select Close (or press the Apple and W keys or the red button at the top left of the clip). Press the Don't Save button. You want to keep the original, unedited clip in case you change your mind about your edits.

11. Repeat this process for all the other clips you make for your movie. For Paul Bibbo's poem "How I Learned to Drive" from Step 1, there will be seven clips in total (Figure 7.20).

Figure 7.20 The seven clips for "How I Learned to Drive" should be named sequentially.

Now you are ready to combine all of your clips into a movie, add a title and ending credits, and upload the film to YouTube and save it on your computer.

12. Open the iMovie application. From the File menu, select New Project . . . (or press the Apple and N keys). In the Project Themes window, select "No Themes." In the right side, name your project "SL Movie," select an Aspect Ratio of "Standard (4:3), select a Frame Rate of "24 fps—Cinema," check the Automatically add box and select "Cross Dissolve," and press the Create button (Figure 7.21).

Figure 7.21 Within iMovie, select the theme, size, and automatic features for your film.

13. From the File menu, select Import and then Movies . . .. Open the folder "SL Movie," select all the clips that you edited earlier, click the Create new Event button and type "SL Movie," check the Optimize video box and select "Full—Original Size," click the Copy files button, and finally click the Import button (Figure 7.22). Your movie now gets processed by the program and will create small thumbnail versions of your clips within the iMovie desktop (Figure 7.23).

Figure 7.22 Create a new movie event and import your clips in this iMovie dialog box. Make sure all of your clips are selected.

Figure 7.23 The iMovie desktop shows your imported clips in the bottom window.

14. Click your mouse on a blank part of the clip window, and from the Edit menu choose Select All (or press the Apple and A keys) to highlight all of your movie clips you imported (Figure 7.24).

Figure 7.24 Make sure all of your imported clips are selected.

15. With all of your clips selected, click the first one and drag the mouse into the Project Window at the top left. Ignore the "Editing Tip" and press Continue. All of your clips should show in the window. Notice the facing triangle icons between the clips. These represent the cross dissolves between them that were set automatically. Press the Play icon at the bottom left of the Project Window to watch your movie (Figure 7.25).

Figure 7.25 Your iMovie desktop now has your clips linked as a film.

16. You need to type the title and ending credit frames. Click the Text icon at the middle right of the iMovie desktop. Click and drag the "Centered" choice to the beginning of your film before the first cross dissolve icon. Click Black as your background choice (Figure 7.26).

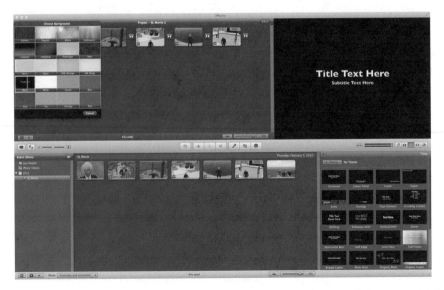

Figure 7.26 Once you learn how to make movies, you can make any choices you think are appropriate for your film.

17. Within the text window at the right, highlight the generic copy and type your own title "How I Learned to Drive" and the subtitle "A Second Life Motion Picture" and press the Done button. Repeat the process for the ending credits except drag the Centered choice with a black background to the end of your movie. Type the title "How I Learned to Drive" and the subtitle "By Your Name Here Based on a photographic essay by Paul Bibbo" and press the Done button (Figure 7.27).

Figure 7.27 Click and drag the generic copy to replace it with your words.

18. Press the play icon to watch the entire movie. If you are happy with it, from the Share menu select YouTube . . .. If you are logged in to YouTube, your Account Name should show in the dialog box. If needed, type in your Password. In Category select "Education," select Title, type "SL Movie," write a description (you can include tags or keywords if you wish), click the Medium size choice if needed, and uncheck the Make this movie personal box. Press the Next button (Figure 7.28).

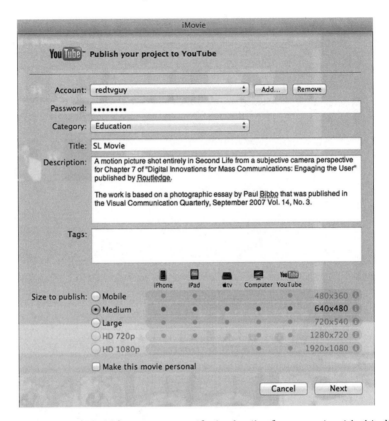

Figure 7.28 Within your YouTube account, specify the details of your movie with this dialog box.

19. The next YouTube window is part of the terms of service for the program. Make sure you only upload your original work. Press the Publish button. You will receive an upload message in which you can "Tell a Friend" or "View" your movie. If not, press the OK button (Figure 7.29).

Figure 7.29 Press the OK button, and in a short time your movie will be added to the vast YouTube collection. Look at it through your personal account. Here is a link to see my humble effort: <http://youtu.be/EeEt5QFLrYo>. I should have used a professional actor's voice.

20. Finally, save your movie on your computer. From the Share menu, select Export using QuickTime . . .. Give your movie a name and press the Save button. You may now quit all of your open programs, put your computer to sleep, and take your dog for a long walk because he has been bugging you to go outside for almost an hour.

Sources

Bibbo, Paul. (September, 2007). "How I Learned to Drive." *Visual Communication Quarterly,* 14, no. 3, 197–204.

Fielding, Raymond. (1970). "Hale's Tours: Ultrarealism in the Pre-1910 Motion Picture." *Cinema Journal,* 10, no. 1. Accessed January 12, 2013. http://www.jstor.org/discover/10.2307/1224994 ?uid=3739560&uid=2129&uid=2&uid=70&uid=4&uid=3739256&sid=21101378983241.

Grove. "A Virtual World. Real Possibilities." Accessed February 5, 2013. http://www.grove-marketing.com/secondlife/.

Head Mounted Displays. Virtual Realities. Accessed February 4, 2013. http://www.vrealities.com/hmd.html.

Immersive Journalism. Accessed January 12, 2013. http://www.immersivejournalism.com/?page_id=2.

Lawnmower Man, The. Internet Movie Database. Accessed January 30, 2013. http://www.imdb.com/title/tt0104692/?ref_=sr_1.

Mashable. "Virtual Reality Journalism Immerses Users in a Public Crisis." Accessed January 12, 2013. http://mashable.com/2012/01/31/virtual-reality-journalism/.

Minecraft. Accessed February 5, 2013. https://minecraft.net/.

Movie Movie. "May 1904: Hales Touring Cars." Accessed January 12, 2013. http://www.moviemoviesite.com/Years/1900–1910/1904%20Articles/hales_touring_cars.htm.

"Nonny de la Peña." Accessed January 30, 2013. http://www.nonnydlp.com/.

Wikipedia contributors. R. Budd Dwyer. *Wikipedia, The Free Encyclopedia.* Accessed January 12, 2013. http://en.wikipedia.org/wiki/R._Budd_Dwyer.

Sundance Film Festival. "Hunger in Los Angeles." Accessed January 12, 2013. http://www.sundance.org/festival/film-events/hunger-in-los-angeles/.

Unity 3D. Accessed January 12, 2013. http://unity3d.com/.

"Virtual Reality." Internet Movie Database. Accessed January 30, 2013. http://www.imdb.com/title/tt0638993/.

"VR Cybersex on Mad About You." Critical Commons. Accessed January 31, 2013. http://www.criticalcommons.org/Members/ccManager/clips/madaboutyouvrchristiebrinkley.mp4/view?searchterm=technocinema.

Waxman, Olivia B. (September 21, 2012). "MinecraftEdu Teaches Students Through Virtual World-Building." *Time Tech.* Accessed February 5, 2013. http://techland.time.com/2012/09/21/minecraftedu-teaches-students-through-virtual-world-building/.

Section III

DATABASE-GENERATED CONTENT

Whether you read a book, a magazine or newspaper article, watch a movie or a television show, click through links on a webpage, or study a promotional pitch, you will become more engaged with the content if it is made more relevant for you. The three chapters in this section use database collections to bring the outside world a little closer.

Suggestive Innovations

Just as with a knowledgeable and observant waiter or store clerk who suggests menu items and products that might suit your specific tastes, book, movie, and online product advertisers, and websites can determine a customer's future choices through past selections. "Amazoning the News," based on a feature of the popular online store, is an experimental program that performs the same function within a journalism context.

Personalization

After a natural disaster occurs in a part of the world thousands of miles from someone's residence, understanding the extent of the tragedy is sometimes difficult. For example, after the 2012 devastation of beaches and homes in New Jersey and New York by Superstorm Sandy, news consumers can be made to care after comparisons between their local communities and the stricken landmasses are displayed. Likewise, empathy can be fostered for any topic—universal health care, immigration, or economics—if database content is employed that moves interest from the large-scale to the individual level.

Mapping

To determine trends within complex stories, computer databases are used to automatically include contextual information to presentations. Examples include crime statistical data and political spending trends. Computer developers and artists have also collaborated to produce informational graphic mash-ups that reveal surprising connections between seemingly unrelated topics.

8   SUGGESTIVE INNOVATIONS

Recommended for You.

Who among us can resist suggestions from someone who seems to know us so well? Take for example:

Books: Based on my recent browsing and buying habits having to do with recommender systems (for this chapter), semiotic signs, and photography, the suggestive program for the online retail giant Amazon thought I might be interested in *Python for Data Analysis* by Wes McKinney, *Data Mining* by Ian Witten, *I Could Tell You But Then You Would Have to Be Destroyed By Me* by Trevor Paglen, *Daring to Look* by Anne Whiston Spirn, and *The History of Photography* by Beaumont Newhall.

Movies: The same is true for Netflix. Because I watched Life During Wartime, a quirky tale of love and hope from director Todd Solondz, the on-demand retailer suggests the movies *The Future, Margot at the Wedding, Me and You and Everyone We Know, What Happened Was. . ., Gainsbourg, Rid of Me,* and *Hello Lonesome,* all relatively obscure indie favorites.

Music: If you type "The xx" within Live Plasma's search window, you get an array of bubbles of various sizes in pastel pink, blue, and green hues with direct links to musical groups of similar styles that include Angus & Julia Stone, Kings of Leon, The Whitest Boy Alive, The Temper Trap, Foals, and Bloc Party. Secondary bubbles feature Bon Iver, Band of Horses, The Postal Service, Vampire Weekend, and Bombay Bicycle Club.

Dating: After you sign up for the free online dating service OKCupid, your search for a companion for the evening or a lifetime soulmate begins with your answers to a series of questions about yourself: Is sex or true love more important, do you smoke, do you like normal or weird, would you date a messy person, would you sleep with someone on the first date, how important is religion and politics, would you date someone with a different skin color, and so on. These questions are paired with what you would accept in another and combined with a rating scale from irrelevant to mandatory. Creators of the program say it takes 100 questions to find a match that is 99.9% right for you (Since I am most happily married, please forgive that I didn't find out who might be my match).

Executives for some of the most popular websites understand this basic and simple human principle:

We tend to like what is similar to what we've liked before.

This principle is actually one that has been around a long time and is rooted in gestalt psychology. Initiated by German Max Wertheimer through research he and others performed while at the University of Frankfurt, it was concluded that the mind likes to organize sensual input into coherent, comfortable, and known entities. The word gestalt comes from the German noun that means form. Our worldview is formed by the arrangement of information we receive through our senses.

Gestalt psychologists further refined the initial work by Wertheimer to conclude that visual perception is a result of organizing sensory elements or forms into various groups. Discrete elements within a scene are combined and understood by the brain through a series of five fundamental principles of grouping that are often called laws. We tend to organize visual elements and verbal concepts because of:

Similarity: Objects and ideas are grouped together that seem alike,
Proximity: Items that are physically near to each other are linked,
Continuation: We like elements that seem linked together, and
Common Fate: Ideas are appreciated when they come to the same conclusion.

Finally, a fifth law of gestalt is most appropriate to this discussion—past experience. Just as misspelled words are sometimes missed when you're editing a paper, familiarity with the whole word can lead us to overlook individual letters. The gestalt law of past experience explains why website producers can successfully predict our future choices based on our previous selections.

The field known as recommender systems attempts to predict user behavior through two methods known as collaborative and content-based (also known as passive, semantic, or social) filtering. With collaborative filtering, a user's previous selections are combined with ratings provided by the consumer. These choices are compared with other customers in order to build a predictable model. An example of a content-based system is the Pandora music website. After an initial choice from a user, Pandora presents songs with similar characteristics.

Joseph A. Konstan and John Riedl, professors of computer science at the University of Minnesota wrote that the recommender system field began in the mid-1990s with just a handful of interested individuals and has now expanded to dozens of research firms and university programs. The two professors note that recommender systems have usefulness for other noncommercial entities. Guidance counselors for universities can employ them to help students find courses and majors while editors can use them to match journal articles with reviewers. Konstan and Riedl use Amazon as an example:

> For example, consider the recommender used for Amazon's online art store, which at last count had more than nine million prints and posters for sale. Amazon's art store assesses your preferences in a few ways. It asks you to rate particular artworks on a five-star scale, and it also notes which paintings you enlarge, which you look at multiple times, which you place on a wish list, and which you actually buy. It also tracks which paintings are on your screen at the time as well as others you look at during your session. The retailer uses the path you've traveled through its website—the pages you've viewed and items you've clicked on—to suggest complementary works, and it combines your purchase data with your ratings to build a profile of your long-term preferences.

As might be suspected, predicting behavior based on past options can be a lucrative aspect of a retail establishment such as Amazon, Netflix, and OKCupid as well as a convenient feature for other website content providers (Figure 8.1). In a *Los Angeles Times* article it was noted, "Analysts say Netflix's recommendation engine is a critical reason the 15-year company has become a powerhouse in home entertainment."

The web portal Yahoo! has an option that aids in customizing the news. From news. yahoo.com, click on "My Y!" (Does everyone who works for that company shout all the time?) and you will get to its "News For You" feature. Thirty current headlines representing stories from national to celebrity news are listed, and you rate each one with a simple thumb up or down icon click.

The search engine Google from its news.google.com website shows two sets of sliders on its "Personalize Google News" page. One set displays eight categories—World, US, Business, Technology, Entertainment, Sports, Science, and Health—plus those you add yourself. You have the choice of eliminating the category to always showing it on your Google news page. The other set shows the sources: *The New York Times*, *Fox News*, CNN, and ESPN with slide arrows that a user can set from never to often. Oddly, however, most newspaper websites do not use recommender systems of any kind. An exception is *The New York Times*. Registered users are shown personalized recommendations based on stories read.

An innovative way of thinking about news presentations within a suggestive, user-generated context is what Ellen Kampinsky, Shayne Bowman, and Chris Willis called "Amazoning the News." The three showed how "traditional news stories might be treated through a design model of Amazon. We contend that a successful news website is a platform that supports social interaction around the story. These interactions are as important as the narrative, perhaps more, because they are chosen by the readers." A news website designed as a popular bookstore might include "guide and direct presentations, reader rankings of stories, reader comments as a part of coverage, links to similar stories, and reader questions." After graduation, the three started their own Atlanta-based design firm, Hypergene Media Solutions, with Radio Shack, American Airlines, and Lockheed Martin among their many clients (Figure 8.2).

Figure 8.1 No books are in sight in this scene in which adults and children select an offering from the on-demand Internet streaming and disc mailing media provider Netflix. However, through its surveys and previous viewing habits, suggestions for the night's entertainment might not be appropriate for young eyes. *Courtesy of Netflix*

Figure 8.2 A sports story in the style of an Amazon page includes the average time it takes to read it, the number of readers who accessed it, and the location of the most interested users. In addition, suggestions for other sports and news stories are included. Could this format be the future for online news services? *Courtesy of Hypergene Media Solutions*

Frédéric Filloux, the general manager for digital operations for the French firm Les Echos Groupe advocates that newswebs employ as soon as possible content-based filtering systems that present stories that have personal interest for a user. Filloux urges publishers to "invest money in a real recommendation engine, tag-based, social, or even semantic filtering. Readers will stay longer on your site, increasing the value of their visits." He also scoffs at tedious long lists of survey questions required by some websites (as with the 100 questions offered by OKCupid), "No one will spend fifteen minutes stating his/her centers of interest by filling a form or checking 20 boxes of news-related preference. Passive Filtering accumulates information from my previous browsing sessions. My navigation patterns draw a profile of my news interest that can be matched with other users, further enhancing the system. The older and thicker my history is, the better the engine will perform."

Another suggestive method involves television viewers. Because it is estimated that 40 percent of those with smartphones or tablets also watch television every day, a promising and increasingly popular technological innovation links television content with these "second screen" devices. Automatic content recognition (ACR) synchronizes the two screens in a seamless way. Charlene Weisler of TV Board explains:

> Imagine that a TV viewer is watching a network while using her iPad, and a commercial airs. ACR recognizes that the ad is on and can then display complementary programming or advertising automatically on the iPad. ACR will also enable programmers to know that their content was consumed on both devices simultaneously, thus potentially facilitating measurement as well as minimizing any audience fragmentation impact.

In addition to advertising purposes, ACR can guide viewers to the Facebook pages and Twitter feeds of entertainment and documentary offerings to find more information and to interact with other interested users.

By knowing your past choices, suggestive systems can predict your future selections and increase your satisfaction with your user experience whether it is for commercial, entertainment, or educational purposes.

■ CHALLENGES, CRITIQUES, AND AMUSEMENTS

- What was the last non-school-related book you bought or movie you watched? If you liked it, did you suggest it to a friend?
- Browse or purchase something from Amazon and check back in a few days. Are any recommendations based on your purchase accurate?
- Get on Live Plasma <http://liveplasma.com> and type in a musical group or performer you enjoy. Did you discover other bubbles of interest?
- Do you use Pandora, Spotify, or some other music player? Do you find new music from those sites or do you use other sources?
- How true is the "like" principle—we tend to like what is similar to what we've liked before—for you?
- Share your good, bad, frustrating, or weird dating experiences made from an online site.
- Check out the definitions for the five gestalt principles of similarity, proximity, continuation, common fate, and past experience. Can you think of any examples in your life in which one or all applied?
- Have you ever used a news recommender website? Why or why not?
- How many items and/or how much time would you spend filling out an online survey?
- Are you a second screener? Do you watch television and get additional information from a tablet?
- Compare top 10 lists on a variety of topics with friends and family members. If possible, try to have a mix of generations and other cultural variables. Are the subjects the same or different from your lists? Why?

■ EXERCISES

Unfortunately, the level of knowledge needed to produce the software coding for an actual working recommender system is well beyond the parameters of this textbook. Even if you could get a program running, in order for any ranking to be credible so the software could offer suggestions, you would need thousands of users as part of a huge database in which they selected their favorite items from the images, products, and stories you have available on a website.

Fortunately, there is an alternative. The website Reddit, a portmanteau of "read it," bills itself as the "Front page of the Internet." Reddit was born in 2005 by two 22-year-old University of Virginia students Steve Huffman and Alexis Ohanian who did their time in the company and left in 2009 to start an online airline and hotel finding website, Hipmunk. In reality, Reddit is simply a bulletin board in which registered users can add links and opinions within more than 60,000 categories (called "subreddits") and make comments about what others have added. The age of the submission, the number of comments received, and whether comments are positive or negative determine whether a post gets a high ranking on the website's main page. It is that feature of Reddit that makes it useful as an exercise for this chapter.

1. Decide on a title, URL, and subreddit for a link you will add to Reddit. I decided to go with the Migrant Mother app that you will learn how to make in Chapter 15.
2. Go to <http://reddit.com> and click on the "register" link at the top right of the page. Fill out the registration form and press the "create account" button (Figure 8.3).

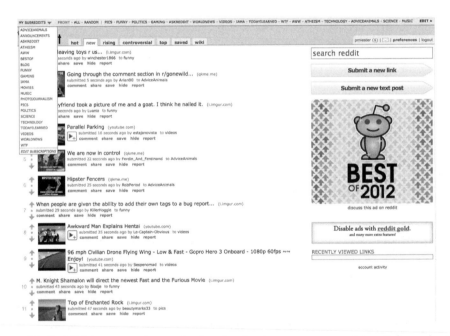

Figure 8.3 Reddit's homepage is an eclectic mix of serious news, entertaining links, and mind-numbing trivia. You can reduce the clutter by selecting the "My Subreddits" pull-down menu at the top, selecting "Edit Subreddits," and unsubscribing to the topics that don't interest you.

To add images to a Reddit post, you must first add pictures to a hosting site. Reddit recommends the free image website Imgur (pronounced "Image-Er," not "I'm Gur" or "I'm Gee, You Are?" which make no sense). However, you should know that Imgur deletes pictures that have not been accessed after six months. It's not the place to store your precious family photos—only those used for Reddit entries.

3. Go to <http://imgur.com>, press the Register link at the top, fill out the form, agree to the rules, and click Register (Figure 8.4).

Figure 8.4 With more than 700,000 pictures uploaded every day, Imgur, seen here in random mode, is a popular place to host images. The social news websites Reddit and Digg both recommend its use.

4. Select "Images" at the top and either the Computer or Web button depending where the picture is located, drag and drop your picture, or Paste it from your clipboard (Figure 8.5).

Figure 8.5 Imgur's simple interface makes it easy to upload pictures and sort them within albums.

5. Click on your uploaded picture and you will see various URLs for different purposes. Copy the first one within the "Link (email & IM)" entry. You will use this URL in Reddit (Figure 8.6).

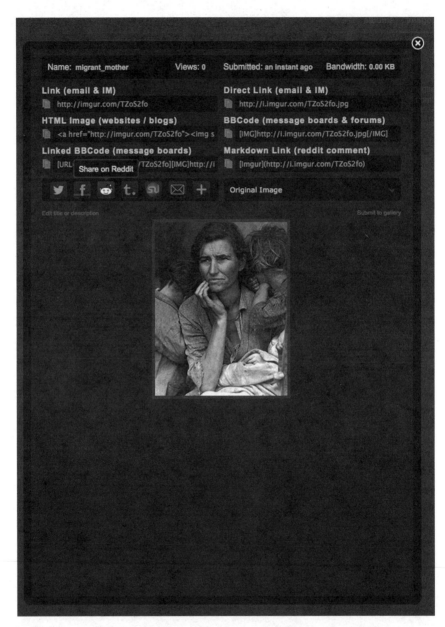

Figure 8.6 All you need from the Imgur interface is the specific URL for the picture you want to use in Reddit.

6. All well and good, however, there is another method for adding images to Reddit. For the Migrant Mother photograph, I want the picture to show up in my post, and then I want interested users to link to a simulation of the app. Consequently, I created a web file in Dreamweaver, added it to my website, and used it as the link in Reddit. As long as the site's homepage only contains the picture, this procedure works fine. It's up to you whether you want to use this method (Figure 8.7).

Figure 8.7 This HTML file as seen in Dreamweaver simply shows a picture named "m_m.jpg" that links to the Migrant Mother app.

7. Back in Reddit, select "Submit a new link" at the right to add content. Make sure the "link" tab is chosen at the top, fill out the form keeping in mind Reddit's rules (click on the links at the bottom), and press Submit (Figure 8.8).

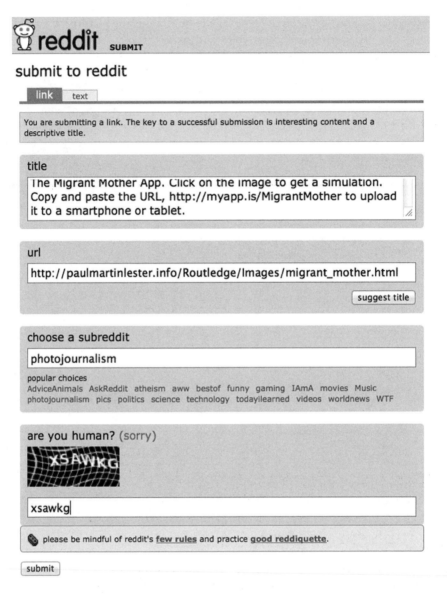

Figure 8.8 Use the title window for more than a few words. You can write a longer description. Within the URL window, I wrote the link from my website, but you could include the URL for your picture from Step 5. Your subreddit must match one of the thousands offered as you type your choice. If it helps, the subreddits that are appropriate for this book include: Advertising, Entertainment, Tourism, Travel, Journalism, PublicRelations (one word), Movies, Television, News, and Photojournalism.

You might consider a Reddit Gold account that you can buy for one month to three years. With Gold, you don't have to see the ads (although they are hardly obtrusive), and you get filtering features to make posts you are most interested in easier to find and perhaps more importantly, access to a members-only lounge where you can chat with others while enjoying your favorite beverage.

8. After a few moments, click the subreddit you chose for your entry to see if your post has been included. If not, sometimes it takes several minutes before one makes it online (Figure 8.9).

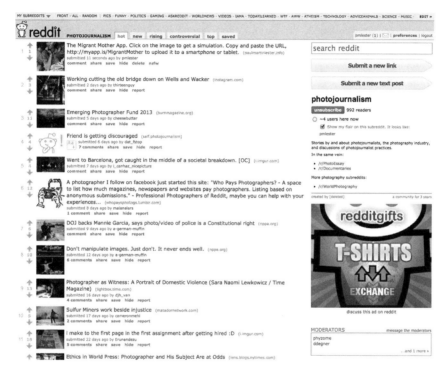

Figure 8.9 At the top of the Photojournalism subreddit is the Migrant Mother App post. However, after 11 seconds, there are no comments. I'm sure your posts will attract more traffic.

9. Now use Reddit to sample opinions about your work—images, stories, ideas, weblinks of interest, and/or opinions. Your blog, newsweb, press release, or website could include a sidebar that shows the number of comments received from Reddit users about the content. Such an addition would add credibility, relevance, and feedback to your message.

Sources

Choate, Brad. "Amazoning the News." Accessed January 12, 2013. http://bradchoate.com/weblog/2001/03/22/amazoning-the-news.

Filloux, Frédéric (Ed.). (February 15, 2009). "Recommendation Engines: A Must for News Sites." Accessed January 12, 2013. http://www.mondaynote.com/2009/02/15/recommendation-engines-a-must-for-news-sites/.

Finkel, Eli J., and Susan Sprecher. (May 8, 2012). "The Scientific Flaws of Online Dating Sites." *Scientific American*. Accessed January 12, 2013. http://www.scientificamerican.com/article.cfm?id=scientific-flaws-online-dating-sites.

Fox, Stuart. "Video: A Company's Algorithms Reveal Hidden Connections Among All that Data." *Popular Science*, November 3, 2011. Accessed January 12, 2013. http://www.popsci.com/technology/article/2011–11/custom-algorithm-reveals-world-hidden-connections.

Fox Trial Finder. Accessed January 12, 2013. https://foxtrialfinder.michaeljfox.org/.

Fritz, Ben. (September 3, 2012). "Movie Buffs Have You Tagged." *Los Angeles Times*, A1.

Google. "Personalization Basics." http://support.google.com/news/bin/answer.py?hl=en&answer=1146405.

Google Systems. (September 9, 2006). "Google Recommendations." Accessed January 12, 2013. http://googlesystem.blogspot.com/2006/09/google-recommendations.html.

Greenfield, Jeremy. "Consumers Like and Trust Amazon Book Recommendations Despite Industry Jitters." DBW. Accessed January 12, 2013. http://www.digitalbookworld.com/2012/consumers-like-and-trust-amazon-book-recommendations-despite-industry-jitters/.

Kampinsky, Ellen, Shayne Bowman, and Chris Willis. "Amazoning the News." *Hypergene*. Accessed January 12, 2013. http://www.hypergene.net/ep2001/ep2001_1.html.

Konstan, Joseph A., and John Riedl. "Deconstructing Recommender Systems." Accessed January 12, 2013. http://spectrum.ieee.org/computing/software/deconstructing-recommender-systems.

Leonhardt, David. (June 7, 2006). "What Netflix Could Teach Hollywood." *The New York Times*. Accessed January 12, 2013. http://www.nytimes.com/2006/06/07/technology/07leonhardt.html?ex&_r=0.

Liveplasma. Accessed January 14, 2013. http://www.liveplasma.com/.

MacDonell, Kevin. (February 8, 2010). "How to do Basic Text-Mining." Accessed January 12, 2013. http://cooldata.wordpress.com/2010/02/08/how-to-do-basic-text-mining/.

Mangalindan, J. P. (July 30, 2012). "Amazon's Recommendation Secret." *CNNMoney*. Accessed January 12, 2013. http://tech.fortune.cnn.com/2012/07/30/amazon-5/.

National Resident Matching Program. "How the Matching Algorithm Works." Accessed January 12, 2013. http://www.nrmp.org/res_match/about_res/algorithms.html.

OKCupid. "Calculating Match Percentages." http://www.okcupid.com/help/match-percentages.

Pariser, Eli. (2011). *The Filter Bubble*. New York: Penguin Books.

Quid. Accessed January 12, 2013. http://quid.com.

Shadid, Tariq. (June 15, 2007). "Yahoo News and Suggestive Journalism." Accessed January 12, 2013. http://zumel.com/index.php?option=com_content&view=article&id=45:yahoo-news-and-suggestive-journalism&catid=15:mediawatch&Itemid=130.

Shardanand, Upendra, and Pattie Maes. "Social Information Filtering: Algorithms for Automating 'Word of Mouth.' " Accessed January 12, 2013. http://www.sigchi.org/chi95/proceedings/papers/us_bdy.htm.

Sheffied, Hazel. (September 10, 2012). "Recommendations from Journalism Profs." *Columbia Journalism Review*. Accessed January 12, 2013. http://www.cjr.org/the_kicker/recommendations_from_journalis.php?page=all.

Stack Overflow. "How does the Amazon Recommendation Feature Work." Accessed January 12, 2013. http://stackoverflow.com/questions/2323768/how-does-the-amazon-recommendation-feature-work.

Sydell, Laura. (May 14, 2012). "Algorithms: The Ever-Growing, All-Knowing Way of the Future." NPR. Accessed January 12, 2013. http://www.npr.org/blogs/alltechconsidered/2012/05/14/152444019/algorithms-the-ever-growing-all-knowing-way-of-the-future.

Tintarev, Nava, and Judith Masthoff. "Similarity for News Recommender Systems." Accessed January 12, 2013. https://docs.google.com/viewer?a=v&q=cache:T0GtLxAvGhYJ:citeseerx.ist.psu.edu/viewdoc/download%3Fdoi%3D10.1.1.102.3571%26rep%3Drep1%26type%3Dpdf+&hl=en&gl=us&pid=bl&srcid=ADGEESjC0jV96ACGj-RQlwos4cPtNw2aJ_Zit-5XyhW4iwjzZMGelTIKV9bxK6VC63t8rXEaJiklFtTe7MPtLOQRocJ7EQd5yyu4LRmkcct_G27mzniTfW4VAUfrXUjqWMC5Jt9Zf4Z4&sig= AHIEtbQePCEl6zavUeZHgscPDRMmk6hkOg.

TNW. (2012). "Google+ Recommendations Across the Web are Rolling Out to all Users Today." Accessed January 12, 2013. http://thenextweb.com/google/2012/07/09/google-recommendations-across-the-web-are-rolling-out-to-all-users-today/.

Weisier, Charlene. (August 1, 2012). "We Need Automatic Content Recognition—Now." *TV Board*. Accessed January 12, 2013. http://www.mediapost.com/publications/article/180050/we-need-automatic-content-recognition-now.html#axzz2GN8RVFsS.

Wilson, Tracy V., and Stephanie Crawford. "How Netflix Works." Accessed January 12, 2013. http://electronics.howstuffworks.com/netflix2.htm.

Yenigun, Sami. (December 28, 2012). "TV Broadcasters Amp Up the 'Second Screen' Experience." NPR. Accessed January 12, 2013. http://www.npr.org/blogs/alltechconsidered/2012/12/28/168163835/tv-broadcasters-amp-up-the-second-screen-experience.

9 PERSONALIZATION

Fifty billion dollars.

That figure represents the estimated total cost of houses, stores, city properties, and infrastructure repairs for the Northeast after 2012's Superstorm Sandy devastated the region. In the southern tip of Manhattan, flooding was as high as six feet. About 650,000 homes were destroyed, 435,300 more than were flooded in New Orleans by Hurricane Katrina in 2005 (Figure 9.1).

Personalizing the cold statistics contained within a news story can help others understand the full extent of a tragedy. For the above example, three sets of numbers are represented: a vast dollar amount, the height of flooded walls, and the number of homes. The key needed to engage a reader who lives far away from the area and might not be concerned is to make the figures relevant for that person.

Suppose a reader lives in Austin, Texas. The federal minimum wage for covered non-exempt employees is $7.25 per hour—the same amount for the state of Texas. If you worked for that salary for 40 hours a week, you would receive a paycheck of $290 a week before taxes. After $50 is deducted for the Federal Income Tax (Texas does not have a state income tax) and fees for Social Security and Medicare, you are able to take home $240. If you work the entire year with a vacation of two weeks, you will make about $14,500. For a family of four, the US Census Bureau defines poverty as an annual income of not more than $23,050. Nevertheless, if you contributed your entire salary to help the victims of Superstorm Sandy, it would take about *three million years* to make $50 billion. Feel free to divide Sandy's bill by your annual salary.

For the second set of numbers, you don't need a calculator. Most interior walls within residential homes in the United States are eight feet high. Ask a six-foot tall friend to come over or you could use a measuring tape. Have that person walk around your abode while you mark with a pencil the height. Notice that almost every object you have in your place on the first floor—all your furniture, appliances, personal pictures, framed art, family heirlooms, and so on will be destroyed.

Finally, let's go back to Austin. I used to live there, so it's a pleasure to virtually return. According to 2010 US Census data, the capitol city has a population of 820,611 persons living in a total of 322,979 households—houses, apartments, and so on. If Superstorm Sandy had set its sights on central Texas rather than the northeastern coastline, no structure within Austin's city limits *twice over* would have been habitable.

Personal Enough for You?

The above thought exercises have their roots in real-world computer applications. Many personalization tools come from the field of informational graphics, sometimes referred to as news graphics, data visualizations, or simply infographics. Interactive and engaging

Figure 9.1 A satellite image of Hurricane Sandy shows the tremendous cloud cover over the northeastern United States. The diameter of the storm at its peak was about 1,000 miles. *Courtesy of the National Oceanic and Atmospheric Administration*

digital innovations can help a user imagine what it might be like to be a part of a news story. Infographics has generated intense interest among producers of print and online presentations since information from databases were combined with graphic design sensibilities and tools. The innovative use of software programs combined with databases allows website producers to create high-quality interactive presentations with moving images and audio.

The informational graphics team at *The New York Times* is known for creating work that is elegant, simple, interactive, informational, and personalized. For example, in "Is It Better to Buy or Rent?" by Kevin Quealy and Archie Tse, after you input your monthly rent and the price of a house you would like to purchase, a graph instantly adjusts to your parameters and reveals how many years it takes before a house becomes a better investment than renting. Other personalized interactive graphics include online pages that calculate your financial recovery, show your household income compared with others, and give you an opportunity to select the supplies you might bring if doomsday approached and you needed to escape a city.

Personalized news services, collectively known as the "Daily Me," a term popularized by Nicholas Negroponte, founder of the MIT Media Lab in his 1995 groundbreaking book *Being Digital,* began with web browser users bookmarking favorite links and expanded as computer science researchers and mass communications professionals discovered their utility. Crayon.net is a user-generated newspaper for the web. You can create your own online newspaper with a title, motto, and a personalized page layout with graphics and links. The result is a series of news and special interest weblinks connected with the zip code and topics provided by the user. Another personalized newsweb took its name from Negroponte. Based in Hollywood, Florida, the "DailyMe" has delivered user-requested news since 2005 (Figure 9.2). Through three

Figure 9.2 Users of the "DailyMe" newsweb can read the top headlines and stories of the day as with any newspaper or personalize the offerings with specific interests from a list of about 200 categories. *Courtesy of Eduardo Hauser*

packages—personalized, socialized, and editorialized—readers can follow the news they select, what others in social networks find interesting, and stories selected by its staff of professionals. In this way, the "DailyMe" creates an experience that is both intentional and serendipitous.

In 1996 for *IBM Systems Journal,* Walter Bender, director of the "News in the Future" research consortium at MIT and three other authors published "Enriching communities: Harbingers of news in the future." The innovative article described four prototypes of online news presentations that change "the relationship between news providers and news consumers" by promoting "an active, *engaged* participant." Based on the work of Lev Vygotsky and his social constructivism theory (see Chapter 2), the authors agree that an individual's ideas about how interest and knowledge is fostered greatly affects that person's connection with the world. Although digital innovations can aid that process, "the network is not the active force; the people are. The critical agency is based entirely upon the prerogatives of the people involved." In other words, if you make presentations that personalize news and information for users, wider social connections become easier to establish and maintain.

The four prototypes were *FishWrap,* PLUM, *The India Journal,* and MUSIC (Multi-User Session In Community).

Named for a slang and slightly derogatory term for printed newspapers, *FishWrap* was a precursor for egocentric presentations described in the previous chapter. An experimental program within *FishWrap* developed at MIT was called "Doppelganger." Doppelganger, explains Bender, "enables your computer to shadow you, get involved in all of the different things you do, and deliver that information to your personal newspaper. My *FishWrap* knows about my email, my calendar, and what I've been doing on the web. And it uses all that information to refine my user profile constantly. Say there's an entry in my computer calendar that shows I'm traveling to Finland. Using Doppelganger, *FishWrap* will smell that out and add a little news section on Finland—local news and what's going on in Helsinki."

For her master's thesis at MIT, Sara Elo designed a database-generated software program called PLUM for the "Peace, Love, and Understanding Machine." It has since been given a computerese name of "Parallel Line with Understanding Mission" by Bender. To determine trends within complex stories, journalists have used computer databases, but such collections of data are not used that often to automatically link contextual information to news stories. PLUM used census data and the *CIA World Factbook,* among other databases, to add comparisons between a local news user's community and natural disasters anywhere in the world. For example, a Boston student could read her personalized newspaper that detailed through a traditional wire service news story a serious flood in China in which 200,000 homes were underwater. With PLUM augmentation, the reader could also see comparative facts in the form of news sidebars and informational graphics that explained comparisons between the Chinese area affected and her local community. In this way, Elo hoped that readers would gain a greater understanding of the complex economic, social, and environmental issues between a local and foreign land. PLUM was eventually incorporated into *FishWrap.*

In 1994, researchers and journalists for the MIT Media Lab and a traditional newspaper, *The Jersey Journal,* teamed to produce a daily on-demand electronic publication, *The India Journal,* aimed at the 10,000 Indian Americans who lived in and near Jersey City, New Jersey. Users could get free versions of the paper from printers located in two groceries and a video store. The most popular features of the *Journal* were "birth and wedding announcements, death notices and obituaries, and, of paramount concern, cricket scores." This experiment proved interest in a personal, "local-to-local connection."

MUSIC was an online bulletin board system that was organized and maintained by local residents of the Four Corners area in Dorchester, Boston's most populated neighborhood. The purpose of this project was "to show that a community network can support the local infrastructure of a typical urban neighborhood and that residents can independently, without technical expertise, use the network as a tool for social constructivism." Besides local news stories, users could also engage each other through synchronous text and voice communications. MUSIC was successful in uniting diverse cultural groups within the neighborhood. It was "used as a publishing vehicle for poetry and drawings. It has also been used to organize potlucks, group trips, and various social gatherings. In addition, it has been used to organize a summer youth program, a neighborhood apprenticeship program, a food cooperative, and a crime watch program." In 1995, MUSIC was expanded to Newark, New Jersey.

The Daily Me concept is not without its critics. *The New York Times* op-ed columnist Nicholas Kristof warned in 2009 that if Negroponte's personalized news concept becomes the norm, "God save us from ourselves. That's because there's pretty good evidence that we generally don't truly want good information—but rather information that confirms our prejudices. We may believe intellectually in the clash of opinions, but in practice we like to embed ourselves in the reassuring womb of an echo chamber." Someone with a liberal frame of mind, for example, might only consider Rachel Maddow of MSNBC as a news source, while conservative thinkers might only want views from Bill O'Reilly of Fox. Any member of an educated democratic society should expose herself to differing points of view. Successful news sites should offer opinions and stories from various sources as well as options for personal choices.

■ CHALLENGES, CRITIQUES, AND AMUSEMENTS

■ Find a news story, television show, or motion picture and make the content personal by comparing your situation with the one featured in the various media. Do the narratives take on new meanings?

■ Either through the media or personal contacts, find someone who lived through a severe firestorm, hurricane, tornado, or some other natural disaster. What hardships did the person experience? What personal items did she most regret losing? What lessons were learned? How does the story of this person's life help you?

■ Austin, Texas. Why does everyone seem to like the city so much? If you attended SXSW, would you be more interested in film, music, or interactive presentations? What does that say about you?

■ What was the worst job you ever had? How much did you make? Did you learn anything from it?

■ *Being Digital* by Nicholas Negroponte is a classic—a must read. So what are you waiting for? You can buy the audio version from Amazon. What is your take on the difference between atoms and bits?

■ Find out what interesting projects are underway at the MIT Media Lab. Which ones particularly attract your attention, which ones seem fit for only rocket scientists, and which ones could be part of a science fiction movie plot?

■ Sign up with the DailyMe <http://dailyme.com> and click on the link, "Personalize your news on DailyMe." Enter at least 10 keywords and select 20 or more categories. Check with the newsweb every day for a week. Did you learn of stories you didn't know about through other media?

■ What concerns might there be with the DailyMe concept?

■ Write a 1,000-word autobiography and convert it into a word cloud graphic with Wordle <http://wordle.net>. What does the display reveal about you?

■ Go to the "The Information is Beautiful Awards" blog <http://www.informationis-beautifulawards.com/>. Find examples that you think have high aesthetic value and those that display personal information. One link should stand out, "Track Your Personal Data." Go to the website of the British scientist Stephen Wolfram and marvel at how he charted his personal emails, computer keystrokes, calls, steps he walked, and other variables *for more than 20 years*. What discipline must it take to produce such detailed personal data, and what does it all mean? Now, get busy and chart your life.

■ EXERCISES

To help personalize the facts presented at the start of this chapter, you will create an interactive informational graphic using the programs Infogram, Excel, and Word.

For the second exercise you will use the free program Vizualize.me to create a résumé in the form of an informational graphic.

The web is almost an infinite source for databases filled with facts and figures from government agencies, public collections, and private individuals. Just about any correlation between seemingly disparate topics can be analyzed by information sources found online. For example, is there a connection within the 50 US states between homicides with a gun, the percentage of residents whom own firearms, and the average annual temperature of the state? The topics you choose and the presentations you make from the data are limited only by the extent of your imagination, curiosity, and tenacity.

1. From the US Department of Labor's website <http://www.dol.gov/whd/minwage/america.htm>, you will discover the minimum wage laws for each US state as of January 1, 2013 (Figure 9.3).

Figure 9.3 Several governmental agencies and other entities have databases you can use to make almost any topic personal for a user. *Courtesy of the US Department of Labor*

2. Scroll down to the bottom and find a table that shows the consolidated state figures. Click and drag to highlight the information within the four columns, and then from the Edit menu select Copy (Figure 9.4).

Consolidated State Minimum Wage Update Table (Effective Date: 01/01/2013)

> Federal MW	Equals Federal MW of $7.25	< Federal MW	No MW Required
AK - 7.75	DE	AR - 6.25	AL
AZ - 7.80	HI	GA - 5.15	LA
CA - 8.00	IA	MN - 6.15	MS
CO - 7.78	ID	WY - 5.15	SC
CT - 8.25	IN		TN
DC - 8.25	KS		
FL - 7.79	KY	**4 States**	
IL - 8.25	MD		**5 States**
MA - 8.00	NE		
ME - 7.50	NH		
MI - 7.40	NJ		
MO - 7.35	NY		
MT - 7.80	NC		
NV - 8.25	ND		
NM - 7.50	OK		
OH - 7.85	PA		
OR - 8.95	SD		
RI - 7.75	TX		
VT - 8.60	UT		
WA - 9.19	VA		
	WV		
	WI		

Figure 9.4 The US states with their corresponding minimum wage figures can be found in a table at the bottom of the webpage. *Courtesy of the US Department of Labor*

3. Open the Excel spreadsheet program and paste the data into an empty worksheet. Click and drag to select all the information. Click on the small formatting icon within the worksheet and select "Match Destination Formatting" (Figure 9.5).

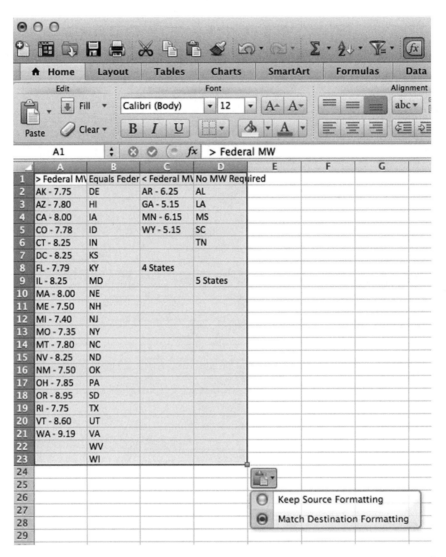

Figure 9.5 You will want to "Match Document Formatting" so that the minimum wage figures are easier to work with in the Excel spreadsheet program.

4. Click and drag to select and then press the Apple and "X" keys to copy the list of state abbreviations in the second column. Skip a space and click in an empty box. Paste the column. Repeat with the four states in the third column. Click on the row number for DC-8.25 and press the Control and K keys to remove it from the list. Now comes the tedious part of this exercise. For each state, type in its corresponding figure next to it in the second column and replace the abbreviation with its full name. Think of this task as a test of your knowledge of the official abbreviations and spelling for each state. To be sure that you don't have any mistakes, copy and paste your state list into a Word file and perform a Spell Check. From DE (Delaware) to WI (Wisconsin), the number is the same—7.25 (Figure 9.6).

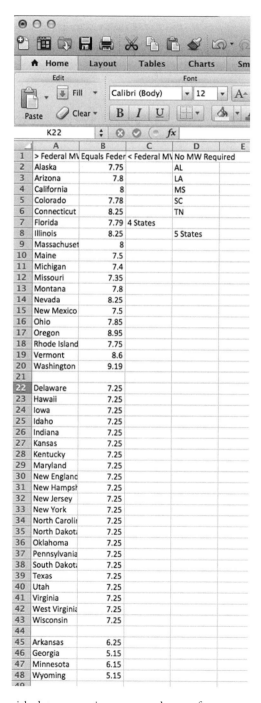

	A	B	C	D	E
1	> Federal MW	Equals Feder	< Federal MW	No MW Required	
2	Alaska	7.75		AL	
3	Arizona	7.8		LA	
4	California	8		MS	
5	Colorado	7.78		SC	
6	Connecticut	8.25		TN	
7	Florida	7.79	4 States		
8	Illinois	8.25		5 States	
9	Massachuset	8			
10	Maine	7.5			
11	Michigan	7.4			
12	Missouri	7.35			
13	Montana	7.8			
14	Nevada	8.25			
15	New Mexico	7.5			
16	Ohio	7.85			
17	Oregon	8.95			
18	Rhode Island	7.75			
19	Vermont	8.6			
20	Washington	9.19			
21					
22	Delaware	7.25			
23	Hawaii	7.25			
24	Iowa	7.25			
25	Idaho	7.25			
26	Indiana	7.25			
27	Kansas	7.25			
28	Kentucky	7.25			
29	Maryland	7.25			
30	New England	7.25			
31	New Hampsh	7.25			
32	New Jersey	7.25			
33	New York	7.25			
34	North Carolir	7.25			
35	North Dakota	7.25			
36	Oklahoma	7.25			
37	Pennsylvania	7.25			
38	South Dakota	7.25			
39	Texas	7.25			
40	Utah	7.25			
41	Virginia	7.25			
42	West Virginia	7.25			
43	Wisconsin	7.25			
44					
45	Arkansas	6.25			
46	Georgia	5.15			
47	Minnesota	6.15			
48	Wyoming	5.15			

Figure 9.6 Sometimes with data processing, you need to perform more typing than you would probably enjoy—the cleaned-up Excel file.

5. Go to the Infogram website at <http://infogr.am/>. Click on the "Sign up, it's free!" button (Figure 9.7).

Figure 9.7 The Infogram website offers an easy way to become familiar with producing personalized interactive informational graphics.

6. Register with a unique username and email address. Input a password you want to use (Figure 9.8).

Figure 9.8 You must register as a user on the Infogram website in order to create infographics.

7. Check your email program and respond to the message from Infogram. You will receive a notice of verification (Figure 9.9).

Figure 9.9 When you click on the link sent to your email account, Infogram will show you this verification message.

8. You will be offered three choices—"New Infographic," "New Chart," and "Library." Select "New Chart" (Figure 9.10).

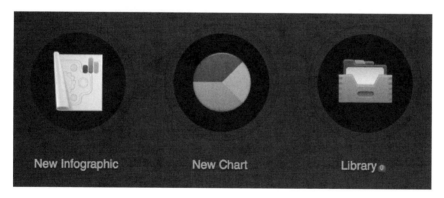

Figure 9.10 I predict that soon your Library will have many examples that you created.

9. From the Chart selection, you will notice many different types of charts, with some having different styles. Feel free to experiment with any of the infographics offered. For now, select "Treemap" and then the "Create chart" button (Figure 9.11).

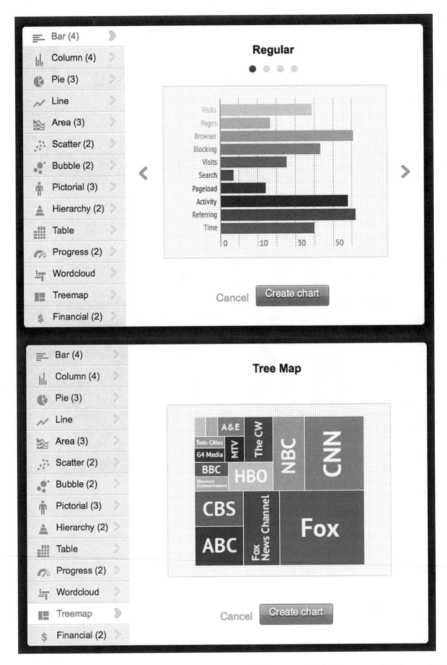

Figure 9.11 Which is it, "Treemap" or "Tree Map"? Either way, it is the type of infographic you will use.

10. You will now replace the generic information from Infogram with the minimum wage data. Double-click the center of the graphic to edit your chart (Figure 9.12).

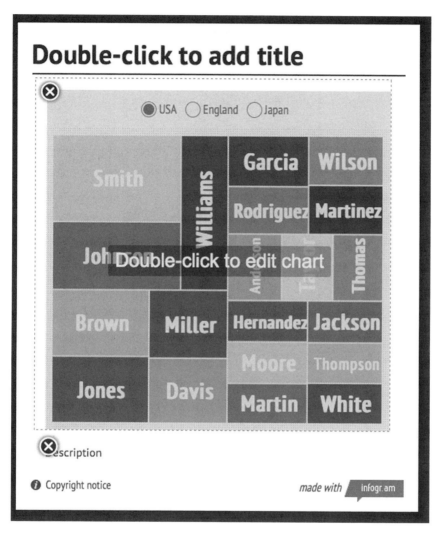

Figure 9.12 I'm not sure what these names from Infogram represent. Does anyone know? At any rate, you will replace them with the minimum wage data.

11. Back in Excel, select and copy the state names and numbers from Alaska to Washington. Return to Infogram. With "Sheet 1" at the bottom right selected, replace "USA" and "%" with "More than the Minimum Wage" and then paste the data from Excel from row 2. In "Sheet 2," type "Equals the Minimum Wage" and paste the data from Excel from Delaware to Wisconsin. In "Sheet 3," type "Less than the

Minimum Wage" and paste the data from Excel that shows Arkansas to Wyoming. Press the Done button at the top (Figure 9.13).

Figure 9.13 You will replace the input from sheets 1, 2, and 3 with the three sets of data from the Excel spreadsheet.

12. Infogram shows you the chart generated from the data. To test the interactive features, press the "Eye" icon at the top to see a Preview. Click in the buttons at the top and within the state rectangles. When finished with the Preview view, press the "Close preview" button (Figure 9.14).

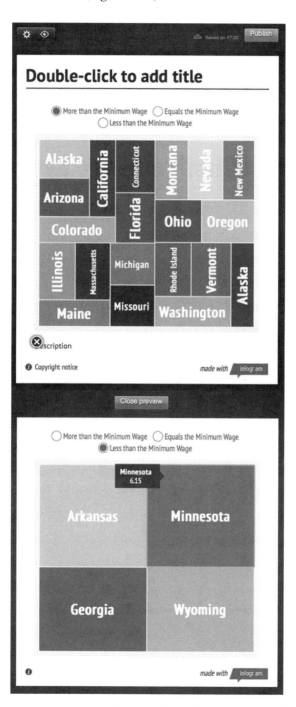

Figure 9.14 The interactive components for this infographic are the major divisions at the top of the first example and the individual rectangles in the second.

13. Now you need to add copy to go with your art. Double-click the Title area and type "Federal Minimum Wage by State" and within the Description area type "The current Federal minimum wage (MW) is $7.25 an hour. Five states do not have a MW requirement: Alabama, Louisiana, Mississippi, South Carolina, and Tennessee." Inside the "Copyright notice" box type "Source: US Department of Labor" (Figure 9.15). Check your interactive informational graphic in Preview and then close the preview.

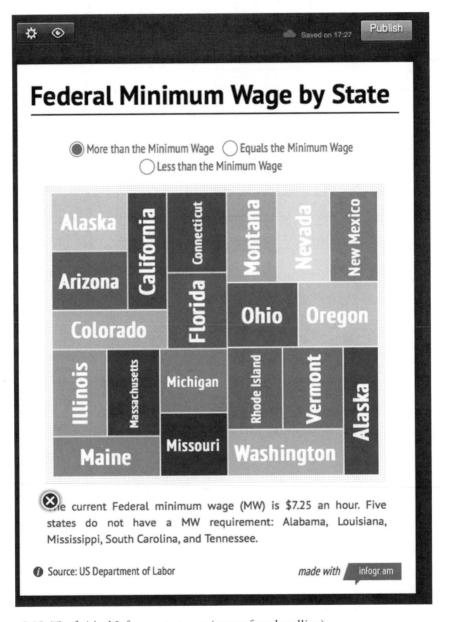

Figure 9.15 The finished Infogram tree map (my preferred spelling).

14. Finally, you need to publish your work. Click the Publish button at the top. The same title and description that you used in the graphic should be shown (Figure 9.16).

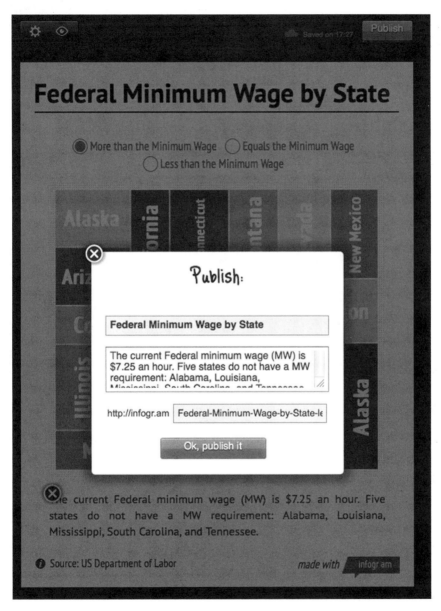

Figure 9.16 The title and description should be included without additional typing (you did enough in Step 4).

15. Decide whether to publish the infographic on a social media site (Figure 9.17). If you choose "View on the web," copy the URL below the button and take a screen shot of your work for your records.

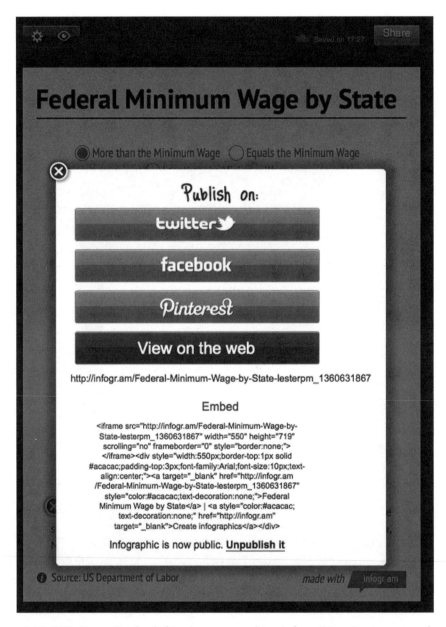

Figure 9.17 Tell all your Facebook friends you are making infographics. But just so you know, I wouldn't. If you want to include your graphic in a website you created, copy all of the code under "Embed" and paste it into your HTML file.

Next, you will create a résumé in the form of an infographic using the free online program Vizualize.me.

1. Go to <http://vizualize.me/> and create your own account (Figure 9.18).

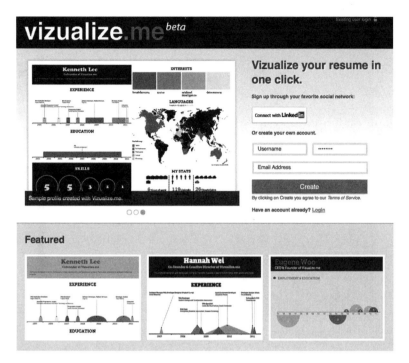

Figure 9.18 Sign up for Vizualize.me through your LinkedIn account or create your own that is separate (probably a better choice).

2. "Pimp up your resume" (not my favorite verb) and add your personal information. Use the Edit buttons at the left to add your experiences, education, skills, and so on (Figure 9.19).

Figure 9.19 Click the Edit button next to the "Profile Summary" menu choice at the left to get started.

3. From the Profile Summary, add the information requested to the boxes (Figure 9.20).

Figure 9.20 Add and then Save your User Information.

4. Do the same for as many of the categories as you wish (Figure 9.21). Click the "+ Add New" button to include more items within a category. When you are finished, press the Save button.

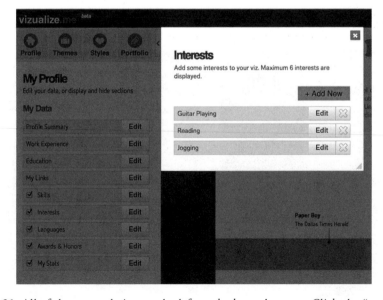

Figure 9.21 All of the menu choices at the left work about the same. Click the "+ Add New" button, and you will see a short form to fill out for each category.

5. You may want to change the theme of your output. Press the Themes button. You have six choices (Figure 9.22).

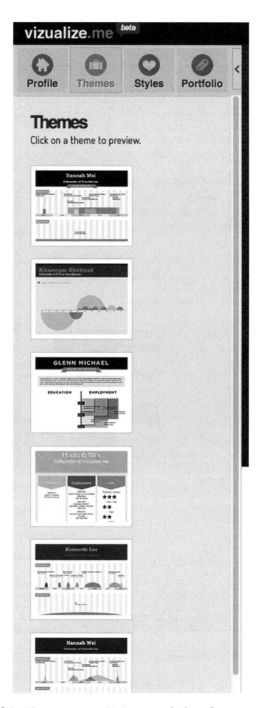

Figure 9.22 Try all of the Themes to see which one works best for you.

6. You can also select the color and typography schemes. Press the Styles button (Figure 9.23).

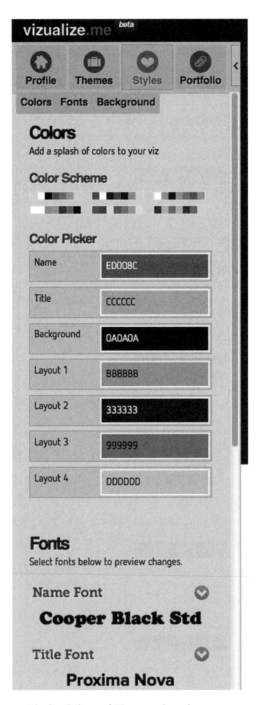

Figure 9.23 Experiment with the Color and Typography schemes.

7. Compare what your finished résumé looks like in different Themes and Styles and make a choice (Figure 9.24).

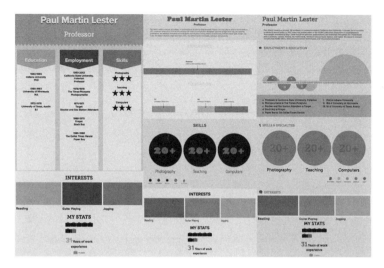

Figure 9.24 I personally prefer the résumé on the right.

8. When you are happy with it, you can share your résumé on various social media (Figure 9.25).

Figure 9.25 It's your choice if you want to publicize your résumé. If you do, Visualize.me will keep track of any hits you receive through the Dashboard button.

9. You can also buy a t-shirt (Figure 9.26).

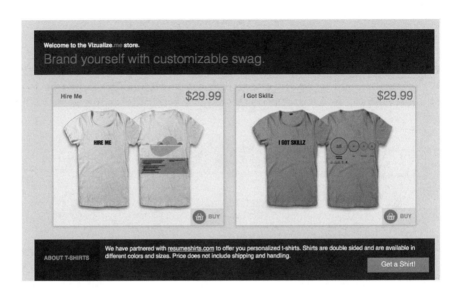

Figure 9.26 I seriously doubt if it will impress a busy executive, but you are offered the opportunity to buy a t-shirt.

Sources

Bender, W., et al. (1996). "Enriching Communities: Harbingers of News in the Future." *IBM Systems Journal* 35, 369–80.

Crayon. Accessed January 11, 2013. http://crayon.net/.

Data Hub. Accessed January 12, 2013. http://thedatahub.org/en/about.

EveryBlock. Accessed January 12, 2013. http://www.everyblock.com/.

Grabowicz, Paul. (January 10, 2013). "The Transition to Digital Journalism." Knight Digital Media Center. Accessed January 12, 2013. http://multimedia.journalism.berkeley.edu/tutorials/digital-transform/mobile/.

Harper, Christopher. (April, 1997). "The Daily Me." *American Journalism Review*. Accessed January 12, 2013. http://www.ajr.org/article.asp?id=268.

Huffington Post. (November 13, 2012). "Highlands N.J. Comes Together, Where Sandy Destroyed 80% of Homes." Accessed January 12, 2013. http://www.huffingtonpost.com/2012/11/13/residents-come-together-in-highlands-nj-sandy_n_2119498.html.

"Japan Quake's Effects." (March 15, 2011). *The Wall Street Journal.* Accessed January 12, 2013. http://online.wsj.com/article/SB10001424052748703597804576194683272395102.html.

Jersey Journal, The. Accessed January 14, 2013. http://nj.com/jjournal/.

Kaplan-Moss, Jacob. (September 12, 2007). "The Sorry State of Database Journalism." Accessed January 12, 2013. http://jacobian.org/writing/db-journalism/.

Kristof, Nicholas D. (March 18, 2009). "The Daily Me." *The New York Times*. Accessed January 12, 2013. http://www.nytimes.com/2009/03/19/opinion/19kristof.html?ref=opinion&_r=0.

Levin, Adina. "Database Journalism—A Different Definition of 'News' and 'Reader.' " Accessed January 12, 2013. http://www.alevin.com/?p=1391.

Liebhold, Mike. "Digital Immersion: Augmenting Places with Stories and Information." Nieman Reports. Accessed January 12, 2013. http://www.nieman.harvard.edu/reportsitem.aspx?id=102426.

Muskal, Michael. (February 13, 2013). "Sandy Is Ranked as Region's Deadliest Storm in 40 Tears." *Los Angeles Times*, A6.

Negroponte, Nicholas. (1996). *Being Digital*. New York: Vintage.

Quealy, Kevin, and Archie Tse. "Is It Better to Buy or Rent?" *The New York Times*. Accessed January 30, 2013. http://www.nytimes.com/interactive/business/buy-rent-calculator.html

Rogers, Tony. "Find the Local Angle." About.com. Accessed January 12, 2013. http://journalism.about.com/od/citizenjournalism/a/localize.htm.

Russ, Hilary. (November 26, 2012). "New York, New Jersey put $71 Billion Price Tag on Sandy." Reuters. Accessed January 12, 2013. http://usnews.nbcnews.com/_news/2012/11/26/15463835-new-york-new-jersey-put-71-billion-price-tag-on-sandy?lite.

Silver, Leah. (June 30, 2011). "Six Tips for Journalists on How to Localize News Stories." Ijnet. Accessed January 12, 2013. http://ijnet.org/stories/six-tips-journalists-how-localize-news-stories.

Spreadsheet Journalism. (August 24, 2012). "Birth Months and Budding Ballplayers: The Little League Thesis Revisited." Accessed January 12, 2013. http://spreadsheetjournalism.com/2012/08/24/birth-months-and-budding-ballplayers-the-little-league-thesis-revisited/.

Swiftly. "Localizing News." Accessed January 12, 2013. http://blog.swiftly.org/post/2905826993/localizing-news.

Tenore, Mallary Jean. (March 29, 2011). "Explainer Maps Locate, Contextualize and Localize News from Libya, Japan." Poynter. Accessed January 12, 2013. http://www.poynter.org/how-tos/newsgathering-storytelling/125206/explainer-maps-locate-contextualize-and-localize-news-from-libya-japan/.

United States Census Bureau. "Austin (city), Texas." Accessed January 12, 2013. http://quickfacts.census.gov/qfd/states/48/4805000.html.

United States Department of Labor. "Wage and Hour Division." Accessed January 12, 2013. http://www.dol.gov/whd/minwage/america.htm#.UPIBc7Z8vuw.

Visual Complexity. Accessed January 12, 2013. http://www.visualcomplexity.com/vc/.

Watling, Meranda. (June 21, 2011). "7 Places to Look for Database Journalism Stories." 10,000 Words. Accessed January 12, 2013. http://www.mediabistro.com/10000words/places-to-look-for-database-journalism-sstories_b4840.

10 MAPPING

You are here.

From creased, torn, and awkwardly folded road maps stuck and stacked within the glove box of a car, to a talking GPS smartphone app with a soothing voice that patiently guides you to an unknown location, digital innovations have propelled the progress of maps and mapmaking.

As an opening joke before a speech I once made to Middle Tennessee State University students and faculty members in the lovely little town of Murfreesboro in 1996, I told a fictitious story. "This morning before I came here," I remarked, "I browsed through a downtown bookstore and bought a city map. When I got outside and opened it, to my amazement, it was printed actual size."

Let's just say that my audience didn't appreciate a joke about the size of their town.

What I didn't realize at the time was how my weak attempt at humor would become true. Today, a map can overlay the actual view from your tablet's camera that not only literally shows you where you are, but includes points of interest nearby while the "street view" feature in Google Maps (called "streetside" in Bing Maps) allows you to take a virtual walk within a map. Yes, today maps are actual size.

The first maps that were made had nothing to do with geographical features found on Earth, but were simple representations of particularly bright stars seen in the night's sky created about 16,000 years ago by Lascaux, France, cave astronomers. The Sumerians about 10,000 years later were the first advanced civilization to make maps. These crude examples were carved in clay and showed a vast agricultural estate in the Fertile Crescent area of Mesopotamia. After the concepts of longitude and latitude for dividing the world into a grid of set coordinates were invented about 2,500 years ago, maps became much more accurate. About 1,500 years after that, a three-foot-square stone was the medium for a detailed map of the eastern coast of China. The map called the "Yü Ji Tu" ("Map of the Tracks of Yü the Great") was produced with a sophisticated grid system for a highly accurate representation. The Spanish mapmaker Juan de la Cosa, who accompanied Christopher Columbus on several voyages, created the oldest known map of the Americas, the "Mappa Mundi," in 1500 (Figure 10.1). Its unique feature is that it shows Cuba as an island. Columbus thought it was attached to the mainland and populated with Tandoori chicken restaurants. As knowledge of lands near and far increased and cartographical techniques improved, locator maps became vital in establishing trade routes, political boundaries, and determining size and distance measurements.

However, locator maps are limited because they stress objectivity, scientific accuracy, and a literal view of the world. Far more interesting and apropos to this textbook are concept maps—presentations that rely on intellectual perceptions and connections.

One of the earliest concept maps was an engraving published in 1649 called "The Tree of Mans [sic] Life," written by the English author Richard Dey and engraved by John

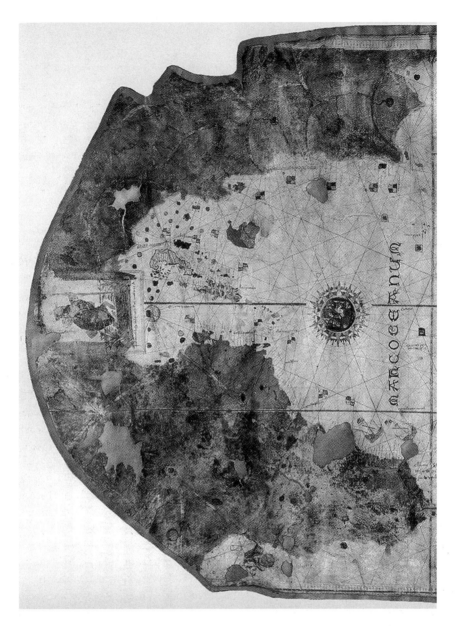

Figure 10.1 Juan de la Cosa accompanied Christopher Columbus on his first voyage to the Indies and later produced the map on leather known as "Mappa Mundi" in 1500. This detail of his handiwork orientated on its side shows the beginnings of land features for Florida, the Gulf of Mexico, the island nation of Cuba, and Central and South America. A picture of Saint Christopher adorns the center, most likely a tribute to Columbus. *Courtesy of the Naval Museum of Madrid*

Figure 10.2 A close-up of a London street map from 1854 shows the dots that British physician Dr. John Snow marked to indicate a death from the latest outbreak of cholera. The X in the center is the location of the public water pump. His infographic clearly showed a problem with the pump, and it was dismantled. However, city officials refused to believe that fecal pollution of the water, as was later proven to be the case, caused cholera. A vegetarian and teetotaler who never married, Snow died of a stroke four years after his water pump finding. *Courtesy of Edward Tufte, Graphics Press LLC, Cheshire, CT*

Goddard. It employed a common metaphor of the time—a tree structure with roots, trunk, branches, and leaves to present a genealogical study of human civilization. If you tried to use this map to get home during a stormy night, you might end up at the Bates Motel. Nevertheless, concept maps gained favor with scientists and historians with two famous examples—one to chart the recent deaths from a cholera epidemic and the other to signify the movements of Napoleon's army.

London in the 1850s, like many overly crowded and unsanitary cities of the day, was often ravaged by outbreaks of cholera. Dr. John Snow, a physician concerned about the cause of the dreaded disease, obtained the names and addresses of about 500 of those who had died during an 1854 epidemic. When he plotted each casualty on a street map, the visual representation of the data clearly showed the deaths clustered around the Broad Street water pump and not any other source (Figure 10.2). Snow asked for the removal of the pump's handle. The plague blizzard ceased.

French engineer Charles Minard in 1869 combined statistical information and a map to tell a complicated story in a simple, direct way. After he told the story of the loss

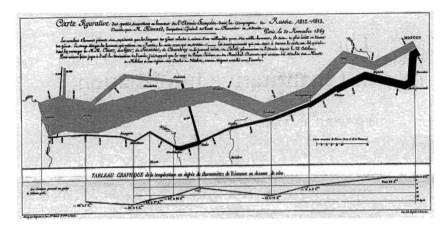

Figure 10.3 Charles Minard eloquently portrays Napoleon's disastrous military advance on Moscow in 1812 in an informational graphic that has been called the best ever produced. The width, shading, and position of the horizontal lines indicate troop strength, direction, and position. This map shows that Napoleon started with 422,000 troops and ended with 10,000, leading to the Emperor's downfall. *Courtesy of Edward Tufte, Graphics Press LLC, Cheshire, CT*

of about 400,000 soldiers and support staff in Napoleon Bonaparte's 1812 disastrous military campaign through a map, Minard showed that a complex story could be reduced to its simplest elements in a compelling visual format (Figure 10.3).

Today's informational graphics designers use creativity, research skills, and advanced technologies to combine complex concepts with locator maps to reveal insights about a community's social problems, entertainment possibilities, and landmarks.

Until his resignation in 2010, Patrick Cain of the *Toronto Star*'s online edition wrote a blog he named "Map of the Week" that recorded 1.4 million page views and about 1,000 comments from readers. Using public data and Google Maps, his infographics detailed the prevalence within the Toronto area of such topics as the number of bedbugs, same-sex marriages, diagnoses of chlamydia, and gun ownership.

The New York Times compiled data from "more than 200,000 facilities that have permits to discharge pollutants and collected responses from states regarding compliance" throughout the United States. Information from the New York City Police Department was used to track homicides from 2003–2011 by month and time of day, race, sex, and age of the victim and the perpetrator, the weapon used, and by borough. In 2003, there were 597 total homicides; in 2011, there were 209. The overwhelming weapon of choice for all homicides for all nine years was a firearm.

Other examples of map creativity can be found on the web. The blog "10,000 Words Where Journalism and Technology Meet" is a showcase for innovative concept map presentations. Meograph lets us create and view interactive stories that "combine maps, timelines, links, and multimedia." With Soundtrack, you select one of 12 locations— from Ramallah, Palestine, to the Samuel P. Taylor State Park north of San Francisco—and listen to recorded sounds as your Google Map marker moves through a specified route. After you type in an address, city, or zip code, the website 2itch identifies restaurants, bars, hospitals, stores, and other activities and services in your area that are open 24 hours. With a free login, users can reveal personal adventures, post reviews, and add pictures, videos, and weblinks. John Voss' LookBack Maps combines map technology with public photographic collections and geotagging to give users a view of history right around the corner or across the country. The Melbourne, Australia, producer of StatPlanet software for the creation of interactive maps lists more than 400 examples that cover "areas such as health, education, drugs & crime, economy, environment, gender and population for all countries" on its page called "Stat Silk."

One more mapping program you should know is Ushahidi's crowd-sourcing application aptly named Crowdmap <http://ushahidi.com/products/crowdmap>. Its website

Figure 10.4 San Francisco's *The Bay Citizen* newspaper maintains a "Data Library" with award-winning examples of informational graphics along with data sets and methodologies to allow readers to make their own interactive maps. *Courtesy of* The Bay Citizen, *http://baycitizen.org*

claims that it can help you "monitor elections, curate local resources, map crisis information, and document a zombie invasion." For the time being, let's assume that the proper authorities have zombies under control. The other uses for the free software product can greatly engage a user with a story you tell and help others during a crisis.

Click on the "Multimedia" link of San Francisco's *The Bay Citizen,* and several pages of mostly mapping projects can be selected. Featured projects include maps that reveal Bay Area county immunization statistics collected from the California Department of Health, the changes in racial and ethnic populations using data from the 2010 Census, and the "Bike Accident Tracker 2.0" in which more than 14,000 accidents are plotted on a map that uses color-coded markers for bike, motor vehicle, and pedestrian mishaps (Figure 10.4). A random click on a green dot reveals a pop-up window with specific information: On June 4, 2006, at 1:25 pm, someone on a bicycle made an improper turn at the corner of Frederick and Stanyan streets and hit a car. There was one injury, no one was killed, and it was not a hit and run. Users can also obtain access to the project's raw data set and discover new combinations of accident factors as well as learn the programs that the creators used to put the information together: Django for web application creation, Highcharts for JavaScript interactive graphs, jQuery that helps in the writing of JavaScript code, Google Maps JavaScript API version 3 that embeds maps into web pages, GitHub's OpenRefine for organizing complex data, Google Fusion Tables for the creation of tables, Google Geocoding API in order to place location-specific markers on maps, and finally, good old-fashioned reporting.

■ CHALLENGES, CRITIQUES, AND AMUSEMENTS

- Find an old paper road map from a secondhand bookstore. Unfold it completely and lay it out on a table. With a stopwatch, time how long it takes you and your friends to fold it back into its original neat rectangle. The loser buys a round of drinks of your favorite beverage.

- Find out all you can about Murfreesboro. Make an anagram of its name and see if you matched the same one used by me at the start of my speech. Email me your answer. If you are the first to match my anagram, I'll send you something.

- Soon after Google executive Eric Schmidt visited North Korea in early 2013, Google Maps included details of the secretive country. What insights can you learn from studying the map?

- Known as the "Hereford Mappa Mundi" created about 1285 and considered the largest medieval map known, it was almost sold for $3.5 million in 1988 to pay for repair work desperately needed for the Hereford (England) Cathedral. Luckily, wealthy donors stepped in to keep the map where it is. The repairs were made and a new library was built where the public can view it. Why do you think the map is such a treasured item?

- From Simon Garfield's book, *On the Map,* without looking, make a quick pencil sketch of a map of your living room, kitchen, or bedroom. Now, create a map of a friend's living room, kitchen, or bedroom.

- Make a map by hand or with a computer of your travel to school or work over a two-month period detailing changes in routes and points of interest or, more interestingly, your various moods as you move along the way. Have your work framed and give it to your friend on her birthday.

- Listen to a 3D sound experiment called "Matchbox" <http://www.youtube.com/watch?v=WYdIidUIbAs> with headphones and your eyes closed. Check out some of the other 3D sound offerings on YouTube. Do you think this technology is, in a way, mapping the space around your head with sound? Can you think of any practical applications for 3D sound and maps?

■ Apply the maps created by Dr. John Snow or Charles Minard to events in your personal or professional life. For example, just before my last class of the fall 2012 semester, the campus was put on lockdown because of criminal activity that involved gunfire. No one at school was hurt. Messages from the police over the auditorium's loudspeaker were confusing. We heard that if we were in a classroom we should stay until authorized to leave, but if we were outside, we should head home. Since my students were adults, I felt that I couldn't demand that they stay. Every 30 minutes from 4 pm until 10:30 pm, I counted how many students were in the room. The counts were: 211, 200, 156, 152, 150, 146, 136, 128, 124, 98, 86, 82, 51, and 43. Use Excel or some other spreadsheet program and make a chart of these figures. Now, do the same for your own data. (Thought I forgot that part, didn't you?)

■ Look over the work in *The Bay Citizen*'s <http://www.baycitizen.org/data/> "Data Library Index." Which informational graphic display is particularly interesting to you and why?

■ EXERCISES

Maps get their life from databases. Dr. John Snow's cholera death classic would simply be a street map of a small section of London if not for the superimposed collection of addresses of those recently killed by the disease. However, there are at least two other factors that bring interest to maps—one more practically oriented than the other. A good map is one in which two or more databases are combined that show surprising connections between seemingly unrelated raw data sets. Knowing where to find those databases and how to process them takes a certain amount of skill and patience. The other more ephemeral aspect of a good map is limited only by your imagination. It is up to you to use an ever-growing array of online tools to think of new relationships between sets of facts.

When the two aspects—the practical and the creative—combine effectively, the user has an "Aha" moment and is engaged with the story the map illustrates. Is there a relationship between homicides and gun sales? Does a location's average temperature have anything to do with the number of domestic violence reports? Is the location of a Starbucks' coffee shop related to the economic status of a neighborhood? Is the number of houses decorated for Halloween connected with the number of children who live in the area? All of these matters—great and small—and many others can be answered.

The exercises for this chapter will show you how to use databases and maps to tell stories. Hopefully, you will go beyond these examples to tell your own. For this first one, you will use the spreadsheet program Excel and the online map generator GeoCommons.

The website for the Environmental Protection Agency (EPA) <http://epa.gov> lists several topics of interest from acid rain to water issues (Figure 10.5).

For this exercise, we will concentrate on what are known as "Superfund Sites." According to the EPA site, "Superfund is the federal government's program to clean up the nation's uncontrolled hazardous waste sites." It dates from the environmental disasters in the 1970s in such locations as Love Canal in Niagara Falls, New York:

> Twenty five years after the Hooker Chemical Company stopped using the Love Canal as an industrial dump, 82 different compounds, 11 of them suspected carcinogens, have been percolating upward through the soil, their drum containers rotting and leaching their contents into the backyards and basements of 100 homes and a public school built on the banks of the canal.

Figure 10.5 The EPA's website contains a vast amount of information for the public and others who wish to make maps from the databases provided. Want to see what bed bugs look like? Click on the link. Keep it to yourself. *Courtesy of the Environmental Protection Agency*

In 1980, the Comprehensive Environmental Response, Compensation, and Liability Act (CERCLA) was passed by Congress after medical horror stories from Love Canal became public. Since CERCLA wasn't a particularly catchy name, Superfund became the common way to refer to the program. With an initial $700 million fund, an attempt was made to clean the initial 799 polluted sites. Since its start, the Superfund has grown to $8.5 billion with more than 1,000 toxic areas.

For the first exercise, you will use a list of Superfund toxic waste sites in the United States and plot them on a map. To make the information a bit more interesting, you will combine that data with the 100 wealthiest US counties to see if there is a visual connection between the two. If you live in a wealthy county, is it likely that your house will be next to a toxic waste dump?

1. Go to the EPA's Superfund page: <http://www.epa.gov/superfund/> and click on the link for "Superfund Sites Where You Live" link." Click on the "Superfund site information" link in the right side search box (Figure 10.6).

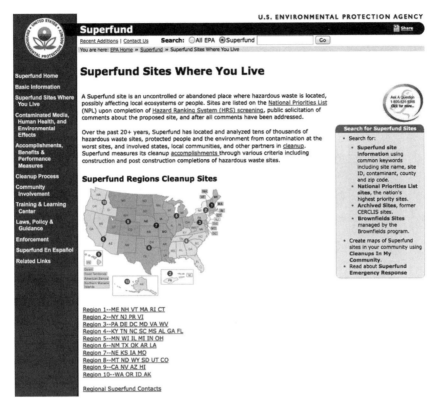

Figure 10.6   It sounds so optimistic, doesn't it? Superfund. It's not just a fund—it's a SUPERfund. With a name like that, it will no doubt clean all of the toxic waste dumps and other messy environmental hazards in no time at all (insert the wink-eyed emoticon here).

2. Click on the link "View a list of all NPL sites (National Priority Locations)" located at the end of the second paragraph (Figure 10.7).

Figure 10.7   Sometimes finding where the databases are linked takes a bit of sleuthing and a helpful guide—true for most governmental and corporate sites.

3. You can now link to a rather long and perhaps depressing list of toxic sites by state. Not to worry. Click the "Save results in Excel format" link and then OK, and the list should open in Excel. Save the file as Superfund_Data_Original.xlsx (Figure 10.8).

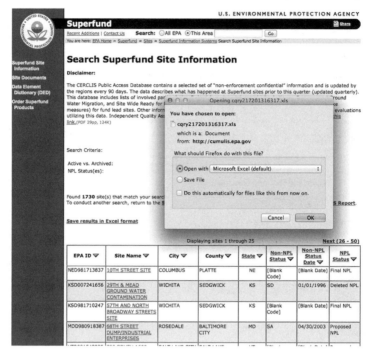

Figure 10.8 You might want to check the box to automatically default to the Excel spreadsheet program with files of this type.

4. The good news: We are done with the EPA website. The bad news: Just as you learned in Chapter 9, many times databases need to be cleaned from errors and extraneous information. First off, resave the file in a format the GeoCommons map program recognizes, a Comma Separated Values (CSV) file, "NPL_Sites.csv. Ignore the error message and press Continue. Keep the original data file for now just in case you need it again (Figure 10.9).

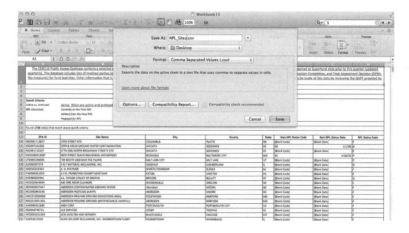

Figure 10.9 As with most software programs, there are many save options available. Always make sure you save work in the proper format for later processing—in this case, a CVS file.

5. Click and drag the row numbers 1–12 and then the Control and K keys to remove those top rows.

6. Notice column H, "NPL Status Code." This is where the government cleverly placed a most important fact—whether a NPL site's status is Final (F, which should be in the list) or Deleted (D) or Proposed (P), which should not be a part of the file. Obviously, you need to remove the D and P sites from the database. Click within the A2 box under the "EPA ID" title and drag over to the right side and then scroll down all the way to the last file. You want to highlight all of the data except the top title row. From the Data menu item, select the first choice, "Sort . . .." Under the Column heading, click the blue line and select Column H. The Order should be from A to Z. Press OK (Figure 10.10).

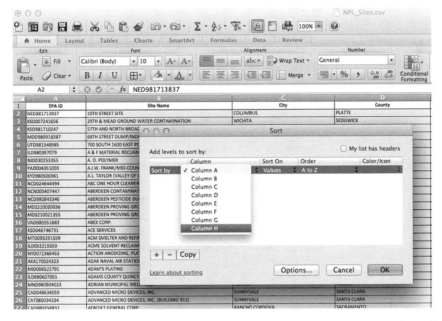

Figure 10.10 Make sure you save yourself some work and not highlight the top title row before you sort the data in Column H.

7. Click and drag the A2 box and highlight all of the "D" files. Press the Control and K keys to remove the entries. Scroll down and do the same for the "P" files. Save. Ignore. Continue.

8. Scroll back to the top and click on the columns F, G, and H to highlight all the data below and again the Control and K keys to remove those columns. You should now have five columns labeled EPA ID, Site Name, City, County, and State. Save. Ignore. Continue.

9. Now you need to process a database that shows the wealthiest US counties. There are 3,141 counties in the United States. Go to <http://en.wikipedia.org/wiki/List_of_highest-income_counties_in_the_United_States> and click and drag to highlight the top 100 highest-income counties—from Loudoun in Virginia with a medium household income of $119,134 to Warren in New Jersey with $66,594 in 2011. By the way, the county with the *lowest* medium household income is

Buffalo in South Dakota with $5,213. By the way, Buffalo County has a population of about 2,000 residents whom mostly live on the Crow Creek Native American Reservation. The unemployment rate is 57 percent. Highlight and copy the five columns for the 100 counties (Figure 10.11).

Median household income

2011

Rank ♦	County ♦	State ♦	Median Household Income[1] ♦	Population[2] ♦
1	Loudoun County	Virginia	$119,134	325,405
2	Fairfax County	Virginia	$105,797	1,100,692
3	Arlington County	Virginia	$100,735	216,004
4	Hunterdon County	New Jersey	$99,099	128,038
5	Howard County	Maryland	$98,953	293,142
6	Somerset County	New Jersey	$96,360	324,893
7	Prince William County	Virginia	$95,146	419,096
8	Fauquier County	Virginia	$93,762	66,320
9	Douglas County	Colorado	$93,573	292,167
10	Montgomery County	Maryland	$92,909	989,794
11	Charles County	Maryland	$91,733	149,130
12	Nassau County	New York	$91,414	1,344,436
13	Stafford County	Virginia	$91,348	132,133
14	Morris County	New Jersey	$91,332	494,976
15	Putnam County	New York	$90,735	99,933
16	Calvert County	Maryland	$89,393	89,256
17	Williamson County	Tennessee	$86,962	188,560
18	Delaware County	Ohio	$85,365	178,341
19	Santa Clara County	California	$84,895	1,809,378
20	York County	Virginia	$84,167	66,134
21	Anne Arundel	Maryland	$84,138	544,403
22	Carroll County	Maryland	$84,117	167,288
23	Suffolk County	New York	$84,106	1,498,816
24	Sussex County	New Jersey	$83,839	148,517
25	Carver County	Minnesota	$83,348	92,638

Figure 10.11 Copy the headings at the top along with all the data in only this first table.

10. Open a new Excel file and paste the county data. Save the file as "Top_Counties. csv" and close the file. Save, Ignore, Continue. (You should know this last bit by now.)

11. Open the file. You will notice that the weblinks have vanished. Unfortunately, the map coordinates for the two Alaska counties are not accurate and must be removed. Click on Row 63 to highlight the entire row and then the Control and K keys to remove the Anchorage entry. Do the same for Row 88, Matanuska-Susitna County. Now, click the angled arrow in the top left corner between the A and 1 boxes (you have a better description?) to highlight all the information. From the Data menu item, select Sort . . . and County under the Column heading. The Order should be from A to Z. Click OK. Next, go back to the file and click in the D1 box and delete "[1]" and then click in the E1 box and delete "[2]" from the ends of the titles. Now, select the D column to highlight all of the dollar amounts. You must remove the dollar signs. Press the Apple and 1 keys to see the Format Cells dialog box. Select Number, use the down arrow to set the Decimal places to 0, and then OK (Figure 10.12). Save and then close the file. (Notice how I am practicing restraint?)

	A	B	C	D	E
1	Rank	County	State	Median Hous	Population
2	93	Alameda Cou	California	67558	1,529,875
3	26	Alexandria C	Virginia	82748	144,301
4	62	Anchorage C	Alaska	72813	295,570
5	21	Anne Arunde	Maryland	84138	544,403
6	3	Arlington Co	Virginia	100735	216,004
7	39	Bergen Coun	New Jersey	79272	911,004
8	88	Boulder Cou	Colorado	68637	299,378
9	70	Bucks County	Pennsylvania	70617	626,854
10	61	Burlington C	New Jersey	72896	449,576
11	16	Calvert Coun	Maryland	89393	89,256
12	22	Carroll Count	Maryland	84117	167,288
13	25	Carver Count	Minnesota	83348	92,638
14	11	Charles Cour	Maryland	91733	149,130
15	40	Chester Cour	Pennsylvania	79160	503,897
16	68	Chesterfield	Virginia	71110	320,277
17	28	Collin County	Texas	82237	812,226
18	55	Contra Costa	California	74353	1,066,096
19	73	Dakota Coun	Minnesota	69902	402,006
20	76	Dallas Count	Iowa	69831	69,444
21	84	Davis County	Utah	69021	311,811
22	18	Delaware Co	Ohio	85365	178,341
23	78	Denton Cour	Texas	69644	686,406
24	9	Douglas Cou	Colorado	93573	292,167
25	57	DuPage Cour	Illinois	74072	923,222
26	91	Dutchess Co	New York	67727	297,999
27	2	Fairfax Coun	Virginia	105797	1,100,692
28	44	Fairfield Cou	Connecticut	77289	925,899
29	8	Fauquier Cou	Virginia	93762	66,320
30	60	Fayette Cour	Georgia	72962	107,784
31	30	Forsyth Cour	Georgia	82209	181,840
32	27	Fort Bend Co	Texas	82271	606,953
33	43	Frederick Co	Maryland	77791	236,745
34	81	Frederick Co	Virginia	69155	79,666
35	66	Gloucester C	New Jersey	71850	289,104
36	35	Hamilton Co	Indiana	80999	282,810
37	94	Hanover Cou	Virginia	67505	100,342

Figure 10.12 With the database in alphabetical order by county, the dollar figures converted to integers, and any extra elements removed, it can now be used within another database (What????).

12. There is one more database that must be addressed. In order to present the boundary of each of the top counties on your map, you must use a database of all the US counties. The bad news: It is no easy task to find a database with all the county coordinates necessary to draw their boundaries on a map, isolate the counties you care about for this exercise (you do care, right?) amid the more than 3,000 possible counties, and delete all the others. The good news: I've done that for you. Go to <http://paulmartinlester.info/Routledge/Top_Counties_Boundaries.csv> and download the file. Now, click on Columns A–E in your file "Top_Counties.csv," copy and paste them into Columns F–J of "Top_Counties_Boundaries.csv" and save and close the file.

13. You can now delete or store in an inactive folder two files: "Top_Counties.csv" and "Superfund_Original.xls." For this exercise, you need two database sets: NPL_sites.csv and Top_Counties_Boundaries.csv.

14. To make your map, go to the GeoCommons website: <http://geocommons.com/>, click the "Sign up for Free" button, and fill out the registration form (Figure 10.13). Good news. We're about halfway through this exercise.

Figure 10.13 The GeoCommons website contains thousands of databases and maps on almost any topic that you can use to create even more engaging connections between seemingly disparate topics.

15. Click the Upload Files button and select the two CSV files you have (Figure 10.14) and then click the Next button. If you already have an account, use the button at the top of the desktop to Upload Data to bring the files into your GeoCommons library.

Figure 10.14 GeoCommons makes it easy to upload files.

16. Click on the Next Step button of the "NPL Sites" name in the dataset window. Select the Geocode choice. GeoCommons uses geocoding to automatically find latitude and longitude map coordinates from addresses and zip codes within CSV files. It would be more accurate if the EPA database included zip codes, but finding them for each site would be more work than you need for this exercise. Nevertheless, extra credit? If you do go to that much trouble, add each site's zip code and maybe a picture and a description while you're at it, in separate columns. The next exercise will tell you how to add those additions. In the following window, click Continue.

17. After the database processes, you will see that there are a number of errors, for example, sites that GeoCommons couldn't find (without zip codes). You need to purge them from the database. Unfortunately, this process is a bit tedious. Check the top box to select all the entries that you can see in the Errors window. Select the Delete Row button at the bottom next page, and then the check box at the top (Figure 10.15). Repeat this process (about 16 times) until all the smelly toxic sites are removed from your database.

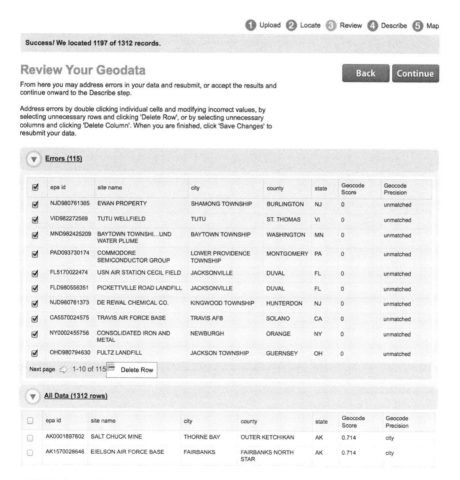

Figure 10.15 Remember the sequence: Check the top box, Delete Row, Next page, and repeat until finished.

18. Select Save & Resubmit and then OK. Your database will reprocess and should show the entries without errors. Press the Continue button.

19. The next step is to "Describe and Share your Dataset." All you really need to do at this point is to name the data. Use the title "NPL Superfund Sites," name the tags "Superfund Toxic Waste Environment," and the description "US Superfund Toxic Waste Locations" (Figure 10.16). You should make the database private by unchecking the boxes Edit, Access, and Find. You will be able to change and add information to this page later. Scroll down and press Save. You will see your data in the form of a simple map. We'll get to mapmaking in a moment.

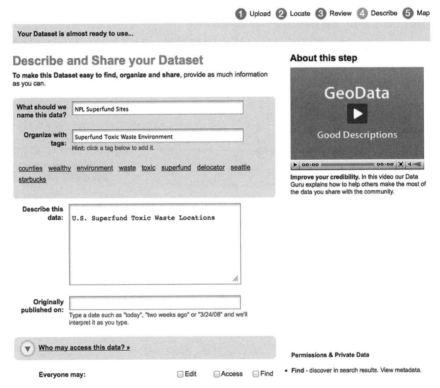

Figure 10.16 GeoCommons provides a video about the importance of selecting quality tags for your databases so others can find them. This feature will be important when you make your finished work public.

20. Now you need to process the other database. From your account pull-down menu at the top, select "Your Library" and press the Pending Datasets button. Find the "Top Counties Boundaries" file and click the Next Step button. Then make the "Join with a boundary dataset" choice. Within the Search window type "Simple US Counties," click the Search button. Hopefully, the entry with the message "uploaded by zfjohnson over 2 years ago" will be one of the top databases shown. Find it and press Select (Figure 10.17).

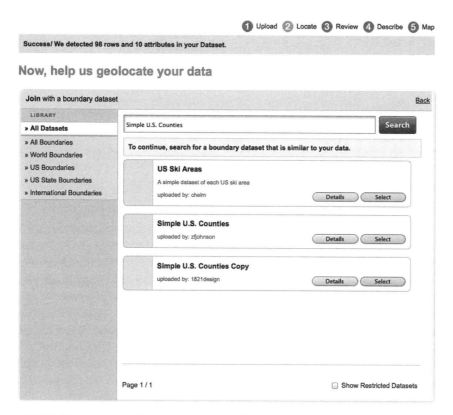

Figure 10.17 There are several choices you can make within GeoCommons that have to do with county boundaries, but the database created by a user named Zachary Johnson fits our needs.

21. In the next window, click on the lowercase "entity" in the left column and the uppercase "Entity" in the right column. Don't ask. You should see an overly exuberant Success message. Calm down and press Continue (Figure 10.18).

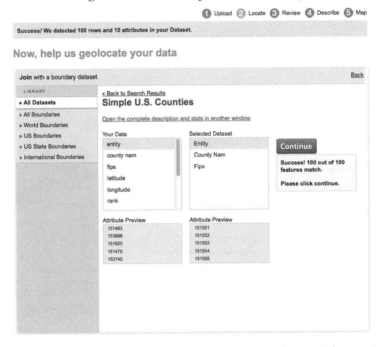

Figure 10.18 Select "entity" and then "Entity" within the two columns. Often, such subtle differences make all the difference to a successful operation.

22. If there are no errors in the database shown in the next window, click Continue. Once again, describe the database. Use the title "Wealthiest US Counties" and press Save. In the next window, double-click in the map a few times to zoom in and see the oddly shaped county boundaries your database file created (Figure 10.19).

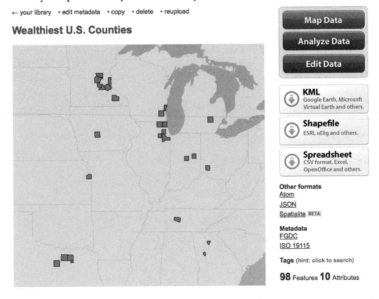

Figure 10.19 In the next few steps, you will learn how to make your map more aesthetically appealing.

23. Click the Map Data button. You should now see an acetate-style map of the country with all of the counties represented (Figure 10.20).

Figure 10.20 The GeoCommons map attributes desktop.

24. In the Style dialog box at the left, ignore Shapes. Click the Color section. Select Single and a green shade (for the color of money). Transparency for the counties should be set at 25%. At the bottom is an icon for Infowindows. These are the dialog boxes that pop up when you click on a map's data point. Within Style Infowindows, click in the Enable Tabs box and *deselect* from the top: entity, county nam, fips, latitude, and longitude (Figure 10.21). Close the Style dialog box (the "X" at the top right of the box).

Figure 10.21 If you forget the meaning of an icon along the left side, simply click on it to produce its dialog box.

25. Now you need to layer in your NPL database. Within the Layers dialog box at the right, press the "+ Add" button. In the Search window, type "NPL sites" and press Search. The database file should be the first one displayed. Click the "Add to map" button and close the window (Figure 10.22). (*Be careful to only click the database file once—sometime it takes a while to process.*)

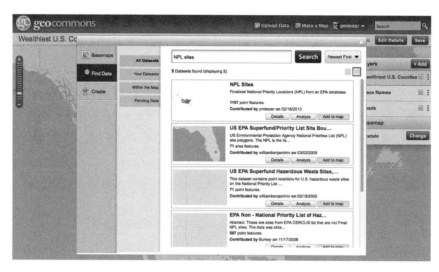

Figure 10.22 If you are interested in this topic, you might want to explore other databases that users have created about the US Superfund. Not now.

26. With the NPL Sites highlighted in green, return to the Style dialog box. In Shape, select a simple round circle. In Color, you might go for a red hue. In Icon Size, slide the bar for a 50% size, skip the Line choices, set the Transparency to 50%, and in Infowindows, check the Enable Tabs box, scroll down, and deselect the two sets of Geocode Score and Geocode Precision choices (Figure 10.23). Close the window. Press Save at the top right.

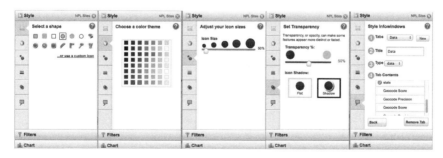

Figure 10.23 Because there are two databases, there are two sets of choices you need to make for your data points.

27. After the files have finished processing, you will see the "Describe and Share your Dataset" page. Type in the title "NPL Superfund Sites and Top US Counties," the tags "Superfund Toxic Waste Environment wealthy counties," and the description "A map that shows the connection between waste and wealth" (Figure 10.24).

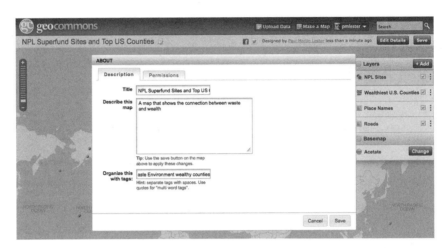

Figure 10.24 You will eventually want to fill out a "Describe and Share" form for your completed map.

28. Double-click to zoom in to see the red toxic points with the green wealthy counties (Figure 10.25).

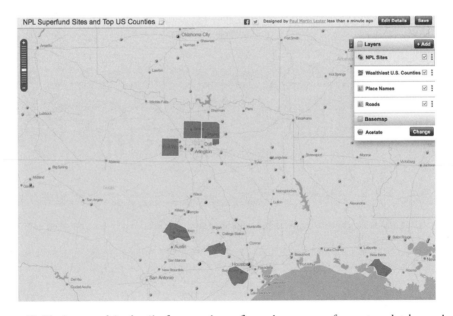

Figure 10.25 A zoomed-in detail of a map that reflects the merger of your two databases shows that most toxic sites are not located in the wealthiest counties. What a shock. For example, all the wealthy counties in Texas have somehow avoided toxic waste issues.

29. Now you need to make your map more visually interesting. Under the Basemap section of the choices in the right-hand box, press the Change button and select your choice of basemaps (Figure 10.26). Close the window and click the Save button at the top. The map will take a few moments to process.

Figure 10.26 For this exercise, I chose the "Microsoft Road" basemap, probably because I don't want to seem too partial to Apple.

30. Finally, pick a part of the map where you live or have a special interest, zoom in, and click on some data points to find out more information. Make a screen shot for your records.

If you feel particularly energized by this exercise you may want to zoom in on your map, click on each county, note its name and how many Superfund sites are within its border, add these figures to your database, and create a new map. Otherwise, just relax and enjoy what you have already created or what I came up with at <http://geocommons. com/maps/236661>.

This next exercise should be a bit more personal. Your clickable map made with Geo-Commons will show all the places you have lived for at least a month or if you haven't traveled that much, the places you have visited. Each map data point will include the city, state, the years you were there, your own pictures, a website, and a brief story.

However, you might want to work on your own ideas. You could make a map of all the top advertising and public relations agencies in your area or country, vacation points of interest, all of the cities visited by Jack Kerouac in his book *On the Road,* locations that might be good as backdrops for your next motion picture, or the locations where you took photographs that are in your portfolio.

Besides your GeoCommons account, you will need a website that you already have or created in the Chapter 1 exercise. The Excel spreadsheet program will once again be the home of your database. You will also most likely need to use Photoshop or an equivalent picture processing program, and Google Maps <https://maps.google.com/>.

1. Open a new file in Excel and give it any name you wish. I used "Places_I_Lived" (never have spaces in file names). Save the file in a .csv format.

2. In the first row, type in the headings—one for each column: city, state, latitude, longitude, years, image, weblink, and story. For each entry, add the city, state (or country), (see the next step for latitude and longitude), number of years (or days or months) you were there, the coding to show a picture of you when you were there with the coding, `<p><a><img src="http://your_website_domain_name.com/file_name.png"alt=",` a brief description of the image, (use small files—not more than an inch wide—in .jpg or .png format), the coding to show a weblink related to you or the location: `<a href="http://URL">, The Website's Name</a>`, and a brief story (Figure 10.27).

Figure 10.27 The unfinished Excel CSV file gives you an idea of the data you will enter for this exercise. The photographic collection at the Library of Congress is a location where many historical links can be found. Don't forget though, you can link to videos too.

3. In order for each location to be as accurate as possible, open Google Maps and type in the location in the Search window (if you know the address, even better). A marker should show on the map. Click the marker with a right-click and select "What's here?" The latitude and longitude coordinates will now show in the Search window (Figure 10.28).

Figure 10.28 Google Maps can give you directions to where you would like to be, but also tell you precisely where you are with the "What's here?" dialog box choice.

4. Copy each coordinate (do not include the comma and don't forget the "-" sign) and place them within the correct Excel file column. Save.

5. You will probably use Photoshop to resize your pictures. The .jpg or .png images you use must then be uploaded to your website. Follow the directions from your provider or use an FTP (File Transfer Protocol) program such as Fetch <http://fetchsoftworks.com/> or FileZilla <http://filezilla-project.org/>.

6. Now, go to GeoCommons (hopefully you finished the first exercise so you know how to use the online mapping program). Click the Upload Files button, select the Excel CSV file, and then click the Next button. Be sure to select the "Locate using the latitude and longitude columns" choice for your data. As long as there are no errors in your data, press Continue until you are ready to select the Make a Map button and then choose the Map Data button.

7. Within the Style dialog box at the left, select the shape, color, icon size, and transparency percentage of your markers. For Infowindows, check the Enable Tabs box and deselect the items you don't want users to see (Figure 10.29).

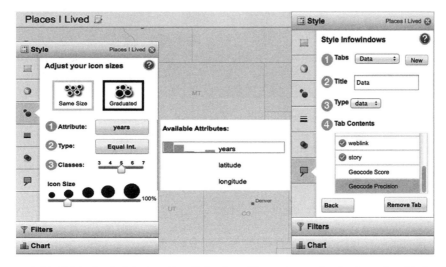

Figure 10.29 With the Style's Icon Size dialog box, if you choose the Graduated and Select buttons and then Years (or another name you used), your icons will reflect the different time periods you included in your CSV file. Also, for Infowindows, be sure to deselect latitude and longitude (or Geocode Score and Precision if you are creating your map for the first time) so the map shows only the data points you want.

8. Make a basemap choice. Close the window and click the Save button at the top, make any changes to the description and access, and press Save again. Don't forget to "Describe and Share your Dataset." The map will take a few moments to process. Make a screen-save and show it off to your friends (Figure 10.30).

Figure 10.30 If you set your access for public viewing, you can email the URL provided by Geo-Commons and make your map available via Facebook, Twitter, your website, or computer hackers from China.

Sources

10,000 Words. (August 28, 2008). "10 Mind-Blowing Maps (and 3 Ways to Create Them)." Accessed January 12, 2013. http://www.mediabistro.com/10000words/10-mind-blowing-maps-and-3-ways-to_b213.

———. "Where to Find the Best Online Interactive Maps." Accessed January 12, 2013. http://www.mediabistro.com/10000words/where-to-find-best-online-interactive_b362.

2Itch Talk. Accessed January 12, 2013. http://talk.2itch.com/.

ABC7. (December 12, 2012). "Cal State Fullerton Lockdown." Accessed January 31, 2013. http://abclocal.go.com/kabc/story?section=news/local/orange_county&id=8918278.

Beck, Eckardt C. (January 1979). "The Love Canal Tragedy." Accessed February 16, 2013. http://www.epa.gov/aboutepa/history/topics/lovecanal/01.html.

Bing. "Maps." Accessed January 12, 2013. http://www.bing.com/maps/.

Cain, Patrick. (July 10, 2010). "-30-." Accessed January 12, 2013. http://thestar.blogs.com/maps/.

Cornell University Library. "Columbia or America: 500 Years of Controversy." Accessed January 12, 2013. http://olinuris.library.cornell.edu/exhibitions/maps.

Crowdmap. Accessed February 26, 2013. http://crowdmap.com.

"Multimedia." *The Bay Citizen.* Accessed January 14, 2013. http://www.baycitizen.org/data/.

Garfield, Simon. (2013). *On the Map: A Mind-Expanding Exploration of the Way the World Looks.* NY: Gotham Books.

Kuro. Accessed January 12, 2013. http://www.kuro.la/.

Lester, Paul Martin. (2014). *Visual Communication: Images with Messages.* 6th Edition. Boston: Cengage Learning.

LookBack Maps. Accessed January 14, 2013. http://www.lookbackmaps.net.

Looney, Margaret. (November 9, 2012). "Mapping Election Results in Real Time." Ijnet. Accessed January 12, 2013. http://ijnet.org/stories/mapping-election-results-real-time.

Meograph. Accessed January 12, 2013. http://www.meograph.com/.

Stat Silk. "World Stats Interactive Maps—Index." Accessed January 30, 2013. http://www.statsilk.com/maps/world-stats-interactive-maps-index

TED. (February, 2010). "Blaise Aguera y Arcas Demos Augmented-Reality Maps." Accessed January 12, 2013. http://www.ted.com/talks/blaise_aguera.html.

Terra Sound. "Soundtrack." Accessed January 12, 2013. http://www.terrasound.org/soundtrack/sanfrancisco.htm.

"Toxic Waters." *The New York Times* (May 22, 2012). Accessed January 12, 2013. http://projects.nytimes.com/toxic-waters/polluters/new-york.

Whitehouse, David. (August 9, 2000). "Ice Age Star Map Discovered." BBC News. Accessed January 12, 2013. http://news.bbc.co.uk/2/hi/science/nature/871930.stm.

Wikipedia contributors. "List of highest-income counties in the United States." *Wikipedia, The Free Encyclopedia.* Accessed February 18, 2013. http://en.wikipedia.org/wiki/List_of_highest-income_counties_in_the_United_States.

Worley, Dwight R. (December 23, 2012). "The Gun Owner Next Door." Accessed January 12, 2013. http://www.lohud.com/article/20121223/NEWS04/312230056?nclick_check=1.

Section IV

SOFTWARE-DRIVEN CONTENT

A media user has many motives—a need to be momentarily entertained, a hedge against temporary boredom, a quick accounting of the day's news, a suggestion for a restaurant and a movie, a way of saving money, and no doubt many others. Content producers must be aware and prepared for several possible consumer incentives that dictate desire. The five chapters in this section use specially designed software that have the potential to satisfy most consumer demands.

Games

Quiz games provide users with tests of their knowledge within a supportive, educational environment in the spirit of social constructivism that encourages collaborative activities. Games related to news stories can be seen in *The New York Times* and other publication websites in which a player competes against the computer or other users. "A Google a Day" challenges participants to find answers to cryptic clues using the popular search engine.

Simulations

With the best simulations, a goal is to help a user understand more fully the complicated aspects of a story by enmeshing the player into a reality different from her own. "City Council" helps a participant understand the journalism process, while "SPENT" explains the effects of poverty on individuals. These two types of simulations, professional practice and issue-oriented, have one aspect in common—they both create engaging first-person experiences.

QR Codes

One of the most prevalent examples of software-driven content is the Quick Response (QR) code. Created by a Japanese company in 1996, the graphic collection of black and white squares printed on billboards, advertisements, window displays, and so on can be links to phone numbers, special offers, videos, and websites for users with a smartphone or tablet app. Graphic designers and artists continue to produce visually creative QR codes within unique contexts—on dinner plates at restaurants that link to drink and dessert specials, behind-the-scene access for the promotion of a movie or television show, and as part of a news photograph that allows users to see video.

3D Displays

As a gimmick to attract attention, the 2009 cover of *Esquire* did its job. With downloaded software and a built-in camera, the actor Robert Downey, Jr. led computer users to the magazine's 3D features. Although many found the "in your face" displays initially charming, the effect had little long-term influence because of the superficial nature of the content. If used more thoughtfully, mass communicators who produce serious stories on social problems might consider this technology as a way to further engage traditional readers.

Apps

Location-specific applications downloaded for free or at a modest cost to a person's smartphone or tablet pinpoint a user's location to provide immediate links to commercial and cultural establishments imposed on a map and/or floating over a view of an area provided by the built-in camera. These environmental-specific apps provided by Acrossair, Junaio, Layar, Wikitude, and others allow users to interact with their environment. Apps could also include a list of news stories that occurred near a smartphone user's location.

11 GAMES

There are usually two types of persons who use computers for the first time in a serious way to complete projects within a mass communications context:

Those who get frustrated early and expect answers to be readily offered and explicit

Or

Those who enjoy the intellectual stimulation in which frustration simply becomes a necessary component of a game-playing exercise.

Once you learn that the use of a computer can be thought of as a game in which the rules change daily, a much more pleasurable and rewarding experience waits—as long as you make regular backups of the work you produce.

Social constructivism theory can help understand your role within a learning environment. Because we acquire knowledge through challenges, designing and playing games have been established as necessary components to a person's education. An individual's specific and separate experiences up to this point dictate how successful the game is.

More importantly, digital innovations as described in this textbook require a collaborative or social approach. Although it is possible to achieve satisfactory results alone, teaming up with another or with members of a discrete group creates the best chance to produce work with lasting impact for others. Consider these two-person teams that were successful because of their collaboration:

- Marie Sklodowska-Curie and Pierre Curie, a married couple that shared a Nobel Prize in Physics for their work on radiology.
- Christo Vladimirov Javacheff and Jeanne-Claude Marie Denat de Guillebon, a married couple known for their colorful environmental artistic displays.
- Elton Hercules John and Bernard John Taupin were a singer and lyricist team that became one of the most successful pop song duos in history.
- Steven Paul Jobs and Stephen Gary Wozniak were cofounders of the Apple Computer Company.
- Sergey Brin and Larry Page were cofounders of Google, Inc.

Consequently, you should never feel you are alone when designing games or other presentations related to your particular mass communications field. In fact, working in a social, collaborative environment within a classroom, lab, or online should be a regular working requirement.

One of the best resources for games is the website of the High School Journalism Initiative (HSJ) with its office at the prestigious Missouri School of Journalism. Established in 2000, it serves to train young reporters as well as educate all in the importance of the First Amendment. HSJ currently is connected to more than 3,500 student news websites.

Several websites offer grammar exercises in the form of interactive quizzes. HSJ offers a "Test Your Skills" game that includes the question:

Which Sentence Has the Error?

- That dog is so ugly it's owner has to walk it in the dark.
- "I think it's a shame," said the Venusian, "that you earthlings don't understand my language."
- The flea could hardly contain his enthusiasm: "More than six square feet of Dalmatian, and it's mine, all mine!"

Whether you are correct or not, there is a brief explanation of the proper use of possessives.

"Newsroom 101" contains more than 2,000 exercises designed for journalism students and professionals who need to learn or take a refresher course in the Associated Press writing style and in grammar, usage, and spelling. Developed by Gerald Grow, a retired professor from Florida A&M University who is better known for his musing on such diverse topics as Buddhism, food, and computers, the elaborate site is a witty exploration of the written rules that makes journalism unique.

Perhaps as a way to encourage more tactical web searches, but more likely a clever marketing strategy, the web browser Google initiated its "A Google a Day" game in 2011. *The New York Times* ran the feature next to its workday crossword puzzle with the questions getting harder as the week progressed. For example, one day's clue was:

> "My name is Robert. One day before my brother Rohan's 19th birthday, our father had an album on the Billboard 200. Name the album."
>   (Try the keywords Robert, Rohan, and Billboard if you don't know.)

Other variations of quiz games included one that was provided by CNN on Beatles trivia while MSNBC and the Scripps Howard newspaper chain offered a "spelling bee" game based on the rules of the National Spelling Bee. Both were included as sidebars connected to a news story about each topic.

While a student at Washington State University, Vancouver, Matt Johnson developed a PowerPoint program inspired by the popular answer-then-question television game show "Jeopardy!" hosted by the amicable Alex Trebek. Depending on your mass communication professional interest, you can use the free website to write specific categories and answers within each dollar amount. To continue with the answers-first format, every Friday, the online magazine *Slate* presents a 12-question news quiz by 74-time "Jeopardy!" winner Ken Jennings. (He couldn't win one more game?) At the end, you can see how your score compared with the average player and one from the magazine. For *Parade* magazine, Jennings also produces a game called "Konnections" in which players answer questions and try to determine the links between them. (It's good that Jennings never encountered a spelling category on the game show.)

For some, checking your score against others is a powerful incentive to play. "The News IQ Quiz" offered by the Pew Research Center, a nonpartisan "fact tank" more known for its polling on various political topics, is a quiz that includes "pictures, maps, graphics and

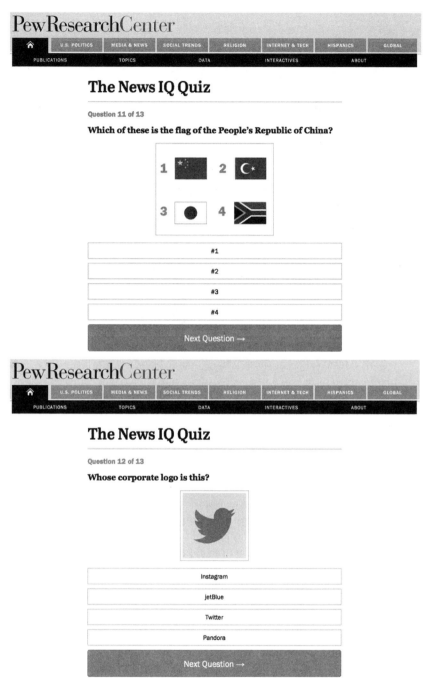

Figure 11.1 Only 57 percent of the players of the Pew "News IQ Quiz" could identify #1 as the flag of China. However, 91 percent of those aged 18–29 knew the Twitter logo.
Courtesy of The Pew Research Center

symbols" (Figure 11.1). "When you finish," the site reads, "you will be able to compare your News IQ with the average American, as well as with the scores of college graduates and those who didn't attend college; with men and women; and with people your age as well as other ages."

Figure 11.2 Funded by the Donald W. Reynolds Journalism Institute at the University of Missouri, "MU Tiger Challenge" was a popular game in which students won cash prizes, but it was also an experiment in the creation of interactive challenges that improved news reading. *Courtesy of Borchuluun Yadamsuren, developed by Joseph Griffin and Michael Haug of Double Maple, and illustrated by Oudvin Cassell*

As a way to get students to read news websites, Dr. Borchuluun Yadamsuren, a user experience researcher in the University of Missouri's School of Information Science and Learning Technologies and the software company Double Maple developed an online game called "MU Tiger Challenge." The Reynolds Journalism Institute, KOMU television station, and the *Columbia Missourian* newspaper sponsored the game that stems from Yadamsuren's work in news user types mentioned in Chapter 2. Fans are challenged and encouraged to submit pictures and videos, to join discussion chat rooms on various sports-related topics, and answer questions about the university's football team (Figure 11.2). While players learn of each week's challenge, news headline links are displayed in a right-hand column that take users to the station's or newspaper's website where they can read the article and, hopefully, other news stories that are provided.

Additional examples of games used to interest readers in stories include news quizzes from the *Chicago Tribune* and *The New York Times*. The *Tribune*'s 10-question "Weekly news quiz" has links to newspaper sections and other online features. However, the "News Quiz" produced by *The Times* that offers five news-related questions is not as subtle. The game starts with the sly message, "See what you know about the news below. To prepare, you might scan the articles or summaries on today's paper" with a link to the top headlines and a reproduction of the front page for the current edition. Nevertheless, after you take the *Chicago Tribune*'s quiz, after every question and answer is a link to a related story that was published on the newspaper's website. Finally, for the Washington, DC, Newseum, an institution devoted to mass communications, its "News Mania" trivia game located on its website asks questions "as fresh as today's headlines." At the end, you can printout a press pass with your name. If you did well on the game, you will be designated an editor.

Yadamsuren's "MU Tiger Challenge" social game experiment resulted in a 16-point list of lessons learned for news organizations that included:

- Market the games early and often;
- Make the games fun, colorful, and interactive;
- Create the site so users want to stay on it;
- Vary the types of challenges that are offered;
- Ask users to include pictures from the community;
- Suggest that game players tell their friends;
- Have readers vote on their favorites;
- Create chat rooms for discussions about the game; and
- Ask for feedback from game players.

The goal of any gaming program should be to use it as an enticement to get users interested in related, but perhaps, more complex, topics.

■ CHALLENGES, CRITIQUES, AND AMUSEMENTS

- What kind of a computer user are you, a whiner or a gamer? Why do you think that is?
- Name some other two-person teams whom couldn't accomplish alone what they could as a duo, but don't include Sacco and Vanzetti, Smith and Hickock (look them up if you have to), or Batman and Robin. What did your two-person teams possess as a team that made them successful that they couldn't achieve individually?
- Do you think news quizzes could be seen as trivializing important events?
- How else could you use the "MU Tiger Challenge" game concept to add interest to other activities such as baseball and basketball teams, the debate club, service learning opportunities, and so on while sneakily exposing users to mass communications stories?

■ EXERCISES

Quizzes can be thought of as games if they are entertaining and engage the user. From a simple interactive "Hang Man" presentation to a multipart news quiz with compelling illustrations, quizzes offer a unique opportunity to reinforce key points and for users to learn more about your topic.

For this exercise, you will create a moderately elaborate multiple choice quiz with as many questions as you like that relate to your professional topic of mass communications using Photoshop, Dreamweaver (or any text-based word processor), and the popular web programming language known as JavaScript.

When University of Illinois student Marc Andreessen famously quit school after creating the user-friendly web browser Mosaic, he formed the Netscape Communications Corporation in 1994 in the better climate of Mountain View, California. An early software programmer hired for the firm was Brendan Eich, who developed the web software code originally named Mocha, then LiveScript, and finally JavaScript, the basis for many popular add-on features to a user's website—from clocks to calendars.

There are several books, YouTube videos, and university courses related to the JavaScript programming language and you are free to investigate those resources. Fortunately for you and myself, I was able to make a variation of a JavaScript named "Simple Quiz" that was developed by Jeremy Rue, a lecturer for the UC Berkeley Graduate School of Journalism.

1. Download the three HTML files you will need for this exercise: <http:// paulmartinlester.info/Routledge/quiz.html>, <http://paulmartinlester.info/ Routledge/quiz_splash.html>, and <http://paulmartinlester.info/Routledge/quiz_ end.html>. Put all the files for this exercise within the same folder.

2. Write at least 10 questions, 5 choices for each one including the correct answer, and find 10 pictures to illustrate the questions.

3. The <quiz.html> has the JavaScript programming for the quiz. Three questions with their images, choices, and explanations are included. Do not change the variable names of "question," "image," "choices," "correct," and "explanation," but you can change the text related to the question. You can add as many questions as you wish. Simply copy and paste all of the information within the brackets for each question. You can also have as many multiple choice answers as you wish. Keep the same format as in the file. **Note:** The correct answer **must** match exactly the choice provided (Figure 11.3).

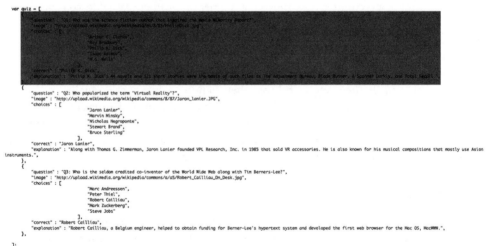

Figure 11.3 The code within the gray box is what you need to copy and paste in order to add more questions to your quiz. After any changes, save your work and reopen the file in a web browser to check it.

4. You should notice that the images all come from Wikipedia. Find a picture that you want to use on the website, click on it, then click the larger file version of the picture, and copy and paste the URL at the top to include in the "image" component of the JavaScript question. If you have your own picture or one from another source, simply include its URL. Be sure to pay attention to quotation marks and commas for the JavaScript to work properly.

5. You now need to change the title for the quiz. Near the top of the <quiz.html> file is a command: var quiztitle="**What's Your Digital Innovations IQ?**"
Simply replace your title (the part in bold) with the one provided. The rest of the programming should remain unaltered.

6. If you want to replace the graphics seen in the exercise, you will need to create the following images all at 72dpi:
File Name Size in Pixels
splash_graphic.jpg 504 x 224
splash_footer.jpg 960 x 50
again_footer.jpg 960 x 50
out_footer.jpg 960 x 50
Otherwise, download the files from: <http://paulmartinlester.info/Routledge/Images/splash_graphic.jpg>, <http://paulmartinlester.info/Routledge/Images/splash_footer.jpg>, <http://paulmartinlester.info/Routledge/Images/again_footer.jpg>, and <http://paulmartinlester.info/Routledge/Images/out_footer.jpg>.

7. Open the file <quiz_splash.html> in Dreamweaver or a simple text file. Scroll to the bottom and replace the title (use the same one as the <quiz.html> file), the headings, and text as you wish (Figure 11.4).

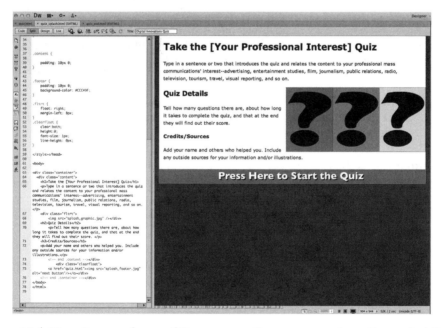

Figure 11.4 The split screen feature of Dreamweaver allows you to see the coding on the left and the design on the right. The structure of the code includes three sections: Title, Quiz Details, and Credits/Sources. Feel free to add or subtract sections as you prefer. You can add as much text as you choose, but be careful not to alter or eliminate any of the HTML coding.

8. Open the file <quiz_end.html> in Dreamweaver or a simple text file. Scroll to the bottom and replace the headings and text as you wish. Notice the code at the bottom:

<a href="http://cnn.com"><img src="out_footer.jpg" alt="out button"/></a></div>. You need to change the "cnn.com" URL to one of your choosing where users will link to after the quiz—perhaps another file on your website or blog. You might also decide to remove one or both buttons from the file. Again, it's up to you (Figure 11.5).

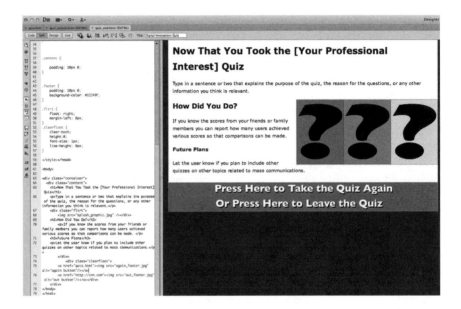

Figure 11.5 As with the quiz_splash.html file, the text at the bottom can be altered as you wish. Be sure to replace the CNN.com URL. After any changes, save your work and reopen the file in a web browser to check it.

9. Within your web browser, open the <quiz_splash.html> file. Make any changes with the text that are needed, save, and reopen the file. If all is well, click on the "Start the Quiz" button.

10. The <quiz.html> file should be open. Go through the quiz and make any changes with the text that are needed in Dreamweaver or a simple text program, save, and reopen the file (Figure 11.6).

What's Your Digital Innovations IQ?

Question 1 of 3

Q1: Who was the science fiction author that inspired the movie Minority Report?

Arthur C. Clarke

Ray Bradbury

Philip K. Dick

Isaac Asimov

H.G. Wells

Check Answer

What's Your Digital Innovations IQ?

Question 1 of 3

Q1: Who was the science fiction author that inspired the movie Minority Report?

Correct! Philip K. Dick's 44 novels and 121 short stories were the basis of such films as The Adjustment Bureau, Blade Runner, A Scanner Darkly, and Total Recall.

Arthur C. Clarke

Ray Bradbury

Philip K. Dick

Isaac Asimov

H.G. Wells

NEXT PAGE »

Figure 11.6 Users click on an answer choice and then the "Check Answer" button (top). If it is correct, the choice will be highlighted in green; if wrong, red. Regardless, the explanation reveals the correct answer with additional information. After the "Next Page" button is pressed, users move to the next question or complete the quiz.

11. When all of the questions have been answered, users see the results page. It should accurately reflect the score without alterations needed. The Continue button takes users to the last page (Figure 11.7).

What's Your Digital Innovations IQ?

You got 3 out of 3 correct for a percentage of:

100%

Press Here to Continue

Figure 11.7 Luckily, I scored 100 on the quiz. It would be really embarrassing if I flunked.

12. If all is well with the beta test of your quiz, upload the three files to your web server and tell your friends the URL so they can start to be entertained, educated, and impressed by your knowledge.

As an alternative to the quiz offered above, you might consider a similar type of user interaction feedback—the survey. Professionals within all the mass communications concentrations need to know what users think about specific presentations and/or campaigns. For example, those in advertising, entertainment, and public relations want to know what consumers think of a product, service, or island resort. Journalists might want to know what readers think of stories and graphic designs. Filmmakers might like to know a viewer's opinions about a motion picture. A 20-item survey might be an easy solution for all. One of the easiest and, consequently, most popular free online survey programs is SurveyMonkey.

1. Go to the SurveyMonkey <http://surveymonkey.com> website and click the "Sign Up FREE" button (Figure 11.8).

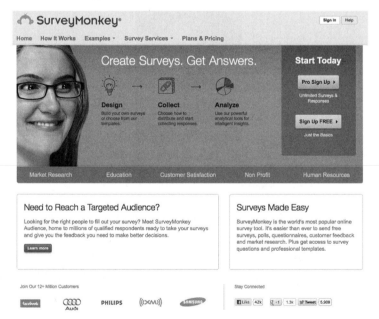

Figure 11.8 With more than 12 million customers, SurveyMonkey is a successful web business. If you don't need any special features, use it for free. Later, you might get your school or company to purchase a PRO account.

2. Fill out the Free Account form and press "Sign Up." On the next page, click on the "+ Create Survey" button (Figure 11.9).

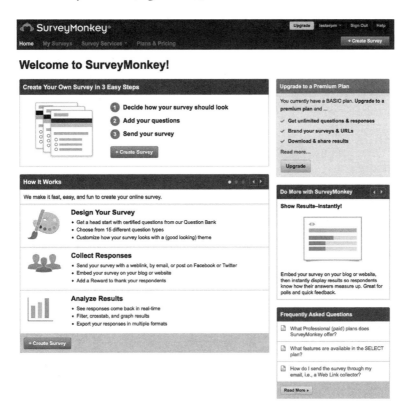

Figure 11.9 SurveyMonkey makes it easy to create, send, and analyze a survey.

3. Make sure the "Create a new survey" radio button is checked. Write a title for your survey. Select a category from the pull-down menu. The "Use an expert template button" is a feature reserved for those listed with a "PRO" account that costs money. Press Continue (Figure 11.10).

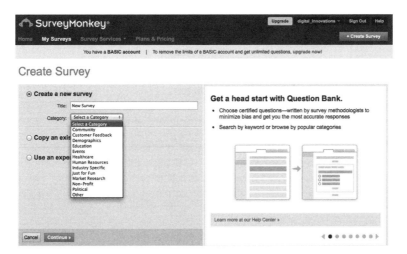

Figure 11.10 Choose your survey category. If you're not sure, simply pick the "Other" category.

4. With the "Design Survey" tab highlighted at the top, choose a color scheme from the pull-down menu. Click on the "+ Add Question" button and you will see the Question dialog box. Type in your question, make it a Multiple Choice (Only One Answer) type, display the choices as buttons, type in your choices, require an answer to the question, and press the "Save & Add Next Question." You can also add demographic questions if you want to know something about those who answer your survey. Repeat the process for all the other questions in your survey and press "Save & Close" (Figure 11.11).

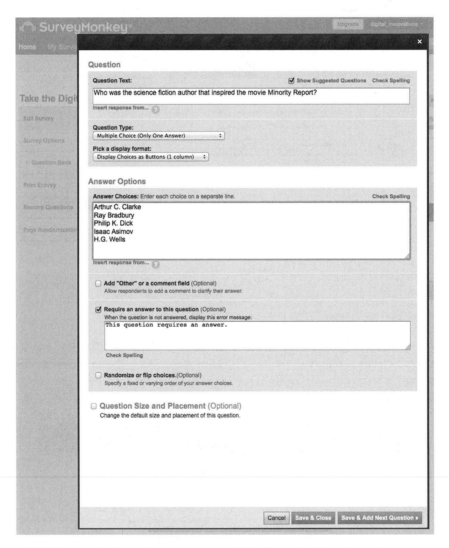

Figure 11.11 As practice in making a survey, use the information from the quiz.

5. SurveyMonkey will return you to the Edit Survey page. You may use the "Preview Survey" button to see how it functions. Press Done to return. If you are happy with the survey, press the "Send Survey" button (Figure 11.12).

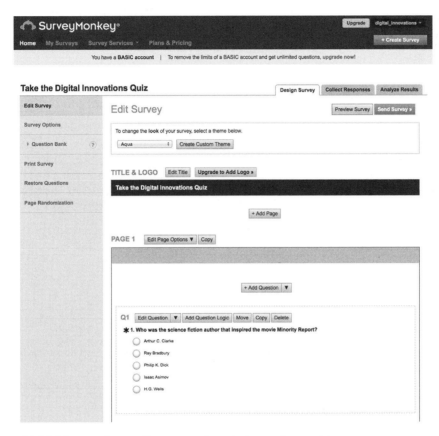

Figure 11.12 You can always edit any question, choice, or the graphic appearance.

6. You will be offered several choices to publicize your survey, including a weblink and Facebook. Copy the URL, place it in a web browser, and take the survey yourself (Figure 11.13).

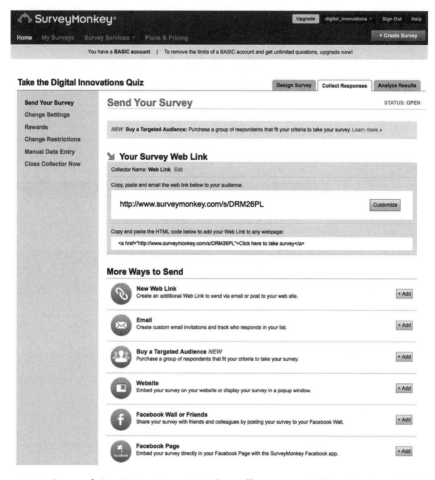

Figure 11.13 Some of the choices SurveyMonkey offers are available only through the PRO account.

7. Once the responses from your survey come pouring in, press the "Analyze Results" tab at the top and see the results (Figure 11.14).

Figure 11.14 SurveyMonkey uses a simple and pleasant graphic style even if there is only one response to your survey. Hmmm. I wonder who that was?

Because a survey is not a quiz, it is difficult to give feedback to an answer, and more importantly, there is no score accumulated for right or wrong answers. However, the basic structure of a survey might be valuable to use in order to learn what your users think of your work. You can easily include the URL for a survey within most presentations.

Writing survey questions is an art form in itself. Make sure you think carefully what you want to ask and how you want your respondents to answer. You might use the questions in Chapter 2 before they see your work if you want to determine whether users can be considered disenfranchised, randomizers, crowd surfers, or active engagers. Once known, you can survey them again to see if you have more users as engaged types. Beta test your survey with those you can trust for their candid opinions before you make the survey public. That way, you have a good chance of obtaining useful results.

Sources

"A Google a Day: The Trivia Game That Encourages Cheating." *The Week* (April 12, 2011). Accessed January 12, 2013. http://theweek.com/article/index/214135/a-google-a-day-the-trivia-game-that-encourages-cheating.

Bogost, Ian, Simon Ferrari, and Bobby Schweizer. (2010). *Newsgames Journalism at Play*. Boston: MIT Press.

burrough, xtine, and Paul Martin Lester. (2013). *Visual Communication on the Web Principles & Practices*. New York: Routledge.

Google. "A Google a Day." Accessed January 12, 2013. http://agoogleaday.com/#game=started.

Grow, Gerald. "Newsroom 101." Accessed January 12, 2013. http://www.newsroom101.com/newsroom101/NR_info.html.

Herbert, Douglas. (September 4, 2000). "Decades on, Beatles' lovers won't let it be." CNN. Accessed January 12, 2013. http://archives.cnn.com/2000/SHOWBIZ/Music/09/04/beatles/index.html.

High School Journalism Initiative. "Game-Based Learning Resources." Accessed January 12, 2013. http://www.hsj.org/Games/index.cfm?menu_id=10.

———. "Test Your Skills." Accessed January 12, 2013. http://www.hsj.org/modules/test_your_skills/index.cfm?menu_id=5&module_id=14.

Jennings, Ken. (December 21, 2012). "Play the Slate News Quiz." Slate. Accessed January 12, 2013. http://www.slate.com/articles/news_and_politics/the_slate_quiz/2012/12/the_slate_quiz_with_quizmaster_ken_jennings_play_the_news_quiz_for_the_week_1.html.

Jeopardy Labs. Accessed January 12, 2013. https://jeopardylabs.com/.

"The Learning Network." (August 7, 2013). Accessed August 7, 2013. http://learning.blogs.nytimes.com/category/news-quiz/.

MY Tiger Challenge. Accessed January 12, 2013. http://mutigerchallenge.com/.

Nelson, Jennifer. (September 21, 2012). "Social Game Promotes Mizzou Spirit While Engaging Young People in News." Accessed January 12, 2013. http://www.rjionline.org/news/social-game-promotes-mizzou-spirit-while-engaging-young-people-news.

———. (January 22, 2013). "Engage Younger Readers in News Through Social Gaming." Accessed January 29, 2013. http://www.rjionline.org/news/engage-younger-readers-news-through-social-gaming.

Newseum. "News Mania." Accessed January 14, 2013. http://www.newseum.org.

Pew Research Center. "The News IQ Quiz." Accessed January 12, 2013. http://pewresearch.org/politicalquiz/.

"Weekly News Quiz." *Chicago Tribune*. Accessed January 12, 2013. http://www.chicagotribune.com/news/nationworld/sns-quiz,0,3775962.triviaquiz.

12   SIMULATIONS

"Last night you covered the regular meeting of the Falconville City Council. Your assignment now is to review your notes, get some follow-up information and write a story for tomorrow's paper."

—City Council

"A five-alarm fire rages late at night in a high-rise apartment in Freeport, a medium-sized city in the Midwest. On the police beat, you hear the report on the police scanner. Your assignment is to cover the fire for *The Freeport News* within a two-hour deadline."

—News Reporting Simulation: A Fire Scenario

"This is not a game. Nobody is keeping score. By playing the role of an aid worker, journalist and survivor, you will be given the opportunity to commit to various strategies, and experience their consequences."

—Inside the Haiti Earthquake

"You are a Darfurian refugee who must forage for water to bring back to your camp. You risk being attacked and possibly killed by Janjaweed militias when you leave the confines of your camp, but you must do it, in order to provide water for your community."

—Dying for Darfur

"You are a pirate commander staked with $50,000 from local tribal leaders and other investors. Your job is to guide your pirate crew through raids in and around the Gulf of Aden, attack and capture a ship, and successfully negotiate a ransom."

—Cutthroat Capitalism

"Over 14 million Americans are unemployed. Now imagine you're one of them. Your savings are gone. You've lost your house. You're a single parent. And you're down to your last $1000. Can you make it through the month?"

—SPENT

The six paragraphs above represent the opening lines of two types of simulations that can be found on the web—professional practice and issue-oriented. The first two interactive programs are designed to teach users how to be better journalists by paying close attention to the facts, knowing who to interview, having competent writing skills, and so on. The next four issue-oriented introductions are a part of simulations, sometimes called "newsgames," that ask you to imagine yourself a participant of a major news story with a difficult set of decision points that help you understand more completely a complex current event.

Originally produced using a now defunct Macintosh computer-specific interactive program called HyperCard, Rich Cameron reworked City Council for the web. With a city's council meeting's agenda, reporter notes, names and telephone numbers of contacts, and basic information about the fictitious city of Falconville, participants learn of real-world political issues that often dominate small towns. Cameron has had a long career teaching journalism and other subjects at various colleges in California and has been called "One of the most prolific journalism advisers" by the Journalism Association of Community Colleges. Written in a simple, direct style with clipart illustrations, the program is a model for easy to produce web-based simulations that nevertheless can be complex depending on the extent of the scenarios offered.

News Reporting Simulation: A Fire Scenario is a much more elaborate presentation that includes photographs, QuickTime videos, and many links to learn the craft of journalism and to aid users in writing a news story. As stated in the credits, the program was "a collaboration among John V. Pavlik (Professor of Journalism and Executive Director, Center for New Media), Melvin Melcher (Professor Emeritus of Journalism at Columbia University and the author of *News Writing and Reporting,* the leading textbook in the field), and the Columbia Center for New Media Teaching and Learning (CCNMTL)." Participants are first advised to try links that provide practice in basic journalistic skills as well as take grammar and math quizzes. With its plain multimedia style, this simulation is another model for those who want to create scenarios that do not require a great deal of expertise.

From the first page of the website for Inside the Haiti Earthquake, a user is aware of the highly professional production values that make this presentation unique. It was produced by PTV Productions, a multiplatform storytelling company based in Toronto, Canada, and is described on the firm's website: "Co-director, cinematographer and composer Nicolas Jolliet travelled to Haiti in January and August 2010 to capture original footage, photos and music for the project." Lauren Kirchner of the *Columbia Journalism Review* writes, "Inside the Haiti Earthquake is designed to challenge assumptions about relief work in disaster situations (Figure 12.1). The footage used to create the simulation was collected for a documentary video series about the Red Cross's relief efforts, called "Inside Disaster." Then you get to see the result, the video footage that "you" produced through the decisions you made, and you get feedback via "text message" from your producer. This might all sound a bit cheesy; somehow, it's not. With stunning footage and tricky decision-points, it's a simulation that not only shows the reality of the chaos in Haiti after the earthquake, but also reinforces the fact that there are no easy solutions to it, whatever one's role may be. Inside the Haiti Earthquake was PTV's first simulation and not surprisingly won the Canadian New Media Award for Best Web-Based Game.

Darfur is Dying and Cutthroat Capitalism are arcade-type, Adobe Flash, first-person simulations but with serious intent. Susana Ruiz, a student at the time of the University of Southern California's Interactive Media Program created Darfur is Dying after attending a "Games for Change" conference in New York City in which an initiative was announced by mtvU, a 24-hour television channel broadcast to college campuses produced by Viacom's MTV Networks. It has been reported that more than two million users have played the program. Reporter Scott Carney's 2009 *Wired* magazine article inspired Cutthroat Capitalism. The introduction states that "The pirates who prowl the Somali

Figure 12.1 "Inside the Haiti Earthquake" is one of several works created by the award-winning Canadian-based PTV Productions. Owned and operated by Andrea Nemtin and Ian Dunbar, PTV is a multiplatform storytelling firm that produces "documentaries, lifestyle, factual series, and digital media." *Courtesy of Ian Dunbar, PTV Productions*

coast aren't just buccaneers—they're also businessmen." Dennis Crothers of Smallbore Webworks, no longer in operation, produced the Flash program. Both simulations have been criticized for trivializing serious social problems and have been praised for their innovative approaches that alert users to important issues.

Chief Creative Officer Jonathan Cude of the Durham, North Carolina advertising agency McKinney brought a pro bono idea of using a simulation program to create awareness about homelessness to Urban Ministries of Durham (UMD) executive director Patrice Nelson. The result was SPENT, a brilliantly conceived and executed presentation "that forces players to make the tough decisions that can lead to homelessness." Users are given a set of choices "from housing to healthcare to unforeseen life circumstances like broken down cars and sick pets" and must try to maintain enough income to survive (Figure 12.2). In 2012, the Association of Fundraising Professionals awarded McKinney the Innovation in Philanthropy award for the project. Because UMD maintains a homeless shelter, Nelson "hopes the game will help it raise funds to support its efforts."

Universities have generally been slow in developing courses and organizing conferences for professionals to teach and share simulation techniques. There is one exception—The Institute for New Media Studies at the University of Minnesota. Among other activities, the

Figure 12.2 Three frames included with "SPENT," devoted to the issue of homelessness created by the North Carolina-based advertising agency McKinney, reveal the educational intent and the emotional impact of the interactive program. *Courtesy of McKinney and Urban Ministries of Durham*

Institute, led by director Nora Paul, conducted a conference titled "Playing the News: Journalism, Interactive Narrative and Games" in which "game creators, game players, journalists, and professors challenged traditional ways of presenting news stories." The conclusion made by many participants was that simulations "should give users a better understanding of the issue, a greater involvement in the story, test the user's knowledge about the story, and keep users on the news entity's website" in order to promote advertising revenue.

The New Media Studies center also won a prestigious $250,000 Knight News Challenge grant to develop a professional practice simulation named "Playing the News" that taught users about the environment, energy policy, farming, world hunger, and the use of ethanol fuel as they pretended to be reporters. More important than the program itself, results of surveys of participants discovered that users preferred different versions. Depending on individual preferences, some liked to play the simulation as an arcade-style game while others liked it as a web-based news story in traditional, topic-oriented, or short story modes.

The lesson learned by the "Playing the News" survey is that creators should design presentations that allow flexibility in user choices.

■ CHALLENGES, CRITIQUES, AND AMUSEMENTS

- Research and report on the current state of Darfur, Somali pirating, and Haiti. Include an interview with an aid worker or journalist who knows each situation. Do you think a simulation can explain the depth of the human misery for each location?

- Have you or someone you know been unemployed for an extended period of time? Share any stories you think are appropriate.

- What lessons can be learned from such immersive computer simulations as Fable, Infamous, Myst, and World of Warcraft? If you don't have one of these simulations, find someone who does and play it. Simulations seem to be more effective when players can imagine themselves in a situation, can affect change based on their own sense of right and wrong, work with others to solve problems, and bring a new skill set to the nondigital world. Do you agree?

- Interview someone who works for the Canadian company PTV Productions, responsible for the "Inside the Haiti Earthquake" simulation and the North Carolina advertising agency, McKenney, that created "SPENT," about the making of each program. How were the projects conceived, and what have been the feedback and results?

- Given the popularity of apps for the presentation of simulations on smartphones and tablets, the Adobe Flash program is less popular than JavaScript for programming because Flash is not operable on many portable devices. Was the previous sentence a mystery for you? If so, it's good you have this book.

- The Knight Foundation funds projects related to journalism innovations. Take a look at some of the work the organization has supported <http://www.knightfoundation.org/grants/>. Do you find any examples that inspire you? Although these projects are related to journalism, could any of them be modified to fit your particular mass communication interest?

■ EXERCISES

Simulations offer one of the best opportunities for your work to go beyond the traditional way most of us consume media—that is, as passive users content with being fed whatever is supplied—and toward presentations that make us personally feel a range of emotions—from anguish to zeal—that give us insights to the subjects of stories. It's a tall order, of course, to create work that a stranger cares about; but if successful, it can move even the most disenfranchised persons toward fully engaged users.

One of the keys of a good simulation—whether elaborately created through animation techniques available with Adobe's Flash program or a much simpler question-and-answer presentation as you will note with this exercise—is the use of personal pronouns. You need a user to imagine being in a situation so she is challenged and educated. Although it's ironic that I used third person pronouns in the previous sentence, you will notice that throughout the simulation (and many times with the exercises provided with the chapters) I evoke and attempt to engage you.

This exercise is deceptively simple. With the six mass communications areas—advertising, entertainment, journalism, public relations, RTVF, and visual reporting—each scenario has only two yes-or-no choices. Nevertheless, the program uses 43 HTML and 25 image files. Luckily, you can download all of them to make it work. Hopefully, you will use this basic structure to create your own variations.

The simulations are concerned with ethical issues (see Chapter 3). Many times we are faced by serious challenges during our personal and professional lives. Most ethical situations revolve around conflicts in values and conflicts in loyalties—we often find ourselves experiencing an ethical dilemma because of a stance we have taken based on what we think is right and wrong (values) and what we hold near and dear to us (loyalties). A full ethics program would contain a great deal of introductory material, at least five separate scenarios for each mass communications field with each one containing several possible choices for the user, a way of calculating and comparing a user's answers with others, and an extensive list of sources for more information.

Of course, you do not need to use the files for an ethical exercise. The structure can be altered to simulate a situation you might want a user to complete in order to learn more about the topic of your story.

1. Create a folder on your desktop where you will store all of the files used for the exercise.

2. Download the six introductory pictures from the file <http://paulmartinlester.info/ Routledge/Images/Intro_Pictures.zip>, decompress them, and place them in the folder (Figure 12.3).

Figure 12.3 Using Photoshop, the pictures chosen were converted to grayscale, slightly darkened in the upper-left region with the burn tool so the copy could be easily read, and resized, and cropped to fit the size of 1440 x 1440 pixels. Don't make any changes to the photographs' file names. *Courtesy of Paul Martin Lester*

3. Download the 19 navigational images from the file <http://paulmartinlester.info/ Routledge/Images/Navigational_Images.zip>, decompress them, and place them in the folder (Figure 12.4).

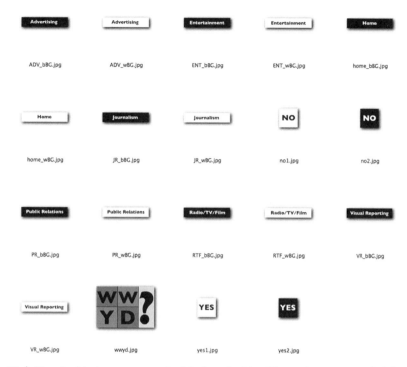

Figure 12.4 The double images, opposite black and white illustrations, are needed for the buttons to display a hovering effect. They were created in Photoshop. Again, don't change their names.

4. Download the 43 HTML files from the file <http://paulmartinlester.info/Routledge/ Images/HTML_Files.zip>, decompress them, and place them in the folder. Make sure you don't have any other file named "index.html." You don't want to accidentally override it.

5. If all the files are within one folder, you should be able to use your browser and open the starting file <index.html> and see the opening page (Figure 12.5).

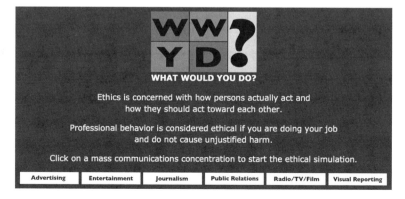

Figure 12.5 Simple and clear text messages and buttons are often the best choices.

6. Click on one of the concentration buttons and advance through the short ethical scenario (Figure 12.6).

Figure 12.6 The public relations simulation is concerned with stereotypes.

7. You should be familiar with the Dreamweaver HTML editing program. Use it or any simple text file to open the <index.html> file. If you are customizing the files, feel free to change the <title> at the top, the text blocks toward the bottom, and the image file names that correspond with new illustrations you created, and any links to other files. Try not to disturb the complex coding text (Figure 12.7).

Figure 12.7 The <index.html> file as seen with Dreamweaver contains CSS (Cascading Style Sheet) formatting, JavaScript functions, and Dreamweaver Rollover Image commands. Dreamweaver makes it easy to make hover-type buttons. From the Insert menu, select Image Objects, and then Rollover Image. Fill out the form and click OK. The necessary coding will be automatically added to the file.

8. If you do plan to create your own multi-question simulation, it is imperative that you plan out the structure and files you will need before you start creating files. For example, even the relatively simple set of scenarios offered here requires planning and an organized structure (Figure 12.8).

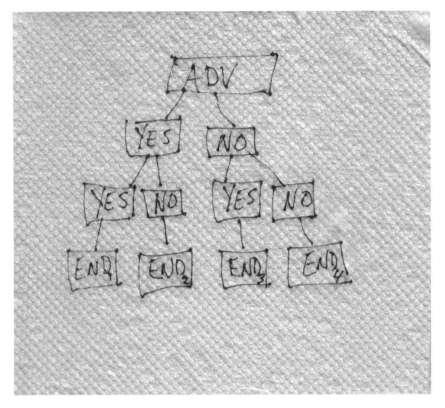

Figure 12.8 This rough sketch was a plan of the ethics simulation. Such a technique makes it easier in the long run to put together the files you need for your presentation.

9. Alter the pictures, text, and questions to make the scenario structure your own. A good idea is to copy and paste all of the text that will be seen by a user into Word in order to run a spell check. You can never be too careful about spelling.

10. Upload all the files to your web server and add the URL with the <index.html> file to a webpage, blog, or to emails to your friends and family.

One of the most impressive simulations on Second Life is "Witnessing History: Kristallnacht, the 1938 Pogroms," created by the US Holocaust Memorial Museum. It offers a virtual experience of the "Night of Broken Glass" and its vicious attacks on German Jews. See the presentation at <http://maps.secondlife.com/secondlife/US%20 Holocaust%20Museum1/1/35/27> (Figure 12.9). Unfortunately, due to budget constraints the Second Life exhibit was closed.

Figure 12.9 The "Night of Broken Glass" on Second Life produced by the US Holocaust Memorial Museum is an interactive, multimedia emotional experience. As your avatar enters the newsroom (top), after you touch a glowing notebook on a desk, you can experience the reproduction of a street scene complete with audio testimony and broken glass on the streets. *Courtesy of the US Holocaust Memorial Museum*

It is beyond the ability of this text to teach how to build such an elaborate simulation. However, you can learn to create objects in a "sandbox" on land reserved for that purpose in Second Life. Use the Search function of the program to find these sandboxes.

Sources

ABC News. "The Conversation: Homeless Simulation Game." Accessed January 12, 2013. http://abcnews.go.com/Technology/conversation-homeless-simulation-game-forces-players-confront-tough/story?id=12931813#.UOOgMLZ8vuw.

Cameron, Rich. "City Council." Accessed January 12, 2013. http://www.rcameron.com/journalism/citycouncil/.

Carney, Scott. (July 13, 2009). "Cutthroat Capitalism." *Wired.* Accessed January 12, 2013. http://www.wired.com/politics/security/magazine/17–07/ff_somali_pirates.

CNMTL. "News Reporting Simulation." Accessed January 12, 2013. http://ccnmtl.columbia.edu/portfolio/journalism/news_reporting_simul.html.

———. "Project Portfolio | Simulations." Accessed January 12, 2013. http://ccnmtl.columbia.edu/portfolio/simulations/.

"Cutthroat Capitalism: The Game." *Wired* (July 20, 2009). Accessed January 12, 2013. http://www.wired.com/special_multimedia/2009/cutthroatCapitalismTheGame.

"Darfur is Dying." Accessed January 12, 2013. http://www.darfurisdying.com/.

"How to Do Simulation Games." Simon Usherwood. Accessed March 2, 2013. https://sites.google.com/site/howtodosimulationgames/home.

Inside Disaster. "Inside the Haiti Earthquake." Accessed January 12, 2013. http://www.insidedisaster.com/experience/Main.html.

Institute for New Media Studies. "Games." Accessed January 12, 2013. http://www.inms.umn.edu/projects/games.html.

———. "Playing the News." Accessed January 12, 2013. http://www.inms.umn.edu/projects/playing.html.

Journalism Association of Community Colleges. "Bio—Rich Cameron." Accessed January 12, 2013. http://www.jacconline.org/contests-awards/bio-rich-cameron-1.527821#.UOORPrZ8vuw.

Kirchner, Lauren. (November 11, 2010). "Inside the Haiti Earthquake: A Simulation." *Columbia Journalism Review.* Accessed January 12, 2013. http://www.cjr.org/the_news_frontier/inside_the_haiti_earthquake_a.php.

Lester, Paul Martin. (2010). "Ethics and Images: Five Major Concerns" in Christopher Meyers (Ed.). *Journalism Ethics A Philosophical Approach.* Oxford: Oxford University Press, 351–358.

PRWeb. (February 9, 2011). "McKinney Creates SPENT, the First Online Game About Homelessness, for Urban Ministries of Durham." Accessed January 12, 2013. http://www.prweb.com/releases/2011/2/prweb8123480.htm.

SPENT. Accessed January 12, 2013. http://playspent.org/.

13 QR CODES

Between Robin Hood Lane and the Sherwood bowling alley at the end of a nondescript shopping mall not unlike thousands of others in small towns across America, is the Marsh Supermarket of Troy, Ohio.

Big deal, right?

As it turns out, it is a big deal.

On June 26, 1974, a new procedure was used for the first time at the Marsh store with equipment provided by the National Cash Register Company when customer Clyde Dawson bought a sixty-seven-cent pack of Wrigley's Juicy Fruit gum from cashier Sharon Buchanan. It was the first item scanned using the now ubiquitous barcode. This simple everyday act introduced the age of information technology. The pack of gum eventually became part of the permanent collection of the Smithsonian Institution's National Museum of American History while the concept of the barcode led to the Universal Product Code (UPC) used by more than a million companies worldwide and a $16-billion annual enterprise.

The code was originally invented in 1949 after Bernard Silver, a graduate student of Philadelphia's Drexel Institute of Technology (now Drexel University) overheard a grocery store manager ask the Dean of Drexel if there was a way to automatically log in prices by a cashier without the use of a cash register. The Dean declined to offer his help, but Silver was intrigued and relayed this idea to fellow student Norman Woodland who quit school, moved to his grandfather's apartment in Florida, and devoted full time to solving the challenge. While relaxing on a beach, he stroked his fingers through the sand to create a longer form of the short dots and dashes common to the telegraph's Morse code. Speaking with *Smithsonian Magazine* in 1999, Woodland detailed the moment:

> What I'm going to tell you sounds like a fairy tale. I poked my four fingers into the sand and for whatever reason—I didn't know—I pulled my hand toward me and drew four lines. I said: 'Golly! Now I have four lines, and they could be wide lines and narrow lines instead of dots and dashes.' "Only seconds later, I took my four fingers—they were still in the sand—and I swept them around into a full circle.

In 1952 Woodland and Silver obtained US patent number 2,612,994 for vertical and bullet style or circle barcode designs. However, scanning technology was of such poor quality that their system was rarely used. Silver graduated and taught physics at Drexel until his death in 1963. Woodland worked for IBM for many years and made improvements on the initial barcode design. In 1992, President George H. W. Bush presented him with the National Medal of Technology and Innovation, during the same ceremony as fellow recipient William H. Gates, III of the Microsoft Corporation. In 1992, Woodland died at the age of 91.

By the 1970s, supermarket executives needed to cut costs and the barcode/scanner innovation was resurrected. The trouble was, by that time there was no standardized barcode symbol food companies could use to make the process efficient. Alan Haberman, a leader in the supermarket field, was asked to head a committee of grocery store business leaders to select a single barcode design that all would employ on their packaging. Haberman and the committee decided upon a design of black-and-white vertical bars, similar to the Woodland-Silver creation. This code was designed by George J. Laurer of IBM and represented 11 digits (today, up to 20) used to identify a product's information.

Twenty years after the pack of gum was swiped over a glass top with a laser scanner underneath, inventors with Denso Wave, a subsidiary of the Toyota Motor Corporation located in the south-central coastal town of Kariya City, Japan, invented an updated version of the barcode for keeping track of cars during the manufacturing process. Denso's Quick Response (QR) codes or tags have a different visual look than the horizontal original barcodes. Their codes are blocky, high-contrast two-dimensional graphic symbols that can be quickly read by laser scanners and smartphones equipped with a QR reader app. These symbols can also store hundreds of times more information than the original barcodes.

A unique feature QR codes have is an automatic error correction function that restores data even if the graphic is dirty or damaged. This attribute allows them to be displayed on outdoor advertisements and within magazine and newspaper pages that are often crumpled after continued use. Consequently, some of the first QR codes from Japan were included on subway advertising posters and billboards along busy streets.

The correction feature also gives artists the freedom to use images and colors within a QR display. Hamilton Chan of Paperlinks.com advises graphic designers to make their QR codes stand out by using color, rounding the harsh corners for a softer visual message, adding depth cues for a 3D effect, and to include illustrations within the code.

QR codes used for advertising, entertainment, and journalism purposes should be more complex than presently configured. They should not merely be used as links to a company's homepage to help advertise and promote a product, service, or point-of-view or by journalists to simply point a user to a newspaper's website. They can also be thought of as examples of artistic expression.

Examples are not hard to find. Chef José Duarte of Boston's North End restaurant Taranta included squid-ink QR codes on his plates that led to links to the ingredients and recipes used to make the dishes. In 2009, *Esquire* magazine featured the actor Robert Downey, Jr. on its cover with a code graphic. After it was scanned, Downey seemingly popped off the page to deliver his introduction. The following chapter will give more details of this type of presentation. For the 10th anniversary of *The New York Times* Sunday magazine in 2010, balloons comprised the QR code on its cover. Denim provocateur Calvin Klein had a giant red QR code printed on the side of a building in New York City with the message, "Get it uncensored." Scanning the code led to a quick-cut video of attractive people who wore jeans and kissed a lot (Figure 13.1). Before a graffiti artist's wall mural was painted over by the property owner, he photographed his creation and placed a QR code over the newly painted surface that linked to the original graffito. In 2013, Chilean weaver Guillermo Bert exhibited blankets that combined ancient tribal lore with QR codes for the Pasadena Museum of California Art. Finally, someone had to do it—the world's largest QR code can be found at the Kraay Family Farm in Alberta, Canada (Figure 13.2). The 309,570 square foot pattern links to the website of the entertainment center, known for its corn maze and other attractions. Trouble is, you need a helicopter to scan the code.

Figure 13.1 Calvin Klein once said, "Jeans are about sex." Consequently, his advertisements for denim pants have often tested the boundaries of what is considered in good taste. Examples include 15-year-old Brooke Shields who seductively asked, "Want to know what gets between me and my Calvin's?," models for commercials in the 1990s with a creepy off-camera adult male's voice asking suggestive questions, and an otherwise plain New York City building displaying a QR code that links to an uncensored video. *Courtesy of Paul Martin Lester*

Figure 13.2 About a 90-minute drive south from Edmonton, Canada, you'll find the Kraay Family Farm, home of the Lacombe Corn Maze "Where Every Day's an Adventure!!" In 2012, Guinness World Records named the 309,570-square foot QR code as the world's largest. *Courtesy of R. Kraay*

Journalist Lauren Rabaino of MediaBistro.com understands that QR codes can do more than simply attract attention. *The Boston Globe* newspaper distributed QR codes around the city as a type of scavenger hunt for users to learn about Boston and to promote the newspaper. Rabaino advises other newspapers to "create an educational, interactive experience for your readers by taking them through a time line of a historical event in their community. Participants could guess answers to questions and be led to the next spot, where they would learn a new fact before heading to the next location." She also advises journalists to include a QR code on their business cards so readers and sources can learn additional details.

With their seemingly ubiquitous penetration in various media, using QR codes in more meaningful ways so that the graphic is part of a story that links to in-depth and thoughtful information about serious social issues is on the rise for many online and print publications.

■ CHALLENGES, CRITIQUES, AND AMUSEMENTS

- Buy some Juicy Fruit gum, have it scanned in the store, make a friend photograph you, and post the picture to your Facebook page. Keep the gum.
- Research the history of the National Cash Register Company and explain why its initials are NCR.
- In 1992, President George H. W. Bush, while campaigning for a second term (he lost to Bill Clinton), was criticized for being amazed at a supermarket scanner. Later that same year, he awarded the National Medal of Technology to Norman Woodland who helped develop the barcode scanner. Was Bush's honor ironic or an attempt to overcome his gaff?
- Bernard Silver, Norman Woodland, and Alan Haberman were responsible for the invention of the barcode. What else did they accomplish in their professional or personal lives?
- Research the Japanese firm Denso Wave. What does the company have to do with robots? How was the company affected by the 2011 tsunami?
- Share as many creative places as you can where a QR code might be useful or attract attention.
- How would you use a QR code for your professional mass communications field?

■ EXERCISES

In this exercise, you will create a QR code and turn it into a personal work of art. You will use a free QR code generator and make a graphic that users can scan with a QR code reader that links to work you have on the web—a website, blog, slide show, video, and so on, or simply text, a phone number, or an email address. To alter the plain black-and-white code, you will need to use the Photoshop and Illustrator programs from Adobe or their equivalents.

1. Go to the Kaywa <http://qrcode.kaywa.com/> website. It's free to generate a simple QR code, but if you want additional features, you can pay for the service. Click a radio button at the top to select the type of information you are coding. With each choice, a different form is revealed. For a website or blog, type in the URL of the site and press the Generate Free button. Move your cursor over the QR graphic,

press the Control and mouse button or pad, and select Save Image As . . . . Give the image a name and save the file (Figure 13.3).

Figure 13.3 The Kaywa website generates a free QR code based on the information you input.

2. You also need a QR code reader. The Kaywa website offers the easiest solution: A scanner app you can use on a smartphone. Click the green "Download Kaywa Reader" button to make that happen. Otherwise, the CNet website <http:// download.cnet.com/1770–20_4–0.html?query = qr+code+reader&searchtype= downloads> offers a number of QR code readers that can be used on desktops and laptops with a camera. Download your choice and follow the directions.

3. Start up Photoshop and open your QR code file. Resize the image as a five-inch square. Either use the scanner software from a smartphone or scan a print of the code and use the program you downloaded to your computer to make sure the code works correctly.

4. Because QR codes have an automatic error correction feature, some of the coding elements in the middle section of the graphic can be removed and replaced with images. The trick is to take out enough of the black squares to include a picture, but not too many or it won't work. In Photoshop, remove a few of the squares and then use your QR reader to make sure the code still operates. If not, revert to the original file and start again (Figure 13.4).

Figure 13.4 Black squares in the center of the original code for the author's website (left) have been removed so an image can be added. *Courtesy of Paul Martin Lester*

5. You can of course use any image to add to your QR code. I happened to decide upon a picture of a sculptured man that I use as my Facebook profile image. In Photoshop, open the picture file, resize it to approximately the empty space you have in your code graphic, select the entire image, copy it, paste it on your QR code, and move it into place. You may need to select the Edit menu and then Transform and Scale to resize the picture. Save your work with a unique name (Figure 13.5).

Figure 13.5 The little man occupies the center of the QR code graphic and doesn't interfere with its operation. *Courtesy of Paul Martin Lester*

6. To give the graphic an artistic quality, you might use choices from Photoshop's Filter Gallery. If so, make sure you select the Flatten Image command from the Layer menu. Save the file with a unique name. With Illustrator, you can also make a high contrast version with the Image Trace command. Open Illustrator, create a New File, place your QR code image on the Artboard, and select the Image Trace button at the top. If you like the look, Export and Save the file as a PNG (Figure 13.6).

Figure 13.6 The effect of Photoshop's "Plastic Wrap" filter (left) and Illustrator's Image Trace function are shown here. I think I prefer the plastic wrap look. *Courtesy of Paul Martin Lester*

7. You can add text to the graphic if you prefer. For my URL, I'm using Gill Sans Regular and the color black in Photoshop. Choose any size you wish. With Transform set to Rotate, I'm making the address run along the right side of the picture. Check with your QR reader to make sure it works. It does! Flatten the image and save it with a unique name (Figure 13.7).

Figure 13.7 With the URL of the website included for those without QR readers, the graphic code is ready for its close-up. *Courtesy of Paul Martin Lester*

8. Experiment with other images and text, different colors for the white background and black squares, and/or see if the code works if you make it out of actual objects—popcorn, tacks, coins, and so on.

9. Put your favorite example (that works) on a t-shirt (either as the graphic itself or a photograph—there are many online shirt companies that will do this for you). Wear it into an Apple store until you get noticed by one of those geniuses.

Sources

"Barcodes Readers and Scanners." (2011). Accessed January 12, 2013. http://www.information-about.com/barcode-industry-uk.htm.

Barnet, Chris. "Why Supermarkets Are Going Bananas Over Computers." *Mainliner.* Accessed January 12, 2013. http://www.atariarchives.org/bcc1/showpage.php?page = 97.

Bellis, Mary. "What is bar code? The history of bar code." About.com. Accessed January 12, 2013. http://inventors.about.com/od/bstartinventions/a/Bar-Codes.htm.

"Bernard Silver." *The New York Times* (August 30, 1963), 21.

burrough, xtine. (October 4, 2011). Designing with QR in Mind." *Design Educator* (blog). Accessed January 12, 2013. http://designeducator.info/?p=626.

CBS News. (July 15, 2010). "Calvin Klein's Bar-Coded Billboards Peek Into and Interactive Advertising Future." Accessed January 12, 2013. http://www.cbsnews.com/8301–505123_162–33248957/calvin-kleins-bar-coded-billboards-peek-into-an-interactive-advertising-future/.

Chan, Hamilton. (April 18, 2011). "How to: Make Your QR Codes More Beautiful." Accessed January 12, 2013. http://mashable.com/2011/04/18/qr-code-design-tips/.

Davis, Phillip. (September 21, 2011). "How to Reach Your Mobile Customer Using QR Codes." *SocialMediaToday.* Accessed January 12, 2013. http://socialmediatoday.com/tungsten branding/358212/how-reach-your-mobile-customer-using-qr-codes.

Denso Wave. (2011). "About." Accessed January 12, 2013. http://www.denso-wave.com/qrcode/aboutqr-e.html.

Design Taxi. (September 11, 2012). "The World's Largest QR Code, You'll Need a Helicopter to Scan It." Accessed January 12, 2013. http://designtaxi.com/news/353564/The-World-s-Largest-QR-Code-You-ll-Need-A-Helicopter-To-Scan-It/.

DVICE. (December 16, 2012). "Joseph Woodland, Inventor of the Barcode, Dies at 91." Accessed January 12, 2013. http://dvice.com/archives/2012/12/joseph-woodland.php.

Fishman, Charles. (2011). "The Killer App—Bar None." *American Way.* Accessed January 12, 2013. http://www.americanwaymag.com/so-woodland-bar-code-bernard-silver-drexel-university.

Fox, Margalit. (June 15, 2011). "Alan Haberman, Who Ushered In the Bar Code, Dies at 81." *The New York Times.* Accessed January 12, 2013. http://www.nytimes.com/2011/06/16/business/16haberman.html?_r = 2&hp.

Gotts, Ian. (May 17, 2011). "Got a problem? Take a photo of a QR barcode." Accessed January 12, 2013. http://iangotts.wordpress.com/2011/05/17/got-a-problem-take-a-photo-of-a-qr-barcode-bpm-qrcode-innovation/.

Hart, Hugh. (October 28, 2012). "Embedded Traditions." *Los Angeles Times*, E2.

"Juicy Fruit." Accessed January 12, 2013. http://www.wrigley.com/global/brands/juicy-fruit.aspx.

Kraay Family Farm. Accessed January 12, 2013. http://www.kraayfamilyfarm.com/.

Lexison. (October 30, 2011). "The Barcode Turns 57 (And Is Still Going Strong)." Accessed January 12, 2013. http://www.lexicontech.com/blog/index.php/2009/10/07/barcode-turns-57-today/.

National Medal of Technology and Innovation Recipients. Accessed January 12, 2013. http://www.uspto.gov/about/nmti/recipients/1992.jsp.

Pavlik, John, and Frank Bridges. "The Emergence of Augmented Reality (AR) as a Storytelling Medium in Journalism." *Journalism & Communication Monographs* 15, no. 1.

Phelan, Kevin. (January 20, 2011). Share21. "Edible QR Codes: High-Tech Gastronomy Hits Boston's North End." Accessed January 12, 2013. http://bostinnovation.com/2011/01/20/edible-qr-codes-high-tech-gastronomy-hits- boston%E2%80%99s-north-end/.

Rabaino, Lauren M. (October 25, 2010). "Five ways journalists can use QR Codes." Accessed January 12, 2013. http://www.mediabistro.com/10000words/five-ways-journalists-can-use-qr-codes_b1386.

Rosenthal, Andrew. (February 5, 1992). "Bush Encounters the Supermarket, Amazed." *The New York Times*. Accessed January 31, 2013. http://www.nytimes.com/1992/02/05/us/bush-encounters-the-supermarket-amazed.html.

Scan2. (February 17, 2011). "Calvin Klein Does QR Code Campaign in Times Square." Accessed January 12, 2013. http://scan2.co/blogs/news/calvin-klein-does-qr-code-campaign-in-times-square/127730.

World's First Barcode." Accessed January 12, 2013. http://thelongestlistofthelongeststuffatthelongestdomainnameatlonglast.com/ first369.html.

YouTube. (April 27, 2010). "Graffyard." Accessed January 12, 2013. http://www.youtube.com/watch?feature=player_embedded&v=4qef08CcLUY.

14 3D DISPLAYS

"Boo-ya. In your face."

So yells the actor Robert Downey Jr. as he points a finger in your general direction and introduces *Esquire* magazine's augmented reality (AR) issue of 2009 from the monitor of your computer. Users could also experience other "in your face" 3D presentations on various pages inside the magazine (Figure 14.1).

Augmented reality is a digital innovation that adds computer-generated images and information between you and the world. These programs can link users with product information, coupons, store locations, and much more as you also watch your surroundings on your smartphone or tablet. For example, at all times during Downey's amusing 3D monologue, you could see yourself in the background with your familiar surroundings holding the actual cover or a print-out of the high contrast graphic "marker" (a stripped-down version of a QR code) that engages a software program previously loaded on your machine that makes the magic happen.

As reported by John Pavlik, a new media author and innovator, David Granger, Editor-in-Chief of *Esquire,* indicated that there were "70,000 downloads of the software to have the AR experience," representing about 10 percent of the magazine's circulation. To his credit, Granger wants to do more with AR than highlight its novelty. He wants to use the technology "to expand on the content of the existing magazine by making it more complex."

Exploitations of the visual cue known as depth date from murals painted on Pompeii walls around 70 CE. The practice became popular during the Renaissance when painters became interested in rendering accurate perspectives on their two-dimensional canvases. By the 17th century, Baroque artists named the effect *trompe l'oeil* (deceive the eye) and used it for paintings on the ceilings of chapels that showed religious figures seemingly ascending to Heaven. Artists also had fun with the technique in which viewers wondered whether something they saw in a painting was actually real. Best known of this genre is the work of Catalan artist Pere Borrell del Caso and his 1874 work "Escaping Criticism" that shows a young boy who leaves the frame of a painting.

Being intrigued by a painting on a wall or canvas is all well and good, but as audiences became more visually sophisticated, more complex methods were used to confound and amaze. An early coinventor of photography in 1839 was the French diorama producer Louis Daguerre who fabricated elaborate 3D scenes for theater audiences. Much more modest versions of the technique can be found today in most natural history museums.

Books were also a popular medium for the 3D effect. Pop-up works were originally intended for adults after a Majorcan mystic Ramon Llull in the 14th century created a spinning wheel to help explain his religious and philosophical theories. It wasn't until the early 1800s that "movables" allowed children to lift flaps in books to show hidden

Figure 14.1 Surrounded by dancing letters explained later as not being used at the moment, actor and *Esquire* magazine spokesperson Robert Downey, Jr. seems to escape from the author's computer monitor. *Courtesy of Paul Martin Lester*

pictures and 1929 that the first pop-up book was published, the *Daily Express Children's Annual,* with "pictures that come up in model form." Pop artist Andy Warhol appropriately produced a pop-up book called *Andy Warhol's Index* with help from Chris Cerf and Alan Rinzler in 1967. Pictures of celebrities and a tomato paste seemingly escaped the pages. In 2007, Matthew Reinhart impressed reviewers with his book, *Star Wars: A Pop-Up Guide to the Galaxy.* A critic for *The New York Times* wrote, "Calling this sophisticated piece of engineering a 'pop-up book' is like calling the Great Wall of China a partition."

The year 2009 is considered a banner year for AR presentations. In addition to the *Esquire* cover, 3D displays could also be found on the covers of *DE:BUG,* a German publication that specializes in technology culture and the American magazine *Popular Science.* In addition, the German AR development company Metaio launched interactive terminals that showed customers what a finished Lego toy set looked like when completed, Topps introduced AR baseball cards, and the US Postal Service announced an application that let customers see if the contents to be shipped would fit within one of their flat rate boxes.

Jump ahead about five years and augmented reality programs are still mainly used to attract attention by publishers of printed publications, to make cute party tricks, arcade-style games, and business cards, and as thinly disguised sales gimmicks for shoppers with a smartphone. For "The Hunter," an album from the heavy metal band Mastodon released in 2011, the instructions of the "Mastodon The Hunter AR" program state, "If you have scanned the deluxe CD cover or deluxe CD insert, your head should turn into the Creature Head and animate with snarls, growls, smoke & spit." How could anyone resist such an invitation? In 2012, British "X Factor" judge and singer Gary Barlow introduced the 25th-anniversary issue of *Hello!,* a weekly publication that concentrates on celebrity news with a 3D cover appearance. The same year Universal Studios for its 100th anniversary released AR DVD cover art versions for 15 of its motion pictures from *Apollo 13* to *Shaun of the Dead.*

What is needed for the innovation to gain respect is for mass communicators to experiment with its use to enhance knowledge about topics of a more serious subject matter. And yet, there are few noteworthy examples from journalism sources. The American national newspaper *USA Today* has been known since its 1982 introduction as a technological innovator with its use of informational graphics (the color weather map is a print publication icon) and its satellite-based printing process that was copied by others. Not surprisingly, the paper has featured several AR presentations. With Universal Studios in 2010, a printed map of "The Wizarding World of Harry Potter," an attraction at the theme park outside Orlando, Florida, became a 3D screen highlight that particularly appealed to younger audiences. In addition, before the 2011 Super Bowl played at Cowboys Stadium in Arlington, Texas, Metaio's Junaio app could be accessed from the paper to get a peek inside the locker room and other features. In addition, the print version of the 2013 Guinness World Records contains 3D AR examples after users download its app and scan a "See It 3D" tag. A giant white shark, for example, seems to jump out of the pages. These efforts were considered a success because of the number of downloads and fan clicks that were recorded. Still, don't look for the Pulitzer Prize committee to update its award list anytime soon for these presentations.

Nevertheless, there are examples of AR programs that might be models for journalism and other areas related to mass communications. Military and airline mechanics use specially designed goggles that "demonstrate each step in a repair, identify the tools needed, and include textual instructions as well." NASA's Jet Propulsion Laboratory in Pasadena developed Spacecraft 3D, an app in which users can "learn about and interact with a variety of spacecraft that are used to explore our solar system, study Earth, and observe the universe." The educational-based program provides 10 different spacecraft that can be manipulated within a user's actual environment (Figure 14.2). Pretend your coffee table is the surface of Mars. Metaio has developed textbooks with "AR elements such as globes that pop up on the pages. The books are printed normally; after purchase, consumers install special software on their computers and point a webcam at the book to see the visualizations."

Experimentations with augmented reality technologies can be found for newspaper presentations. For example, Dave Miller, a postdoctoral researcher at the University of Bedfordshire, England, along with Dave Moorhead and Professor Alexis Weedon, developed a model for the inclusion of 3D-augmented images with sound for graphic novels and newspapers in their collaboration, "Sherwood Rise." When a smartphone or tablet with the Junaio app scans a mock newspaper called *The Truth,* 3D elements seem to jump off the page and enhance the story (Figure 14.3).

To truly engage consumers of mass communications with 3D digital innovations, it might take more than spacecraft toys and digital versions of pop-up books. And yet, what is thought of as merely a literary gimmick for children may be a hint of the future for this technology for educational purposes. After all, with 3D displays, an illustration within a chemistry, physiology, or geology book can become a pop-up revolving molecule, a beating heart, or the inside of a volcano.

There should be no reason, other than a lack of creativity, that a newspaper or magazine page, a press release, an advertisement, or a website cannot include a 3D informational graphic, an organization's director introducing a new service, a behind-the-scenes look at a newly released motion picture, or an interactive map that pops up valuable information in the face of an engaged user.

Figure 14.2 Named for the American astronomer Edwin Hubble, who was one of the first scientists to surmise that the universe is expanding, the Hubble Space Telescope was placed into Earth's orbit in 1990. As seen in this photograph, it now hovers over the author's computer keyboard. *Courtesy of NASA*

Chancellor goes green

Day One of a bright new four-day experience. Max 35C, min 30C. Always sunny?

Chancellor George Nottingham has decided to travel the five miles from his home to Parliament by bike. A statement released by the Conservative Party confirms the decision was made out of concern for the environment and in the hope that others across the country may follow suit.

Crisis crushes council estate

Forgotten hero paints worrying picture

David Moorhead, Northern Editor

Work harder! That was the demand from the Chancellor, George Nottingham, yesterday. But for millions, it seems to be an impossible task.

We are used to seeing the falling figures of the stock market, the rising figures in unemployment and closed shops, but what we rarely look at is the people themselves.

In Sherwood Rise unemployment is nothing like the national average of eight per cent - it's far closer to 80 per cent.

Even so, Sherwood Rise is not the exception, there are council estates like this all across the country. With cuts to handouts

as a banker with a bulging bag of cash on his back, notes and coins spilling to the floor as he makes away with the booty. His name tag says "Barclays Bank". Is this an indication of how the residents here feel and who they believe is responsible for their current situation?

There are children playing in the stairwell, instinctively dodging the broken glass and avoiding the ranting drunk. Having adapted to their environment, they are as happy as any children playing anywhere at all. Their game shocks me as much as anything I've seen here - one child leaps from the stairs shouting "suicide bomber" while his pals scatter as quickly as they can to avoid the

Not the exception: Ordinary people are struggling to survive on Sherwood Rise and similir council estates all across the country

Gisbourne approves big public cash cuts

Steve Dumbleton, City Editor

The Government has been handed some welcome relief by senior banker Sir Guy Gisbourne, who has given their polices his personal stamp of approval.

Gisbourne has reassured people that the public sector cuts will pay off in the long term. He also encouraged the Government's emphasis on keeping big business in Britain.

With much of the country calling for a clamp-down on tax avoidance by big business, and with families all across the

Figure 14.3 In the augmented reality experiment called "Sherwood Rise," after the Junaio AR app scans the front page of *The Truth* (top), the seemingly typical newspaper comes alive with a 3D picture of "a gang of hacker outlaw terrorists." *Courtesy of Dave Miller, a UNESCO Chair in New Media Forms of the Book* <http://itsthetruth.org>

■ CHALLENGES, CRITIQUES, AND AMUSEMENTS

- You should know the life and work of actor Robert Downey, Jr., but what about his father?
- Is *Esquire* magazine particularly known as being digitally inventive?
- Ever seen the work of the British sidewalk artist Julian Beaver? Check it out.
- Did you have pop-up books as a child? Write an original children's story or find a fairy tale from the Grimm brothers. Convert it into a pop-up book and give it to a child.
- Gary Barlow? Talk.
- What do you think is the future for 3D films and television?
- Why don't we see more 3D displays in print publications?
- How could 3D displays be used for your mass communications professional interest?

■ EXERCISES

Knowing how important the depth cue is for visual communication, for this chapter you will create a 3D image that can be seen with a smartphone or tablet using the free Onvert. com program. You can use your own image or the one provided with this exercise. However, it is advisable that you follow the instructions here before you attempt your own picture, but it's up to you.

This effect has the potential of being thought of as a bit cheesy if it is simply used to catch a user's attention without offering additional information. Always try to employ a 3D picture to maximize a user's understanding of a topic and not simply as window dressing.

The 3D presentation requires four pictures: Target image—a high contrast graphic illustration, and three layers: Background Layer 1—it fills a 512-pixel (7.111 inches) square size and forms the background for the other two layers, Background Layer 2—a part of the picture that sets in front of Layer 1, and Background Layer 3—another foreground picture that adds to the illusion of depth.

1. Your first task is to create a high-contrast and graphic target image that will be scanned by the Onvert app to display the 3D image. This illustration should be a 512-pixel (7.111 inches) square. The one I am using can be downloaded from <http://paulmartinlester.info/Routledge/Images/target.png> (Figure 14.4).

Figure 14.4 The Onvert website gives a visual tutorial of the type of image that is best for a target illustration (left). My choice is part of a QR code picture created for the previous chapter.

2. The most complicated part of this exercise is creating the three layers for your 3D picture. Ideally, you want to choose an image that has significance for your mass communication interest, accompanies a story about your specific field, and has elements that can be cut out and included within the layers you need to make the effect work. Using a lasso tool in Photoshop to isolate parts of a picture and perhaps a cloning tool to fill in those parts you've cut out from the background requires a certain degree of expertise with the picture-altering software. You also need to save your layers as PNG transparent images.

3. If you don't feel particularly ambitious or confident, you can simply take a picture as your background and take two other close-ups that comprise your foreground images without worrying about cutting them out in Photoshop. You can also use the images available from my website.

I decided to work with a photograph that is part of one of the most famous portraits in the history of photography. Known as "The Migrant Mother," the close-up of Florence Thompson and her three children taken by Dorothea Lange in 1936 is an icon for those worrying about economic hard times and a mother's responsibility to care for her children (Figure 14.5).

Figure 14.5 "The Migrant Mother" by Dorothea Lange. *Courtesy of the Library of Congress*

The second photograph Lange made of the sad encampment located in Nipomo, California, is an overall view of the family and environment. It is this picture I will use for the 3D effect (Figure 14.6).

Figure 14.6 Pea-picker's camp, Nipomo, California, 1936 by Dorothea Lange. *Courtesy of the Library of Congress*

4. Download my versions of the photograph that will be used as the three layers: <http://paulmartinlester.info/Routledge/Images/background.png>, <http://
paulmartinlester.info/Routledge/Images/leanto.png>, and <http://paulmartinlester.
info/Routledge/Images/family.png> (Figure 14.7).

Figure 14.7 The background and two other layers for the 3D effect are presented here.

5. You will need to have a website address in order to upload text or images about
your 3D picture, story, or product. Users will link to that URL if they want more
information. For this exercise you can download the original photograph from
<http://paulmartinlester.info/Routledge/Images/migrant_mother.jpg> and then
upload it to your personal website.

6. Go to the Onvert website at <http://onvert.com> and click the "create an onvert" button at the top (Figure 14.8).

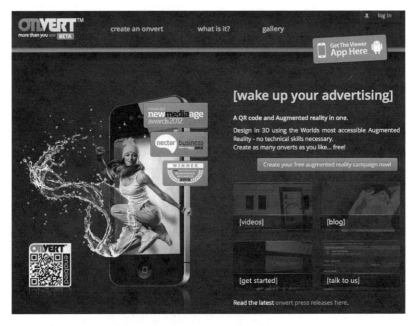

Figure 14.8 Notice that the Onvert website stresses their program for primarily advertising purposes. That's fine, but it's up to you to think of other uses.

7. Onvert asks you for basic information: Title, Link, and Link Name. For the link, use the address where you updated a web file, video, image, or so on so users can receive additional information (Figure 14.9). Press the Create Onvert button.

Figure 14.9 You will receive an error message if all three blanks in this form are not filled.

8. Now is a good time to obtain yet another piece of this 3D puzzle. You need to download the free Onvert app to a smartphone or tablet so you can see your finished work. Click either the Apple App Store or Google play button at the bottom of the Onvert website. For Apple, press the "View in iTunes" button and download it after typing in your password (Figure 14.10).

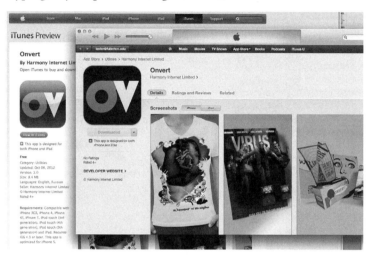

Figure 14.10 The Onvert 3D viewing app is available in English and Russian. Whatever.

9. That done, return to where you left off on the Onvert website. The second step of the process is to include the images previously taken, processed, or downloaded. Click each Choose File button, find the corresponding file for the target and the three layers, and double-click them. You don't need a soundtrack or stock animations. When finished, press Upload. The pictures will show in the order you directed (Figure 14.11).

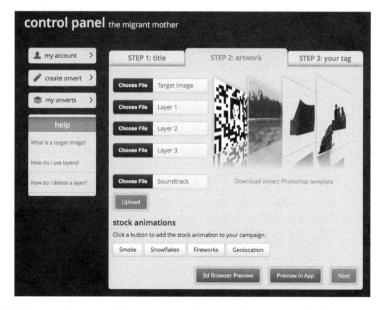

Figure 14.11 Remember to make Layers 2 & 3 a little smaller than the background picture so the background is clearly visible behind them.

10. Click on the "3D Browser Preview" button and move your mouse to see the 3D effect (Figure 14.12).

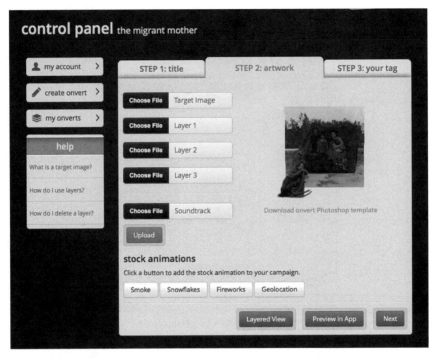

Figure 14.12 As you move the mouse to see the 3D effect, if the foreground images are not separated enough from the background, make them smaller and reload the new versions.

11. To see what your picture looks like on a smartphone or tablet, press the "Preview in App" button. Open your recently downloaded Onvert app and first point it to the graphic at the right with the Onvert logo. After confirmation, move it over to the Target Image and see the 3D picture. Make sure the link to more information works as well. If you prefer, the app allows you to share your work with your Facebook, Twitter, and email friends (Figure 14.13).

Figure 14.13 The Target Image and the Onvert tag are displayed at the top. When a smartphone or tablet with the Onvert app scans the two graphics, the image seems to pop out of the screen as seen on the author's monitor through a smartphone.

12. If you are happy with your preview, close the Preview in App window (the "X" at the top right) and press the Next button. From this last Onvert step, press the "Download Tag" button to receive a high-quality version (Figure 14.14).

Figure 14.14 The Onvert tag and the Target Image need to be included with a printed or screen piece so the effect will occur.

13. Create a magazine, newspaper, website, or blog page that pertains to the topic of your image. The Onvert and Target tags can be as small as one-inch square and still be picked up by the scanner's app. Download the layout from <http://paulmartinlester. info/Routledge/Images/migrant_mother_layout.jpg>, print it out if you wish, and with a smartphone or tablet with the Onvert app running, hover over the graphic tags at the bottom (Figure 14.15).

The Migrant Mother
A Portrait of Courage and Dedication

Once you see the forlorn face of Florence Thompson, you will never forget her. With furrowed forehead, a faraway look, hand cupped to her chin in a gesture of uncertainty, two children shyly hiding their faces in the warmth of her shoulders, and an infant sleeping on her lap, the photograph is more than a simple portrait of a family. Here in black and white is a real-life symbol for all parents struggling to survive and feed their families during the Great Depression and for all uncertain economic times. "Migrant Mother" is probably the world's most reproduced photograph in the history of photography because it makes people care about this mother on a deep, personal level.

Tired, hungry, and anxious to get home after a month-long project taking pictures in central California, Dorothea Lange drove her car north along the cold and wet Camino Real Highway (101) in February 1936. Along the way she noted a migrant workers' camp of about 2,500 people outside the small town of Nipomo. On the side of the road someone had placed a sign that simply proclaimed, "Pea-Pickers Camp." These sights were all too common, with poor people from all over the country forced to stop for lack of money and gasoline for their cars and earn a few dollars picking local crops.

Lange retrieved her press camera, a portable version of the tripod-bound, large-format camera, and immediately found Florence Thompson sitting in the barely adequate shelter of an open tent with her daughters. With the crop destroyed by a freeze, there was no work at the camp.

When she returned to her home in Berkeley, Lange made several prints and gave them to an editor of the *San Francisco News*, where they were published on March 10 under the headline, "FOOD RUSHED TO STARVING FARM COLONY." Two of Lange's photographs accompanied the story that detailed the situation of the migrants and the efforts of relief workers to bring food and cleanup crews to the camp. The famous close-up was not published. Because of the story and pictures, the camp residents received about 20,000 pounds of food from the government and contributions of cash from the public, but Thompson and her family had left before help arrived.

The picture soon became an American classic with a life of its own. Newspapers across the country reproduced it. When John

Steinbeck saw the picture, it inspired him to write *The Grapes of Wrath*. In 1941, the Museum of Modern Art in New York City exhibited it. Without question, the photograph made Lange famous.

When she first saw it in print, Florence Thompson didn't like the image and tried to get it suppressed. When that effort failed, she tried to get Lange and/or the government to pay her for being in the picture. In 1979, 44 years after the picture was taken, Thompson was still bitter about the fact that the photograph made Dorothea Lange famous but didn't improve her life.

In 1983, Thompson suffered from cancer and heart disease. She couldn't pay her medical bills. Family members alerted the local newspaper and a national story was published about her situation. Readers who saw the story and remembered the emotional image were moved to send money to her—more than $15,000 ($33,500 today)—before she died. Many of the letters that contained money noted how the writers' lives had been touched by Lange's close-up portrait of "Migrant Mother."

Figure 14.15 The story of "The Migrant Mother" photograph is told in art and copy with an interactive, 3D feature to help put the user in the place where Dorothea Lange took the photograph—a field in Nipomo, California, in 1936.

Sources

2010 Horizon Report. "Two to Three Years: Simple Augmented Reality." Accessed January 12, 2013. http://wp.nmc.org/horizon2010/chapters/simple-augmented-reality/.

Augmented Reality. Guinness World Records. Accessed March 4, 2013. http://www.guinness worldrecords.com/GWR-2013/augmented-reality.

AVForums. (April 21, 2012). "Universal 100th Anniversary—UK Augmented Reality Editions." Accessed January 12, 2013. http://www.avforums.com/forums/blu-rays-dvds-download-services/1621625-universal-100th-anniversary-uk-augmented-reality-editions.html.

Brogan, Danny. (May 28, 2012). "Hello! Magazine Features 3D Augmented Reality Gary Barlow Front Cover." Accessed January 12, 2013. http://www.pocket-lint.com/news/45819/hello-magazine-features-3d-augmented-reality-gary-barlow-front-cover.

Carpenter, Thomas K. (December 27, 2009). "Augmented Reality Year in Review—2009. Accessed January 12, 2013. http://thomaskcarpenter.com/2009/12/27/augmented-reality-year-in-review-2009/.

De:Bug. Accessed January 12, 2013. http://de-bug.de/mag/9443.html.

"Escaping Criticism." National Gallery of Art. Accessed January 26, 2013. http://www.nga.gov/exhibitions/2002/slideshow/slide-176–9.shtm.

"Welcome to the Esquire Augmented Reality Issue." Esquire. Accessed January 12, 2013. http://www.esquire.com/the-side/augmented-reality.

Inbar, Ori. (December 21, 2012). "Augmented World Expo Opens Call for Proposals. Accessed January 12, 2013. http://gamesalfresco.com/.

Jardin, Xeni. (July 20, 2012). "Spacecraft 31323D: Nifty Robotic Space Travel Augmented-reality App from NASA JPL." Boing Boing. Accessed January 12, 2013. http://boingboing.net/2012/07/20/spacecraft-3d-nifty-robotic-s.html.

Lester, Paul Martin. (2014). Visual Communication Images with Messages. 6th Edition. Boston: Cengage Learning.

Mastodon. Accessed January 12, 2013. http://www.mastodonrocks.com/ar/.

Metaio. "Popular Science 3D Magazine Cover." Accessed January 12, 2013. http://www.metaio.com/solutions/web/popular-science-3d-magazine-cover/.

Miller, Dave. Augmented Reality & the Future of the Book. Accessed February 2, 2013. http://augmentedwonder.blogspot.co.uk/.

Miller, Stephen. (November 24, 2009). "The 'King of the Pop-Ups' Made Books Spring to Life." The Wall Street Journal. Accessed January 12, 2013. http://online.wsj.com/article/SB125902884513660749.html.

Pavlik, John, and Frank Bridges. "The Emergence of Augmented Reality (AR) as a Storytelling Medium in Journalism." Journalism & Communication Monographs 15, no. 1.

"Peek at Harry Potter's World as it Takes Shape." USA Today (January 28, 2010). Accessed January 12, 2013. http://www.usatoday.com/travel/wizarding-world-of-harry-potter-preview.htm.

Pogue, David. (November 11, 2007). "A Galaxy in Your Face." The New York Times. Accessed January 12, 2013. http://www.nytimes.com/2007/11/11/books/review/Pogue-t.html?_r=2&ref=authors&oref=slogin&.

Swaminathan, Nikhil. (July 9, 2010). "Are Augmented Reality Textbooks on the Horizon?" Accessed January 12, 2013. http://www.good.is/posts/are-augmented-reality-textbooks-the-future-of-learning/.

Taub, Eric A. (March 8, 2009). "Webcam Brings 3-D to Topps Sports Cards." The New York Times. Accessed January 12, 2013. http://www.nytimes.com/2009/03/09/technology/09topps.html?_r=2&.

Townsend, Allie. (February 16, 2011). "Pop-Up Books." Time. Accessed January 12, 2013. http://www.time.com/time/specials/packages/article/0,28804,2049243_2048646_2048993,00.html.

YouTube. (March 27, 2012). "Esquire's Augmented Reality Issue: A Tour." Accessed January 12, 2013. http://www.youtube.com/watch?feature=player_embedded&v=LGwHQwgBzSI.

15 APPS

"I would eat an oyster from the NY Harbor."
- Yum!
- No way!
- Maybe in 80 years.

Don't answer too quickly. Your opinion may change after you experience the augmented reality smartphone or tablet app "Oyster City," a walking tour that tells the story of oysters in the New York City area (Figure 15.1). Hopefully the answer won't make you lose your app-etite.

Unlike the famous neon sign within the New Orleans' French Quarter seafood institution Felix's that glows yellow with the mysterious message, "Oysters R in Season" in which you must ask someone knowledgeable its meaning (the sign is a clever way of saying, "It's best to eat oysters from the area during the eight months out of the year that have an "R" in their names"), the Oyster City app will clearly educate you about the past, present, and future of the bivalve mollusk as if you are walking with a well-informed personal tour guide.

Created by interactive documentarian Meredith Drum, nonlinear storytelling and psychogeography adjunct professor at Hunter College Rachel Stevens, and media artist and application programmer Phoenix Toews, Oyster City is described in the introduction:

> When Henry Hudson sailed into the bay in 1609, 350 square miles of wild oyster beds surrounded Manhattan and adjacent islands. NYC became the world's largest producer of oysters until industrial pollution and over harvesting depleted the oyster population in the late 19th and early 20th centuries. Colorful lore detailing how oysters were cultivated, monetized, distributed, prepared and consumed reveals interconnections between ecological, social and economic systems. Recent interest in planting oyster reefs is playing a role in the regeneration of shoreline ecosystems and water quality. For *Oyster City*, sites in NYC are being populated with AR elements enabling participants to learn and play as they interact with their immediate environment.

Although smartphone and tablet apps for commercial and entertainment purposes have been available since 2009, programs for educational purposes are a fairly new concept. Writer Thomas K. Carpenter chronicled AR highlights for 2009: AR programs could be made with Adobe's Flash software program; Patty Maes of MIT introduced the inexpensive "SixthSense" portable AR device; author Bruce Sterling's novel *The Caryatids* was introduced with augmented features; Amsterdam-based Layar, an AR development

Figure 15.1 Oyster City cocreator Meredith Drum listens to a narration through her Sony head-phones while she points her tablet along a New York City street where oyster beds once were plentiful before they were replaced by concrete. *Courtesy of Oyster City, an AR Project by Meredith Drum, Rachel Stevens, and Phoenix Toews*

firm, began operation; Sterling gave the keynote address at an AR convention sponsored by Layar; AR companies Wikitude and Layar offered smartphone versions; and Metaio's free smartphone app, Junaio, was introduced. As with most digital media, location-based or locative consumer apps were produced to attract the attention and funding from deep-pocketed companies with advertising agencies that exploited their earnings potential.

With almost two million apps available from Apple and Google with many of them free, there is a download for everyone (Figure 15.2). Apple lists 11 categories of apps: cal-culate, entertainment, games, news, productivity, search tools, social networking, sports, travel, utilities, and weather, but we all know there are more categories available from other companies. For the purposes of this book, there are essentially two types of apps: Those created to provide users with useful programs and entertaining distractions and those created to help professionals do their jobs more efficiently and effectively.

As with the Oyster City app, augmented reality locative apps such as Acrossair, Junaio, Layar, and Wikitude are glorified search engines (Figure 15.3). Paul Hartsock of *MacNews-World* writes that these apps use your smartphone's camera and look "out at the world, the sensors figure out which way you're pointing, the app overlays information about nearby things of interest, and you see a land bedecked with signs and clickable links." Links pop up on the screen for "sponsored entries from the likes of FedEx, YouTube, Beck's, etc. (finding store locations, videos shot near you, and nearby live music, respectively). Others will show you what people around you are tweeting, the Foursquare activity in your vicin-ity, Wikipedia entries on nearby points of interest, and a car-finder that can guide you back to your parking spot after a long night's wandering." In 2012, *Time* magazine listed the 50 best apps. The locative entries included: Find My iPhone, GasBuddy (local stations and their prices), MapQuest 4, iMapMyRun+ (tracks your route), FourSquare and Find My Friends (geosocial networks), and Smart Ride (public transit system information).

Figure 15.2 "What Happened Here?" is a locative app under development for a smartphone that gives a user information depending on that person's location. In the left panel, news events that occurred in the immediate area are highlighted. The center panel features important cultural or historical events that occurred. The final panel is programmed so users can input their own stories about a location that others can read through the app or on Facebook. *Courtesy of Paul Martin Lester*

Mass media executives have finally caught on to the importance of apps to convey their publication's content. With newspaper and magazine print editions fading from memory and local and national news television shows declining in viewership, these traditional mass communications outlets have necessarily switched to online platforms. Nevertheless, an interest in news, regardless of age, is still a strong desire among many. Consequently, according to Pew Research Center polls, there has been recent interest for news-oriented websites, social media, and apps—especially those that offer breaking news alerts on their smartphones. In 2012, the "Old Gray Lady," a nickname for *The New York Times* because of its traditional graphic design appearance (it wasn't until 1997 that it first published a color photograph on its front page), introduced an app that was free for subscribers. Anyone else can get the "Top News" section for free and then can chose to pay for additional content. Other news organizations, the Associated Press, National Public Radio (NPR), CNN, and MSNBC, among others, also have popular smartphone apps with push notifications for breaking news events, videos, and articles. In addition, news app aggregators such as the Fluent News Reader and Newspapers amass stories from many different sources. The Newspapers app allows a user to choose from more than 6,000 online publications throughout the world for a personalized list of news accounts.

Advertising, entertainment, journalism, public relations, RTVF, and visual reporting apps help harried professionals perform their duties better. Alejandro Martinez, writing for the Knight Center, offers five types of apps that all professionals within the mass communications field should own. For Martinez, you need apps in which you can access your saved work from anywhere, perform picture editing functions, manage your social networks, organize your content, and allow for live streaming.

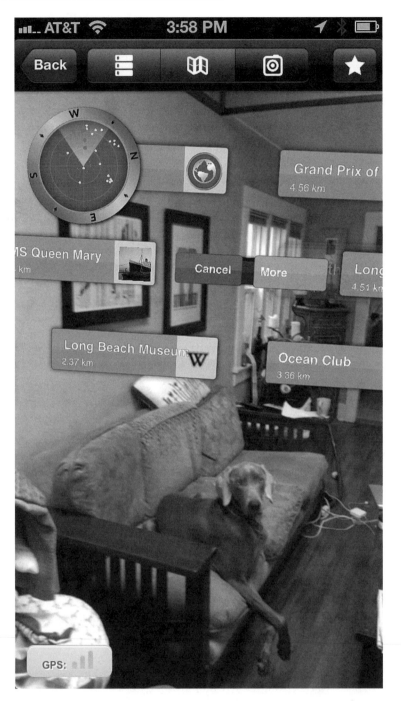

Figure 15.3 As the author's Weimaraner, Nietzsche, sits unaware, Wikitude's interface reveals points of interest available in a northern direction—the Queen Mary and the Long Beach Museum. Perhaps a walk is in the dog's future. *Courtesy of Paul Martin Lester*

For advertising industry professionals, the PR apps are useful with these additions: AdMall (for account representatives), Action Method (task management), Webex (conference calls), Dragon Dictation (voice notes), Expense Tablet (bill tracker), Project Planner (multitasking aid), Keynote (presentations), Web Projector (external screen output), Pages (word and spreadsheet processing), and Idea Sketch (doodle aid).

Besides the apps mentioned elsewhere, Dr. Jim Collison of the Entertainment and Tourism Studies concentration for the Department of Communications at California State University, Fullerton, recommends these apps for those who work in the travel and tourism fields: Hipmunk (flight planning), Kayak (flight, hotel, and car rental planning), GateGuru (updated airport information), TripAdvisor (reviews), Yelp (user reviews), The World Clock, Dark Sky (weather data), INRIX Traffic (automobile traffic source), and Borderlines (USA-Mexico and USA-Canada crossing information).

Lauren Maffeo of *The Next Web* also has a specific list of apps she finds are essential for journalists: Bambuser (live video streaming), Dropbox, iA Soundnote (dictation), Viddy (video package production), Wikipanion (Wikipedia access), Writing Prompts (writer's block help), Audioboo (sound sharing), Evernote and freeDive (data sharing), and The Reddit Edit (pro version of Reddit).

For smartphone journalists, students at the University of California, Berkeley Graduate School of Journalism offered five apps: Filmic Pro (improves video capabilities), ProCamera (improves picture quality), Camera Awesome (exposure improvements and filters), Hindenburg Field Recorder (audio recorder and editor), and 1st Video–Video Editor (video and audio editor). For interviews, Ryan Lytle of *10,000 Words* recommends: Dragon (voice to text transcriber), SoundCloud (recorder), and WriteRoom (note writing).

MediaMiser is an app for beginning public relations and marketing professionals who need a resource for industry terms, activities, planning, and reports. James Hudson of *PR News* stresses 13 apps PR pros should have on their smartphones: AP Mobile (news), Dropbox (file sharing), Evernote (note taking), Facebook (updating information), Free Wi-Fi Finder (Internet sites), Instagram (picture posting), LinkedIn (networking), OpenTable (restaurant reservations), Pinterest (visual storytelling), Twitter (news updates), Skype (client chats), and TripIt (travel reservations). James Chupick of PRNewser adds five more to the list: Flipboard (converts content into magazine spreads), Phoster (poster creation), Splashtop (desktop synch), Hootsuite (Twitter content management), and Cozi (task organizer).

RTVF executives, according to *Skye Production News* should have Action Log Pro (keeps track of reel names and time codes for up to 25 cameras at once), Cinemek Hitchcock (storyboarding), Movie Slate (notes, clapper board, digital slate, and shot log features), IMDB (Internet Movie Database for film and television facts), Red Laser (barcode scanner with price comparisons), Skype, and Pro Camera Guide (movie making basics).

Chicago Tribune visual reporter Alex Garcia recommends a list of apps for serious photographers: Skylights (lighting diagram aid), Evernote and Sun Seeker: 3D Augmented Reality Viewer (sunlight direction for any day, time, and location), Hootsuite and Photosync (image transfers), Dropbox, Filterstorm Pro (picture editing), Adobe Carousel (picture library access), and Blurb (multimedia essay production).

Brian Storm maintains one of the premiere websites to see multimedia presentations that include still and moving images, voice-overs, natural sound, music, and interactive navigation features. With a master's degree in photojournalism from the prestigious University of Missouri and experiences as the former director of multimedia for MSNBC and vice president of News, Multimedia & Assignment Services for the picture agency Corbis, Storm runs a New York City-based multimedia production studio that presents stories created by journalists throughout the world. He also trains professionals and academics in making their own multimedia programs. On his MediaStorm website, as of this writing, there is only one app offered, Above & Beyond: George Steinmetz. With still and video pictures, narration, satellite imagery, and technical details about each photograph, Steinmetz, a *National Geographic* magazine photographer and Stanford geo-physicist, explains the use of a paraglider he used to take pictures throughout the world. It is an example of the best an app is capable of presenting.

Whether for multimedia presentations intended to educate, entertain, and persuade users or to help make more efficient professional practices, apps are invaluable for mass communications. As such, apps will probably overtake the web in importance within our increasingly shared media environment.

■ CHALLENGES, CRITIQUES, AND AMUSEMENTS

- Oysters! How many different kinds are there? Where do restaurants get them? Are they endangered?
- Read Bruce Sterling's *The Caryatids*. Start a book club and discuss it and the influence Sterling has had through his science fiction writings.
- How many apps do you have on your smartphone or tablet, and what are your favorites for personal and professional uses?
- Imagine an app you would like to have that no one else has created. Sketch out its features and graphic style on paper.
- What do most news apps have in common?
- How much would it cost if you downloaded all the apps mentioned for your mass communications field in this chapter?
- Write a detailed scenario in which you would need all the apps mentioned for your interest in this chapter. For example, you might consider the planning and filming of a Super Bowl commercial, a series of vacation spots related to a season of "The Amazing Race," a complex investigative story that involves several countries, or the inauguration of a charitable organization to help homeless persons.

■ EXERCISES

To create a smartphone and tablet app from software code is way beyond the intention of this textbook. After all, if a chapter were devoted to picture alterations, you wouldn't be expected to create a Photoshop-like program from scratch. There are numerous how-to books, college classes, and YouTube tutorials that might help you create your own app, but you would be working on it for several months with no guarantee of success. Fortunately, there are several free and simple app maker programs such as TheAppBuilder <http://theappbuilder.com>, ShoutEm <http://shoutem.com>, Appsbuilder <http://apps-builder.com>, and Appsbar <appsbar.com>.

For this exercise, you will use TheAppBuilder from JamPot Technologies out of Belfast, Northern Ireland. TheAppBuilder has 21 app templates within the categories of business, education, events, groups, music, social, and sport. There is also a "Build Your Own" category in which you can customize your effort in any way you choose. Whether you are an advertising, entertainment, journalism, public relations, RTVF, or visual reporting student or professional, you can find a category that will fit the story you want to tell.

Regardless of the purpose of your app, before you get started you will need to make at least 12 images saved as 72dpi JPG or PGN files. The illustrations are needed for four purposes—App Icon, Splashscreen, Home Image, and Banner Image. The App Icon is a picture that acts like a logo. It should be graphically simple and interesting to stand out among other apps on a user's smartphone or tablet. The Splashscreen is seen while the app loads and is sized to fit a variety of platforms. The Home Image helps illustrate the content contained in the app. The Banner Image runs along the top of the app to help link all the pages stylistically.

Below are the pictures you will need, their size in pixels, and the recommended file names:

Picture Name	Size in Pixels	Recommended File Name
App Icon	512 × 512	appicon.jpg
iPhone 3/3G/3GS	320 × 480	iphone3.jpg
iPhone 4/4S	640 × 960	iphone4.jpg
iPad 1&2	768 × 1024	ipad2.jpg
iPad 3	153 × 2048	ipad3.jpg
Android Small	320 × 426	androidsmall.jpg
Android Medium	320 × 470	androidmedium.jpg
Android Large	480 × 640	androidlarge.jpg
Android XLarge	720 × 960	androidxlarge.jpg
Windows Phone 7	480 × 800	windows.jpg
Home Image	1024 × 1024	home.jpg
Banner Image	640 × 88	banner.jpg

(Note: As of this writing, there is no Splashscreen for the iPhone5, but it works fine on that device.)

For all your choices, you can easily change your mind and edit your app with different pictures.

1. Select an image you want as the App Icon that will reside on the desktop of a user's smartphone or tablet. If you are recreating the example included with this exercise, download the Migrant Mother picture from <http://paulmartinlester.info/Routledge/Images/the_migrant_mother.jpg>. Save the original. All of your other files will be based from it.

2. Open the photograph in Photoshop and pull down the Image menu item and select Image Size. Make sure the Constrain Proportions and Resample Image boxes are checked. Within the Pixel Dimensions area at the top input the width size. The pixel size of the height will set itself automatically. For TheAppBuilder, the dimensions do not have to match the size recommendations in the above table exactly. This procedure will be used throughout this section of the exercise (Figure 15.4).

Figure 15.4 Use the Image Size command to set each picture's size by conforming to the width or height of the size you need. This procedure avoids distortion or cropping of the photograph.

3. For all of the Splashscreen size variations, you will use the same picture. I have elected to have the picture I am using for the App Icon also as my Splashscreen pictures. You can, of course, use a different illustration. As with Step 1, set the size of the width and save each Splashscreen picture according to the table above.

4. Decide on a Home Image, size, and save it. Again, I am using the same picture.

5. The Banner Image can be a picture or a typographical display. Its small width perhaps lends itself more to copy than art. I created a new file in Photoshop set to the size needed, used the Paint Bucket tool to make the background black, wrote the copy with the Text tool set to the color white with a 60-point Gill Sans Bold typeface, moved the line where I wanted it, flattened the image using the Layer menu, and saved the illustration (Figure 15.5).

Figure 15.5 As the name implies, the Banner Image runs along the top of the app. Because its background is black, the same color background for the text is advised. However, you have the option to change the color scheme as you wish once you start the program.

6. Go to TheAppBuilder's website <http://theappbuilder.com> and press the "Start—It's Free!" button (Figure 15.6).

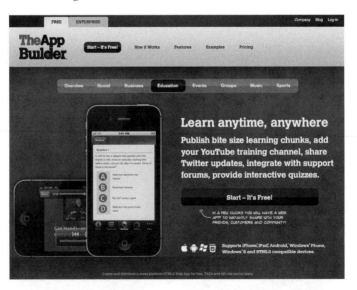

Figure 15.6 The developers of TheAppBuilder have added a number of tutorials to help you create apps. You should take advantage of their expertise.

7. Explore the different categories of apps available with their features. For this exercise, select the "Build Your Own" category and then the Next button (Figure 15.7).

Figure 15.7 Although you can customize any of the app templates the program offers, the "Build Your Own" selection gives you the most choices.

8. Within the "What type of things do you want to include in your app?" dialog box, check the Web Page, Gallery, and Feedback boxes. Press Next (Figure 15.8).

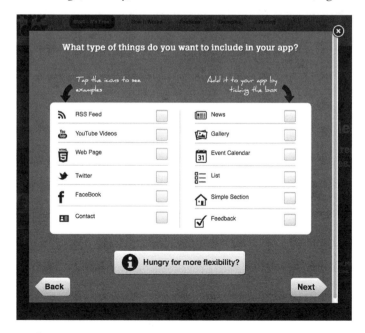

Figure 15.8 Feel free to explore the icons with the examples provided by the developers and choose the features you feel are appropriate.

9. In the dialog box that follows, add your blog or web address and your email address to receive user feedback. You can change or eliminate any element you wish later. Press Next (Figure 15.9).

Figure 15.9 The generic Gallery images will be eliminated a bit later.

10. At this point, you need to register with the free program. Enter your specific data and press Next. Your app based on your previous input will be created (Figure 15.10).

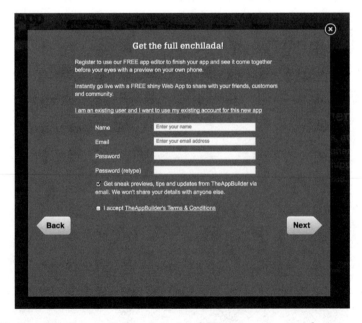

Figure 15.10 Complete the standard registration form—the only price for using the free program. You might consider checking the previews, tips, and updates box to stay current with the developers' innovations.

11. Press the "Draft App" menu choice at the top of the left menu and fill out the form:

App Name: MigrantMother (Note: Whatever name you use, make it short, relevant, and without spaces. This is the name that will be a part of the URL for the app).

Description: Photographer Dorothea Lange's 1936 compelling portrait of Florence Thompson with three of her children is a classic image from America's Great Depression. This app includes photographs, text, plans for a marker to commemorate the location in Nipomo, California, and other features to help you understand the importance of the moment preserved for all time.

Keywords: Dorothea Lange, Migrant Mother, Great Depression, Nipomo, California

Use the procedure explained by Chapter 10's exercise to find the latitude and longitude coordinates for the location you want to plot. For this exercise, use 35.046687, -120.492364. Press Save at the bottom of the page (Figure 15.11).

Figure 15.11 Keywords are included so that others might find your app. The maps you use will be included within a Maps feature we will add a bit later.

12. Press the Customize menu choice at the left and then the Icon & Splashscreen button. With the Icon tab selected, click and drag the square 512-pixel appicon.jpg picture to the upload box. Press Save (Figure 15.12).

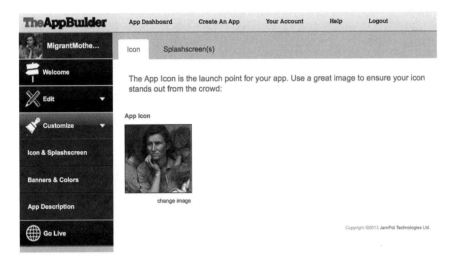

Figure 15.12 TheAppBuilder makes it easy to change your mind about a picture choice—simply replace one image with another.

13. Select the Splashscreen(s) tab. Within each image rectangle, press the Click to Upload box and drag the appropriate version of the picture to the drop area. Ignore the red warning message if the image is too small or too large. Press Save. Repeat for all the size variations for the three devices (Figure 15.13).

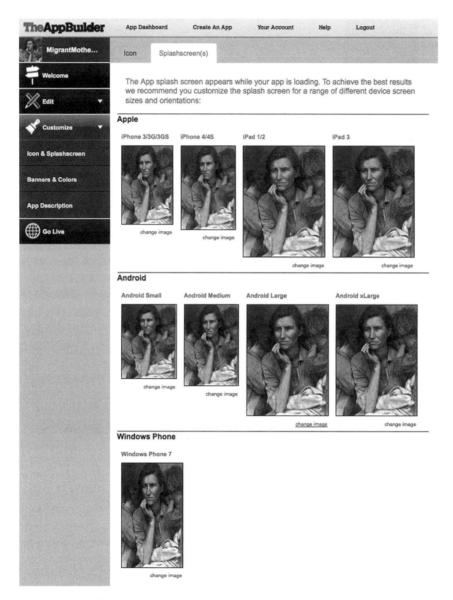

Figure 15.13   The different sizes of Dorothea Lange's portrait reflect the different uses put to the splashscreens. Ironically, because most users have quick wireless speeds, a splashscreen is seldom needed.

14. Select the Banners & Colors menu button and click within the drop box. Drag your banner into the perforated rectangle. Click Use. I selected a black background to match the color used as the border for most smartphone and tablet apps. Change colors if you wish (Figure 15.14).

Figure 15.14 The banner image should probably be a short text message that helps to contextually and graphically link the pages of your app.

15. There is no need to press the "App Description" button because you completed the form in Step 11. Press the Edit menu choice and then "Edit Sections." Press the "New Section" button at the top and then the "Choose Section Type" button. Select the first icon, Simple. Press Save (Figure 15.15).

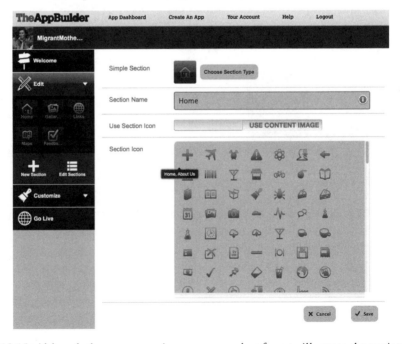

Figure 15.15 Although there are many icons you can select from to illustrate the section type, it is best to maintain a professional appearance.

16. Within the Home dialog box, upload a picture, type in a title, and include a description of your app. This page will be the first your users see (Figure 15.16).

Figure 15.16 In the Description window you can add as much information as you feel users need in order to understand the purpose of your app.

17. Return to Edit Sections and click on the Web Page title. Change the title to "Links" and include the URL link. I created a simple webpage where users can get more information (Figure 15.17).

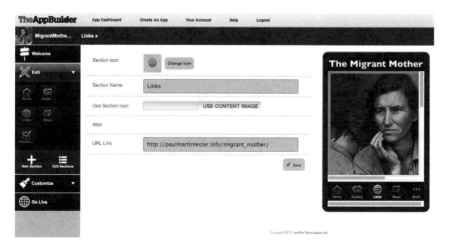

Figure 15.17 The preview screen at the right lets you see changes made to the app before it goes public.

18. Return to Edit Sections and click on the Gallery title. When you add an image, you can delete all the generic pictures that come with the program. Download the following file from <http://paulmartinlester.info/Routledge/Images/App_Folder. zip>. After you decompress the folder, click the "Add Item" button and the "change image" link to upload the picture. Write a caption, a brief description, and then Save for each one.

Use the following text:

Picture: mother.jpg

Caption: "Migrant Mother," 1936, by Dorothea Lange.

Description: The disturbing and touching story line of a woman alone with her children during the height of America's Great Depression spurred many to help others. But is she posing or wishing the photographer would leave?

For this photograph you also need to include the Item Location. Press the "add location" button and the map coordinates of 35.046687, -120.492364 as before.

Picture: migrants.jpg

Caption: "Family Between Dallas and Austin, Texas," 1936, by Dorothea Lange.

Description: The Library of Congress's caption for the photograph reads, "The people have left their home and connections in South Texas, and hope to reach the Arkansas Delta for work in the cotton fields. Penniless people. No food and three gallons of gas in the tank. The father is trying to repair a tire. Three children. Father says, 'It's tough but life's tough anyway you take it.' " During the Great Depression, the Farm Security Administration of the US government produced numerous classic documents, such as this "Migrant Mother" alternative.

Picture: exodus.jpg

Caption: The book jacket of *An American Exodus: A Record of Human Erosion*, by Dorothea Lange and Paul Taylor

Description: The cover shows a typical sight along the roads during America's Great Depression—a truck filled with household goods. With Lange's pictures and Taylor's words, the two documented the migration of many from ruined Dust Bowl farms to migrant worker camps out West.

Picture: image1.jpg

Caption: Photojournalists call the first picture taken at a scene a "cover shot," but not related to a magazine page.

Description: If you are asked or are forced to leave, at least you have something. With the older girl avoiding the camera, the younger one smiling for the lens, and Florence Thompson looking back at a daughter hiding behind her, this image is almost a snapshot—not a particularly telling moment.

Picture: image2.jpg

Caption: A formal portrait of the family group

Description: The older Viola strikes a model's pose as she sits awkwardly on the cane rocking chair as (from left) Ruby, coaxed from behind her mother and wearing a wool cap, Katherine, Florence, and baby Norma are inside the lean-to tent. Lange is now obviously stage-managing this situation, an ethical violation for documentary and news photographs by today's standards.

Picture: image3.jpg

Caption: Dorothea Lange moves in a little closer.

Description: Five-year-old Ruby unnaturally rests her chin on her mother's shoulder, is not wearing her wool cap, and the tent flap has been pulled back, probably by Viola. All of this stage-managing was no doubt suggested by Lange.

Picture: image4.jpg

Caption: If "Migrant Mother" had never been taken, this photograph would have been revered as a powerful portrait of migrant life, with probably as much attention given to it as its famous cousin.

Description: Florence looks just as forlorn as in "Migrant Mother" and little Ruby now seems more comfortable with one hand on her mother's shoulder as she grasps the pole with the other, but this image also contains more information with the addition of the simple metal plate and worn trunk used as a table and the outside, forbidding farm field beyond the tent's inadequate shelter.

Picture: marker.jpg

Caption: The Proposed Migrant Mother Marker

Description: City leaders from Nipomo, California, with academics, authors, photographers, and interested parties are working to erect a historical marker that commemorates the site of the famous photograph. The location of the marker will most likely be at the proposed Jim O. Miller Memorial Park. In addition, include a map with this picture. Press the "add location" button and the map coordinates of 35.039853, -120.480603.

When finished uploading all the pictures, writing the captions and descriptions, and including the maps, take a break and congratulate yourself for a good job with your favorite beverage, but not before you press Save (Figure 15.18).

Figure 15.18 Add as many images as you wish. But make sure they are your own, in the public domain, copyright free, or you have permission to use them.

19. Click on the New Section button at the left and then the "Choose Section Type" button to select Maps. Let TheAppBuilder know your location if you wish (I personally don't even like my mother knowing where I am). Check the box for "Show a map with pinned content" and the Select box for the Gallery so the marker.jpg picture will include the map for the user (Figure 15.19).

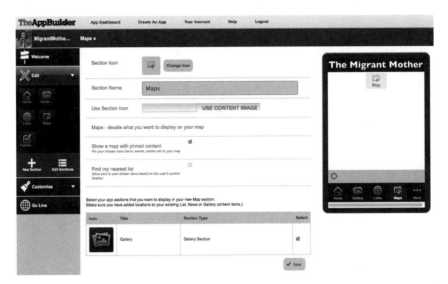

Figure 15.19 The Map feature will automatically place markers at the locations you specify.

20. Return to the Edit Sections editing page and click on the Up and Down arrow buttons to order the titles as Home, Gallery, Links, Maps, and Feedback (Figure 15.20).

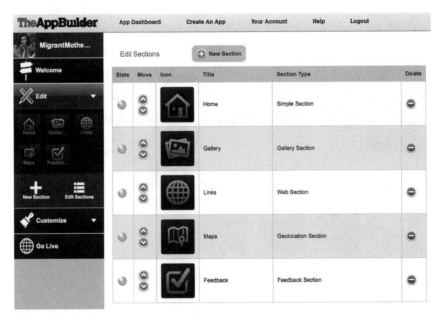

Figure 15.20 Only four sections will be displayed along the bottom of the app. Others, including the mandatory link to TheAppBuilder's website, will show within the More area.

21. You are now ready to see your app on a smartphone or tablet. Click on the "Go Live" menu choice, make a copy or remember the URL for the app, and press the "Publish Changes" button (Figure 15.21).

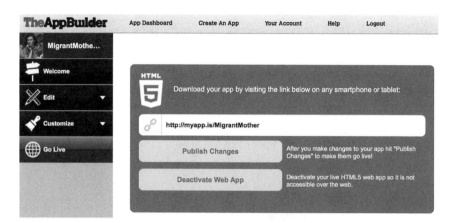

Figure 15.21 This is the location where you learn your app's URL so you can tell your friends how to download your work, where you make your app public, and where you eliminate it if you no longer need it.

22 Select a browser on a smartphone or tablet, type in the URL of your app, and then choose Search. When it shows on the screen, select the email icon and then the "Add to Home Screen" button. A user has the option to rename the app, but it shouldn't have more than 15 characters or the title won't fit under the icon. Spaces between words in the title are now allowed (Figure 15.22).

Figure 15.22 (Left) After inputting the URL for the app, users click on the email icon and then the "Add to Home Screen" button in the center. Once the app is added, users can type whatever name they wish for the app. Most, however, will use the name you use.

23. Once the app is downloaded to the device, position it amid all the other apps that are typically collected (Figure 15.23).

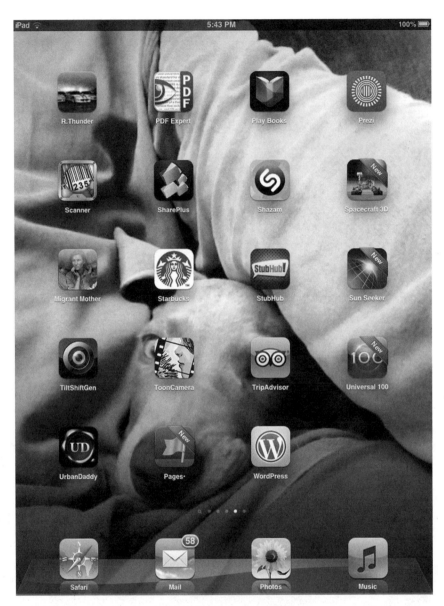

Figure 15.23 On an iPad, the Migrant Mother app stands out from the other apps (and a Weimaraner puppy in the background) by its compelling human content and the black and white tones.

24. Click on the app's icon and look through all the elements to make sure they operate. If there is a problem, you find a typo, or you want to add or subtract features, return to your TheAppBuilder account, edit the page, and republish the changes. In that way, updates come from you—a user doesn't have to decide to perform an update (Figure 15.24).

Figure 15.24 The Migrant Mother's gallery page as it looks on an iPad.

Sources

About.com. "Top 6 iPhone News Apps." Accessed January 12, 2013. http://ipod.about.com/od/bestiphoneapps/tp/top-iphone-news-apps.htm.

Augmented Mountain. "Oyster City." Accessed January 12, 2013. http://www.augmentedmountain.com/oyster_city/.

Carpenter, Thomas K. (December 27, 2009). "Augmented Reality Year in Review—2009. Accessed January 12, 2013. http://thomaskcarpenter.com/2009/12/27/augmented-reality-year-in-review-2009/.

Chupick, Jason. (August 25, 2011). "Five 'Must Have' iPad Apps for PR." *PRNewser*. Accessed January 12, 2013. http://www.mediabistro.com/prnewser/five-must-have-ipad-apps-for-pr_b26050.

Collison, Jim. (January 8, 2012). "Apps for Travel and Tourism Professionals." Personal Email.

Connected Creativity. "Top Ten Apps for the iPad Powered Advertising Executive." Accessed January 12, 2013. http://connectedcreativity.tumblr.com/post/11318951653/top-ten-apps-for-the-ipad-powered-advertising.

Farber, Dan. (September 27, 2012). "Pew Study: News Consumption Up Via Mobile, Social Media." *CNet*. Accessed January 12, 2013. http://news.cnet.com/8301–1023_3–57521694–93/pew-study-news-consumption-up-via-mobile-social-media/.

Garcia, Alex. (November 15, 2011). "iPad Apps for Photojournalists." *Chicago Tribune*. Accessed January 12, 2013. http://newsblogs.chicagotribune.com/assignment-chicago/2011/11/ipad-apps-for-photojournalists-tuesday-tips.html.

Hartsock, Paul. (July 29, 2010). "Acrossair: Getting There Is Half the Fun." *MacNewsWorld*. Accessed January 12, 2013. http://www.macnewsworld.com/story/70502.html.

Hudson, Jamar. "Lucky 13: Mobile Apps Every PR Pro Must Have." *PRNews*. Accessed January 12, 2013. http://www.prnewsonline.com/watercooler/Lucky-13-Mobile-Apps-Every-PR-Pro-Must-Have_17219.html.

Journalist's Toolbox. (November 25, 2012). "Mobile Journalism." Accessed January 12, 2013. http://www.journaliststoolbox.org/archive/mobile-journalism/.

Lytle, Ryan. (November 1, 2012). "5 iPad Apps Journalists Should Try for Interviews." *10,000 Words*. Accessed January 12, 2013. http://www.mediabistro.com/10000words/5-ipad-apps-journalists-interviews_b16039.

Maffeo, Lauren. (September 29, 2012). "The Best Apps, Communities & Tools for Writers and Journalists." *The Next Web*. Accessed January 12, 2013. http://thenextweb.com/apps/2012/09/29/the-best-apps-communities-tools-writers-journalists/.

Marshall, Sarah. (August 17, 2012). "22 Tools and Apps Every Journalism Student Should Know About." Accessed January 12, 2013. http://www.journalism.co.uk/news/22-tools-and-apps-every-journalism-student-should-know-about/s2/a550112/.

Martinez, Alejandro. "5 Apps Every Journalist Should Have on His/Her Smartphone." Knight Center. Accessed January 12, 2013. http://knightcenter.utexas.edu/blog/00–11837–5-apps-every-journalist-should-have-hisher-smartphone.

Mashable. (July 24, 2012). "5 Road-Tested iPhone Apps for Journalists." Accessed January 12, 2013. http://mashable.com/2012/07/24/iphone-apps-for-journalists/.

Media Miser. "Resource Apps." Accessed January 12, 2013. http://www.mediamiser.com/resources/resource-apps.html.

MediaStorm. Accessed January 12, 2013. http://mediastorm.com/.

———. "Apps." Accessed January 12, 2013. http://mediastorm.com/store/apps.

Newman, Jared. (February 15, 2012). "50 Best iPhone Apps 2012." *Time*. Accessed January 12, 2013. http://techland.time.com/2012/02/15/50-best-iphone-apps-2012/.

Oliver, Sam. (September 26, 2012). "Google Android Store Reaches 25 Billion Downloads, 675,000 Apps." *Apple Insider*. Accessed January 12, 2013. http://appleinsider.com/articles/12/09/26/google-android-reaches-25-billion-downloads-675000-apps.

Oyster City. Accessed January 12, 2013. http://oystercity.org/.

Oyster City Preview. Accessed January 12, 2013. http://oystercity.org/preview/.

Sterling, Bruce. (2009). *The Caryatids*. New York: Del Rey.

Section V

IMMERSIVE EXPERIENCES

One of the most innovative and promising digital media uses can combine physical items in a store, objects found during a walk along a trail or urban area, or museum exhibits with overlaying data provided by apps and other software programs and additional commentary and information from participants who use social media.

With transmedia experiences, it is possible for users to find out about a political cause, service, product, or social challenge through all the possible media of presentations learned in the previous chapters.

Transmedia storytelling is a hybrid of presentations that contains information about stories with relevant content and interest for a passive consumer, but it is presented in such a way that may attract even a disenfranchised media type. An object of good storytelling is to help people understand how their view of themselves and their place in the world is a part of a larger societal context. Technology should be employed not only to help people learn about a story, but to help them *feel* a story. Creators of this type of media presentation understand that a user can only feel a story if she becomes a part of it.

16   TRANSMEDIA STORYTELLING

Academic, advisor, bald, bearded, consultant, ego-maniac, fan, funny, genial, influential, long-winded, lucky, married, mild-mannered, nearsighted, oxymoron, parent, professor, prolific, short, suspender wearer, workaholic (Figure 16.1).

These words and others have been used to describe one of the greatest thinkers concerned with the cultural impact of digital innovations, Henry Jenkins III.

Born in Atlanta, Georgia, in 1958, as a child he read such cultural touchstones as the humor magazine *Mad* and the fanzine *Famous Monsters of Filmland,* started the same year as his birth. Not surprisingly, he was an early avid reader of comic books and science fiction, experimented with monster makeup, wrote scripts for Super 8 movies, and collected television-themed toys. A product of three state universities—Georgia Tech, Iowa, and Wisconsin for his undergraduate, master's, and PhD degrees—he has taught exclusively at highly respected private institutions. For a decade, he was the director of the MIT Comparative Media Studies Program and a Professor of Humanities. In 2009, he moved to the University of Southern California to become the Provost's Professor of Communication, Journalism, and Cinematic Arts. He and his wife Cynthia are parents of a 20s-something son, Henry Jenkins IV, who wrote with his father " 'The Monsters Next Door': A Father-Son Dialogue about Buffy, Moral Panic, and Generational Differences."

Single-authored and with others, Jenkins has written books that have helped explain the almost inconceivable ways digital media have altered human experience forever. Such titles as *Spreadable Media: Creating Value and Meaning in a Networked Culture* (2013), *Textual Poachers: Television Fans and Participatory Culture* (2012), *Convergence Culture: Where Old and New Media Collide* (2008), *Rethinking Media Change: The Aesthetics of Transition* (2004), *Democracy and New Media* (2003), and *From Barbie to Mortal Kombat: Gender and Computer Games* (2000) give substantial clues to his emphasis and impact.

"We are living in an age when changes in communications, storytelling and information technologies are reshaping almost every aspect of contemporary life—including how we create, consume, learn, and interact with each other," writes Jenkins. "A whole range of new technologies enable consumers to archive, annotate, appropriate, and recirculate media content and in the process, these technologies have altered the ways that consumers interact with core institutions of government, education, and commerce." He first called this new age, "media convergence." Now he prefers, "cultural convergence."

As might be expected, Jenkins has much to say about transmedia storytelling. For him, it is "a process where integral elements of a fiction get dispersed systematically across multiple delivery channels for the purpose of creating a unified and coordinated entertainment experience." However, for our purposes, this definition needs a remix: Transmedia storytelling is a method to distribute the key audible, textual, and visual components of a narrative through digital innovations that enhance the learning experience. As such,

Figure 16.1 Henry Jenkins III *Courtesy of Joi Ito*

it is a culmination of all the background knowledge, assignments, and tools previously discussed, but gets its inspiration from a much older form of presentation—the museum.

Type in a Google search "best museums in the world" and you will more than likely get a similar list to that of the travel and tours blog Touropia: The Rijksmuseum Museum in Amsterdam, the National Museum of Anthropology in Mexico City, the National Palace in Taipei, the Museum of Modern Art in New York City, and the Hermitage in Saint Petersburg, Russia.

What makes these museums so special? They each are highly respected repositories that offer thousands of pieces in their numerous collections from throughout the world from several centuries with most works sitting safely behind glass cases. But moving through the floors and chambers with their constant low murmur, directional lighting, and controlled temperature and low humidity settings can be a bit numbing as favorite pieces are crowded, textual explanations get only a fast scan, and unique items are often missed. To enhance the experience, you might wait for a tour guide from an educated and hopefully personable docent or purchase an audio tour and walk among the exhibits safely isolated from others within an audible cocoon.

In *Place is a Palimpsest Augmented Reality and Experience of Place*, Aaron Justin "Phoenix" Toews, who created the software for "Oyster City" detailed in the previous chapter described such tours as primitive AR experiences:

> A visitor to a site is given some form of audio playback device and is presented with a pre-recorded spoken commentary that guides her. These programs are

typically institutional, ideologically "clean" narratives that give the officially recognized account of the works or places being represented. The visitor is told where to go, and what to look at, perhaps given some historical perspective or surface level analysis, but has little chance to deviate from the official perspective without disengaging from the device by pausing or switching it off.

To "deviate from the official perspective" is a key to the success of the technologies described in this book. The task is tricky for a producer. The user must feel free enough to make personal choices, but confined enough to ensure that important details and major contributions are not missed. In addition, the design of digital innovations must allow a certain degree of serendipity where "Aha" moments make exciting and unexpected connections between the various presentations. Such is the promise and challenge of truly engaging works.

Why this emphasis on museums, one of the oldest and most traditional places devised by humans to convey cultural awareness, stability, and power? Simple. A growing number of these nondigital showcases with their packaged tours have hired digital innovators who have been freed to exemplify the possibilities when the real and the virtual combine. The lessons learned will help in the creation of all types of storytelling needed by mass communications students and professionals.

A relatively simple example of transmedia storytelling can be found at San Diego's Museum of Photographic Arts. Some of the works by the Dutch artist Ruud van Empel in his "Strange Beauty" show included QR codes on label cards so that users could see additional text and videos that would be difficult for a tour guide to include. A more elaborate example comes from Coventry University northwest of London. Its "Eye Shakespeare" app is meant to augment a tour of the museum maintained by the Shakespeare Birthplace Trust located at the birthplace of the playwright, Stratford-upon-Avon. A guided tour includes an interactive map, photographs, audio, and video clips. Geotagged information guides help visitors as they walk along the historic streets with a smartphone or tablet while a 3D visualization of Shakespeare's last home, New Place, is featured.

Tim Ventimiglia teaches a seminar on museum design practices at the Parsons School of Design in New York City titled "Museum Lab." He also maintains the "Museum Design Lab" blog with posts that help his students. Under the heading, "Social Immersive Media," Ventimiglia writes:

> Over the last decade a wide array of technologies have found their way into the museum including GPS (global positioning systems), RFID (radio-frequency identification), infrared cameras and other locative sensors as well as networked objects, tablets, smartphones and other devices. These technologies when paired with large-scale, immersive interfaces have allowed designers to create experiences that reinforce the value of the museum as a physical site of social interaction and learning.

Ventimiglia appreciates the work of Snibbe Interactive that creates museum exhibits in which participants use various technologies to interact with displays on screens, floors, and tables (Figure 16.2). Digital artist Scott Snibbe's company includes such software program names as "Arctic Ice," "Wonderwall," "Our Environment," "Galapagos," and "Height and Arm Span." "SocialShare" allows videos made by users during an exhibit to become available to their Facebook friends. "SocialStage" allows museum-goers to become digital characters in a James Cameron's *Avatar* motion picture exhibit. Similarly, at the 2013 International Consumer Electronics Show in Las Vegas, 3M introduced a

Figure 16.2 The website for Snibbe Interactive hints at the worlds of wonder that are possible when creative minds combine with digital innovations for data visualization and interactive storytelling. *Courtesy of Snibbe Interactive*

touch-screen table that enable museums to offer comfortable interactive experiences for patrons.

A powerful immersive experience is compelling when combined with a seamless delivery system worn as eyewear, such Vuzix's iWear VR920 or Recon MOD ski goggles. However, more elaborate displays have been devised.

At the 2009 Technology, Entertainment, and Design (TED) conference held in Long Beach, California, Pattie Maes and Pranav Mistry of MIT's Fluid Interfaces Group demonstrated a $350 wearable computer that includes a webcam attached to a small portable projector with a wireless connection to a smartphone and web access that can project images and other types of information on any surface (Figure 16.3). Called "SixthSense," a user can use her hands in a framing gesture to take a picture, use a finger to make a circle on a wrist that turns into a watch, and get product information by simply looking at an item on a store's shelf. In 2013, Google released a beta commercial version, Google Glass. However, there are concerns that the data overlays might be too distracting for driving

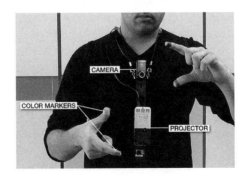

Figure 16.3 With a relatively inexpensive investment of about $350 in equipment, software, and instructions generously provided by the SixthSense team at MIT, a user can build an interactive computer system that can be used to provide additional information from objects in the real world. *Courtesy of Pranav Mistry, MIT Media Lab*

and walking. Nevertheless, in the not too distant future these wearable computers may become what we call smartphones.

However, if a story is compelling, technology can be minimized and still achieve emotional responses. An overpowering transmedia storytelling experience is demonstrated by the Holocaust Museum in Washington, DC. Even the museum's architecture signals a relationship between the exhibits and the viewer. Architect James Ingo Freed, of Pei Cobb Freed & Partners, writes, "Its architecture is intended to engage the visitor and stir the emotions, allow for horror and sadness, ultimately to disturb. It must take you in its grip." For example, design features in the Hall of Witness "summon more directly the tragic themes of the Holocaust. Crisscrossed steel trappings seem to brace the harsh brick walls against some great internal pressure. Inverted triangular shapes repeat in windows, floors, walls, and ceilings. The Hall's main staircase narrows unnaturally toward the top, like receding rail tracks heading to a camp. Exposed beams, arched brick entryways, boarded windows, metal railings, steel gates, fences, bridges, barriers, and screens—all 'impound' the visitor, and are disturbing signals of separation." The Los Angeles Museum of the Holocaust includes digital innovations by Variate Labs, a firm that specializes in architecture and interaction design. Its motto is "Digital Meets Physical." With wall and touchscreen monitors, improved audio guides with more user controls, and traditional photographic and object-filled exhibits, the immersive experience becomes individualized (Figure 16.4).

If you, as a mass communicator, can produce work in which users feel a one-to-one connection with the material, the barrier between subject and viewer is erased. The museum planning and design firm Gallagher & Associates created interactive exhibits for the National World War II Museum in New Orleans. Individualization is accomplished through confrontational scenarios that make participants imagine themselves as a young

Figure 16.4 For the Los Angeles Museum of the Holocaust, the oldest Holocaust museum in the United States, patrons can interact with the museum's content because of the newest digital innovations from Variate Labs, also based in Los Angeles. *Courtesy of Robert Miles Kemp, Variate Labs*

Japanese American man having to decide whether to stay in an internment camp or fight for the country that put him and his family behind barbed wire or as a photojournalist during the liberation of the Dachau concentration camp who must choose whether to keep photographs taken of American soldiers committing a war crime. Other situations include dilemmas concerned with railroad lines bombed in France and Belgium before the D-Day invasion causing a large number of civilian casualties and whether an African American man who was treated rudely at a recruitment office should still volunteer to fight? The ethical and moral choices are personalized after a viewer's decisions are recorded on touch screens and compared with others. For a "multisensory simulation" exhibit of the story of the USS *Tang* submarine in which only nine sailors survived its sinking, each visitor is given the name of an actual crew member. At the end of the experience, it is learned what happened to that person.

Creating an environment on a single subject in which a visitor becomes a participant is no doubt costly. However, the lessons learned by the interactive methods employed to tell a complex story within a museum environment can be translated to smaller gallery spaces and with online computer presentations. Transmedia simulated experiences hold the most promise in turning passive viewers into active engagers.

■ CHALLENGES, CRITIQUES, AND AMUSEMENTS

- Find out all you can about Henry Jenkins through his writings, interviews, and third-person profiles.
- Read at least one of the books Jenkins has written and critique it.
- Jenkins charts the development of digital innovations as leading us from media convergence to cultural convergence. Is that a totally positive change? Shouldn't we also celebrate our differences?
- In your opinion, what makes a good museum?
- When you visit a museum, do you stay for hours studying every piece on every floor, pay extra for an audio tour, and attend the special movie showings and presentations or do you head for the restaurant for lunch, maybe see one or two works, and leave as fast as you can? Tell us more.
- Have you ever had an immersive museum experience in which you were so intrigued by the content that you lost track of time? If so, what made it special? Do you think the techniques and technologies used could be employed for any type of content?
- One of my favorite museums in the world is the Museum of Jurassic Technology in Culver City, California. If you are ever in the Los Angeles area, put it on your list of sights to see <http://mjt.org/>. Even the website is, well, a bit odd.
- Create a nondigital or digital museum with personal items from your home. Don't forget the glass cases, respectful lighting, and information cards.

■ EXERCISES

The exercises presented here are the culmination of the knowledge you have learned in all the previous chapters. As such, you will want to employ as many of the procedures as possible to tell a story that is complex and yet compelling because of its clarity and level of engagement. Consequently, you need to decide on a story that has multiple components or chapters that lends itself to the digital innovations discussed in this book. You also should realize that such a project shouldn't be accomplished alone. You need a team composed of enthusiastic, organized, thoughtful, tenacious, and relatively egoless members.

Before starting, review all of the procedures and software programs discussed in the previous exercises:

Name	Major Function	Purpose	Chapters
Dreamweaver	Web Editor	Production	8, 11, & 12
Excel	Spreadsheet	Production	9 & 10
GeoCommons	Map Creation	Production	10
Google Maps	Map Creation	Production	10
Illustrator	Graphics	Production	13
iMovie	Film Editing	Production	7
Infogram	Infographics	Production	9
iShowU	Screen Saves	Production	7
JavaScript	Web Code	Production	11 & 12
Kaywa	QR Code	Production	13
Onvert	3D Imaging	Production	14
Photoshop	Image Processing	Production	4, 10, 12, 13, 14, & 15
Pixel Resort	Icon Creation	Production	4
QuickTime	Video Processing	Production	7
Second Life	Virtual World	Production	3, 6, 7, & 12
SurveyMonkey	Survey Creation	Production	11
TheAppBuilder	App Creation	Production	15
Word	Word Processing	Production	9 & 12
Blogger	Blog Production	Publicity	2 & 5
Facebook	Social Media	Publicity	1
Imgur	Picture Hosting	Publicity	8
LinkedIn	Social Media	Publicity	1
Reddit	Recommendations	Publicity	8
Twitter	Social Media	Publicity	1
Vizualize	Résumé Creation	Publicity	9
Wikipedia	Social Media	Publicity	1, 5, 10, & 11
WordPress	Social Media	Publicity	2 & 5
YouTube	Social Media	Publicity	1 & 5
JustGive	Charity Support	Fundraising	16
Kickstarter	Project Support	Fundraising	16

As the table makes clear, this book uses, and for some of you, introduces, 30 programs—18 for production, 10 for publicity, and 2 for fundraising. Your team should be composed of members with a variety of skill sets—computer use, creative ideas, editing, empathy, management and delegation, publicity generation, reporting, still and moving image production, user perspective, writing, and so on. In other words, digital innovations take cooperation and require collaboration. Working with others is no vice. It often leads to new connections and ideas that make the story produced—whether for commercial, educational, or persuasive purposes—more engaging and useful.

1. Within your mass communications professional field, find a topic of national interest that is also important for those where you live. As the former Speaker of the House of Representatives Tip O'Neill famously orated, "All politics is local." Translated for our purposes, any story, no matter how remote, can be shown to affect you and those near you. Such hot button topics as congressional stalemates,

gun control, the war in Afghanistan, the death penalty, abortion, global warming, education reform, gay marriage rights, health care, and many others have national and local implications. With each one of these stories you can find connections with your professional field (Figure 16.5).

Figure 16.5 The Political Guide website <http://thepoliticalguide.com> visually represents important topics on its webpage. Each picture is a link to more information about the issue.

2. Assemble a team to help you tell a story from a personal, local angle.
3. Select team members to oversee the compilation of the various components, conduct research, collect still and moving images, make recorded interviews, write stories, edit and process the work, and publicize the completed project.
4. Create a blog using Blogger or WordPress.
5. Create a website with Dreamweaver.
6. Write stories using Word.
7. Edit photographs with Photoshop.
8. Create a Second Life simulation.
9. Make videos and edit them with iMovie, iShowU, and QuickTime.
10. Include maps using Excel, GeoCommons, and Google Maps.
11. Add informational graphics with Infogram.
12. Make QR codes that point to additional information with Kaywa.
13. Include a 3D display with Onvert.
14. Create buttons and icons for your website and app with Illustrator and Pixel Resort.
15. Make an app using TheAppBuilder.
16. Design and implement a quiz to test users' knowledge of the topic using Dreamweaver and JavaScript.
17. Write an opinion survey to evaluate your work using SurveyMonkey. Remember that a goal of digital innovations for mass communications is to move those whom might be considered disenfranchised, randomizers, and crowd surfers to active engagers. You should include the questions in Chapter 2 that help determine which type of user is attracted to your work.

18. Apply for funding to continue your efforts after the class is completed with Kick-starter. In this era of media downsizing and conversion to online presentations, you often must become as entrepreneurial as possible in order to make a living in mass communications. Go to <http://kickstarter.com> (Figure 16.6).

Figure 16.6 A link on the Kickstarter homepage explains that a funding effort cannot be used for charity organizations but is reserved for obtaining financial support for projects. Click the "Start your project" link, create an account, read the guidelines for approved projects (and those that are not allowed), and fill out the form about your project including the funding duration and goal.

19. Register with Just Give and find a charity where users can make donations that help those who told their stories to you and others related to the topic of your presentation. Traditional journalists might object to this step, but it is often the ethical action to take when someone needs help. Go to <http://justgive.org> (Figure 16.7).

Figure 16.7 On the JustGive homepage, click on the "Act Locally" tab within the "Find a Charity" window. Type in your zip code and press Go. Scroll down the list and find a charity that coincides with your project's topic. If you don't find one, click the Registries tab at the top, Charity Registry, and then "Create a Charity Registry." After you obtain an account, you can create a registry with a specific URL so others may provide funding for a charity you want to sponsor. Use the URL to publicize your funding efforts.

20. Once your project is completed, publicize all your hard efforts through Facebook, Imgur, LinkedIn, Reddit, Twitter, Wikipedia, and YouTube.

21. And finally, don't forget to add your project's name and your role in creating it to your online résumé with Vizualize.

At the début of your presentation, invite your friends, family members, and all those who participated in making the work. Include your research and interview subjects. Make the occasion nice. Provide food and drinks in a relaxed setting. Take pictures and send me something.

Sources

Arnsdorf, Isaac. (August 18, 2010). "The Museum Is Watching You." *The Wall Street Journal.* Accessed January 12, 2013. http://online.wsj.com/article/SB10001424052748704554104575435463594652730.html.

ArtFund. (May 16, 2012). "What Makes a Good Museum?" Accessed January 12, 2013. http://www.artfund.org/news/2012/05/16/what-makes-a-good-museum.

Blair, Elizabeth. (January 12, 2013). "World War II Exhibit Asks Visitors, 'What Would You Do?'" Accessed January 12, 2013. http://www.npr.org/2013/01/12/169081431/world-war-ii-exhibit-asks-visitors-what-would-you-do.

Bruggeman, Seth. (October 4, 2009). "What Makes a Good Museum?" *Travels Through History* (blog). Accessed January 12, 2013. http://stevenhistory.blogspot.com/2009/10/what-makes-good-museum.html.

Chang, Andrea. (January 8, 2013). "Gadget Makers Embrace Connectivity." *Los Angeles Times,* B1.

Ellis, Sarah. "Keeping an Eye on Shakespeare by David Hopes." Accessed January 12, 2013. http://myshakespeare.worldshakespearefestival.org.uk/keeping-an-eye-on-shakespeare-by-david-hopes/.

Gallagher & Associates. Accessed January 12, 2013. http://gallagherdesign.com/.

Herschthal, Eric. (December 16, 2010). "What Makes a Museum Good?" *The Jewish Week.* Accessed January 12, 2013. http://www.thejewishweek.com/blogs/well_versed/what_makes_museum_good.

Immersive Journalism. "You Are Here." Accessed January 12, 2013. http://www.immersivejournalism.com/?p = 54.

Jackson, John M. (2011). "Jenkins on Transmedia Storytelling." *Ink and Vellum.* Accessed January 12, 2013. http://inkandvellum.com/blog/2011/08/jenkins-on-transmedia-storytelling/.

Jenkins, Henry III and Henry G. Jenkins IV. "'The Monsters Next Door': A Father-Son Dialogue about Buffy, Moral Panic, and Generational Differences." Accessed January 12, 2013. http://web.mit.edu/cms/People/henry3/buffy.html.

———. "Publications." Accessed January 12, 2013. http://web.mit.edu/cms/People/henry3/holodeck.html.

———. "Who Do You Think I Am: My Life as a Cartoon Character." Confessions of an Aca-Fan. Accessed January 12, 2013. http://henryjenkins.org/2008/04/who_do_you_think_i_am_my_life.html.

———. "Who the &%&# Is Henry Jenkins?" Confessions of an Aca-Fan. Accessed January 12, 2013. http://henryjenkins.org/aboutmehtml.

Joselit, Jenna Weissman. (December 15, 2010). "Liberty Bells and Whistles. Accessed January 12, 2013. http://www.tabletmag.com/jewish-arts-and-culture/53430/liberty-bells-and-whistles-2.

Kerr, Dana. (January 1, 2013). "Google Glass Development Charges Ahead." Accessed January 14, 2013. http://news.cnet.com/8301–1023_3–57561525–93/google-glass-development-charges-ahead/.

"Media Convergence." Accessed January 12, 2013. http://web.mit.edu/cms/People/henry3/converge.html.

Museum Design Lab. (September 13, 1009). "Social Immersive Media." Accessed January 12, 2013. http://museumdesignlab.wordpress.com/2009/09/13/social-immersive-media/.

Museum Next. Accessed January 12, 2013. http://www.museumnext.org/conference/museumnext_barcelona_programme.html.

Perennial Student. "What Makes a Good Museum." Accessed January 12, 2013. http://paulinege.wordpress.com/2010/08/23/what-makes-a-good-museum/.

Predavec, Evan. (March 4, 2011). "Searching the World for the Perfect Science Museum." *Wired.* Accessed January 12, 2013. http://www.wired.com/geekdad/2011/03/searching-the-world-for-the-perfect-science-museum-the-winners-so-far/.

Schofield, Jack. (July 11, 2002). "Birth of a Medium." *The Guardian.* Accessed January 12, 2013. http://www.guardian.co.uk/lifeandstyle/2002/jul/11/shopping.technology.

Serious Games Institute. Accessed January 12, 2013. http://www.seriousgamesinstitute.co.uk/showcase/default.aspx.

Snibbe Interactive. Accessed January 12, 2013. http://www.snibbeinteractive.com/.

———. "SocialScreen." Accessed January 12, 2013. http://www.snibbeinteractive.com/platforms/socialscreen/products.

TED. (March 2009). "Pattie Maes and Pranav Mistry Demo SixthSense." Accessed January 14, 2013. http://www.ted.com/talks/pattie_maes_demos_the_sixth_sense.html.

Toews, Phoenix. "Place is a Palimpsest Augmented Reality and Experience of Place." Accessed January 12, 2013. http://www.academia.edu/640542/Palimpsest_Augmented_Reality_Browser.

Touropia. "14 Best Museums in the World." Accessed January 12, 2013. http://www.touropia.com/best-museums-in-the-world/.

United States Holocaust Memorial Museum. Accessed January 12, 2013. http://www.ushmm.org/museum/a_and_a/.

Variatel Labs. Accessed January 12, 2013. http://variatelabs.com.

Visit Britain. "Top 10 Interactive Museums." Accessed January 12, 2013. http://www.visitbritain.com/en/Travel-tips/Britain-for-kids-and-families/Top-10-interactive-museums.htm.

World War II Museum, The. Accessed January 12, 2013. http://www.ddaymuseum.org/.

You Have Found Coney. Accessed January 12, 2013. http://www.youhavefoundconey.net/.

YouTube. (June 27, 2012). "Google Glasses Demonstration." Accessed January 14, 2013. http://www.youtube.com/watch?v=MP1gvGcXcLk.

———. (September 25, 2012). "Strange Beauty: Souvenir #2, 2008, with Ruud van Empel." Accessed January 12, 2013. http://www.youtube.com/watch?v=QbOdeuIHBus.

CONCLUSION

Tell Stories That Engage

I once had a delightful conversation with my 100-year-old great-grandmother in which I asked her what she thought when she first learned about automobiles as a child. She laughed and explained, "My first thought was, how could everyone have their own train?"

The idea amuses her because all she knew as a young girl was one mode of modern transportation—steam-powered trains that were set on tracks that noisily divided her town. When she first heard of cars as a new technology, she couldn't comprehend at first that they offered independent, flexible, innovative, and empowering movement from one point to another that trains couldn't supply. She also couldn't anticipate that automobiles would fill people with consumer desire conveyed in advertising, carve up the countryside with roads, increase governmental bureaucracy with legal restrictions and rules, spread the popularity of music through dashboard radios, and add untold costs to the environment through the burning of fossil fuels and in lives injured and lost through accidents. Innovations always create new paradigms and problems.

We all tend to evaluate and anticipate technology based on previous experiences—cars must be like trains. In the same way, we think of the web as an extension of what we know—books, newspapers, radio, movies, and television. However, the future of mass communications probably has little to do with our understanding of our past or present uses of the web. Nevertheless, we are stuck in this moment thinking about how professionals in the field of mass communications will communicate their messages in eras yet to come while we wear our metaphoric traditional print and screen media blinders that are difficult to shed.

Take journalism as an example. Traditional news offers a daily edited diary of events that reporters and editors determine to be of the most interest and the most important to the most people. In other words, news is a combination of what news producers say it is and what news consumers say they want. If news producers continually provide news that is not needed or desired, consumers lose interest and subscription rates and ratings decline—a situation not unlike what is currently happening as newspaper readers drop out, advertisers put their money into other media, websites become more vital, and print publications go bankrupt.

News media managers that want to improve their rates and ratings have tried to incorporate controversial innovations—increased use of images and graphics, market-driven commercially based stories, live-action set-ups, special effects learned from motion picture technologies, and so on. They have focused on what people want, sometimes to the detriment of what they need.

These commercially driven innovations are based on a traditional model of stories and storytelling—the one-to-many model of mass communications in which news is pushed to waiting, grateful, and passive consumers. The flaw in this approach is that decisions are based on the presumed generalized characteristics of a target audience (ideally people with infinite resources and inclinations toward consumerism) and not the true specific characteristics of individual consumers of news and information. Like train travel, traditional mass media producers seek to take the majority of consumers somewhere close to where they would like to go in the most efficient and cost-effective way possible while they ignore the family speeding past the engine in its comfortable Audi. Traditional mass media managers find it difficult to conceive of other models—one-to-one, many-to-one, or even many-to-many—because these models are outside the commercial paradigm they have carefully constructed over many years in order to deliver a product efficiently and inexpensively. Within the commercial paradigm, traditional media function with three goals in mind—entertainment, persuasion, and information. As long as audiences are content with this mix of functions, there is no incentive to innovate. And when a new technological innovation is discovered—the web, for example—there is no incentive to have it look and feel any differently from what is known and comfortable. Consequently, the web "cars," which seem modern and trendy are in actuality another version of a train—safe, but ultimately unsatisfying just as with those found in the "Autopia" ride at Disneyland.

Whether you think of the web as a car, train, or timesaving tool that helps you avoid a trip to the library, it can be more than the sum of its parts. It should be a device that not only gives us more media message choices, but also allows us to influence what we find. When we are given the ability and responsibility to affect what we see, hear, and read, the gap between producer and consumer closes like two Venn circles that move toward each other until they completely overlap. When that happens, producers and consumers collaborate. We all are the media.

Albert Borgmann in *Technology and the Character of Contemporary Life* writes, " . . . the acquisition of skills, the fidelity to a daily discipline, the broadening of sensibility, the profound interaction of human beings, and the preservation and development of tradition. These traits we may bring together under the heading of engagement. Engagement would not only harmonize the variety among people but also within the life of one person."

When consumers become producers, unanticipated relationships are established. There is more interactivity between all the possible combinations—producers and consumers, producers and producers, and consumers and consumers. Such engaging interactivity perhaps can lead to an increase in:

1. A person's self worth,
2. Societal, environmental, and cultural understanding,
3. The overall population's knowledge base on a wider range of topics,
4. Technological innovations that foster interactivity and empowerment, and
5. To what has been called "the good life."

Digital innovations foster engagement that can lead to unanticipated and serendipitous connections between users, the persons that are a part of a story, and the producers of the work. At its best, mass communications allows users to care more fully about those involved with any narrative—whether for persuasive or educational purposes. The technologies featured in this book should be part of the gear within a mass communicator's toolkit that facilitates that process.

When you know how communication innovations grew from past developments, the types of persons whom are repelled and attracted by your presentations, the ethical and legal considerations that guide the production and use of new technologies for positive purposes, and the use of typography and illustrations that best display words and images for maximum attention, literacy, and understanding, you will be prepared to create works that can educate, entertain, and persuade.

On the desk of my workstation at home I have an eclectic mix of objects related to my work and personal lives—HP and Apple laptops, a cable for an electric guitar, a pine cone from a walk in the woods, two Flip cameras, an expired driver's license, a small replica of the Rosetta Stone, a bag of little dog treats, a bumper sticker from a popular restaurant, collections of rocks, coins, and shells, an external hard drive, family pictures, and a pair of headphones. These mementos (and many others) each have a personal story associated with them. Whether remembered or forgotten, they are powerful symbols of my past. They remind me of where I came from, the person I have become, and those who have helped me along my journey. When something as esoteric as a computer program helps to link myself with other, unknown strangers, like the possessions on my desk, I am reminded of our shared humanity.

Regardless of whether the purpose of a digital innovation is to serve advertising, entertainment, journalism, public relations, RTVF, or visual reporting, the field of mass communications has one, overriding responsibility—to tell stories.

Effective storytelling that engages others can be as simple as a knowledgeable elder sitting around a campfire's glow with the awe and admiration seen by the flickering firelight on her listener's faces or as complex as a 3D display that seemingly jumps off the screen of your tablet and makes you think of your world in a new and totally unexpected way. Whether by text, voice, or picture, a presentation is only as good as the way the story is told.

If a user is attracted, entertained, and educated by a compelling tale, for that person the tools used to accomplish that feat should become irrelevant and even invisible. As the scientist and novelist Sir Arthur Charles Clarke once wrote, "Any sufficiently advanced technology is indistinguishable from magic."

Make stories. Make magic.

Sources

Borgmann, Albert. (1984). *Technology and the Character of Contemporary Life: A Philosophical Inquiry.* Chicago: The University of Chicago Press.

Briggs, Mark. (2010). *Journalism Next.* Washington, DC: CQ Press.

APPENDIX

VIRTUAL PHOTOGRAPHY

When Images Become Real

By Paul Martin Lester

The universe is not only stranger than we imagine, it's stranger than we can imagine.

—J. B. S. Haldane, biochemist

As an experimental technology available within the well-financed halls of military installations, a few large universities, and corporate institutions, virtual reality is quickly becoming known by the general public. It has recently been boosted by print and broadcast reports as the next major breakthrough in mass communications. It will allow architects to pre-plan their complicated structures by giving them the ability to "walk through" their buildings on the computer. It will be used as a tool for training future surgeons who will perform practice operations on virtual reality patients without the need for smelly cadavers. It has recently been introduced at some shopping mall arcades where, for $1 a minute, consumers can blast their computer-generated counterparts. Much has been promised from this new technology. Will virtual reality be the revolution in mass communications that some in the industry have forecast or will it disappoint consumers on the same scale as holography? The answers at this early stage in its development are far from readily available. What follows is a fictionalized account of the possible uses and problems that one may have to confront once virtual reality technology becomes as common as a photographic teaching tool.

It's 30 minutes before Dr. Mark Premack's advanced photojournalism class. Premack, a tenured professor at a California liberal-arts commuter school with about 45,000 students, walks into the area that contains a virtual reality workstation.

Called a VR-3000 by the manufacturer, virtual reality technology has revolutionized the way students and professionals produce images for advertising and commercial purposes. Funding for this workstation, and the 11 in the multipurpose room shared by advertising, entertainment studies, film, journalism, photography, public relations, and television classes came from lottery money designated for education purposes and grants from the manufacturer and the software producers. Each workstation costs about $10,000. But each software program cost only about $100. The manufacturer saw tremendous success in the entertainment operation of its virtual reality machines at arcades and at homes and wanted to establish educational benefits for the technology. Consequently, the company provided similarly equipped virtual reality workstations at drastically reduced prices for five universities. Located at Premack's school and in Missouri, Texas, New York, and New Jersey, the five colleges are linked through optical fibers that keep all of the instructors up-to-date on successes and problems with the systems.

A technological breakthrough in computer processing about five years ago caused renewed interest in the technology. Because of advances in using atomic-size, light-based microchips, computers are able to process information at speeds approaching that of light itself. Users can use preexisting films and videotape combined with holographic effects for true, three-dimensional realism. There is life-like, real-time movement with no delays as in the earlier models. Interactions between the players and computer-generated characters and objects seem much more real because of the highly detailed graphics. There are even sensory detectors built into the gloves and leg wrappings so that a player has the sensation of actually holding an object—the user can feel the weight of the object. The playing field itself is much improved as the backgrounds and foregrounds are almost completely realistic and can be changed at the whim of the user.

Social scientists warned that players would think that these new and improved products would be mistaken for actual reality and become addicted. This technology, they argued, would further alienate society as members of a culture would prefer their computer-generated interactions to face-to-face contact. Because of the extreme cost of the technology, they warned, virtual reality would also drive a further wedge between those in society who could afford such new technological toys and those with less money to spend and who would become disenfranchised even further from society. Critics called virtual reality the "hallucinogenic of the next generation" because it would act like an addictive drug that altered a user's sense of reality. Religious leaders saw a threat from pornographic programs that would influence culture in negative ways.

Counterarguments were just as numerous. Psychologists argued that with every new technology there is a danger that some users will become addicted and isolate themselves from society. While it may be true that some addictive individuals have trouble, most players have no problems. These "alienated society" arguments, they explained, were the same charges leveled initially against radio, television, computers, and even rock and roll music. All new forms of communication undergo an initial stage of social criticism until quality programs are introduced and the educational benefits of a new technology are clearly understood and disseminated among the citizens of a culture. This phenomenon is why the manufacturer of the VR-3000 invested a large amount of resources to permit educational institutions to experiment with the technology.

Premack has mostly positive opinions about this new form of communication. But after seeing a videotape of a young user at a computer arcade who had a nervous breakdown because he thought the images were too real and killed some actual customers waiting in line for their turn on the machine, Premack believes that virtual reality must be closely monitored. He and three of his colleagues introduced a number of failsafe mechanisms for the machine three years ago that have since been adopted. These failsafe devices include:

- Keyboard commands can be activated at all times during a session. Students can easily find the stop key on the computer keyboard and end the lesson.
- Monitors built into the helmet, gloves, and leg wrappings chart brain activity, the pulse rate, and the blood pressure of each student. The program automatically stops for the student if those measures become too high.
- There is an automatic time-out function that is set by the instructor. Premack sets the time at 15 minutes and doesn't think anyone should use the system any longer. After the time limit, all of the workstations end their programs.
- In order to remind users that they are only watching a glorified movie, a pressure sensitive device is located on the right-hand glove of every participant. It is a small bar that continuously applies intermittent pressure to the student's arm. As a check on reality, it is an annoying mechanism that all the students complain about, but reminds the user of the real reality outside of the program.

- There is a graphic display that is superimposed upon the picture that the student can read throughout the program. The messages flash a student's physiological condition, the time spent viewing the program, the actual time, and any message the instructor wants to add. Premack finds, however, that rather than typing a message on the keyboard, he can simply talk loudly during a lesson and the students will respond to his words. That way he doesn't have to take off his helmet to type a message.

- Finally, there is the gray zone. The gray zone is the edge of the program—where the graphics stop. It is that portion of the program that does not contain graphic illustrations. If a user looks at the extreme left or right side of the program, a clearly defined gray-colored area can be seen. At any time, a student can walk through the gray zone and end the program. In a group situation as during a class, any time one person walks through the zone, the program stops for everyone. Consequently, a student should not walk through the gray zone unless it is a real emergency.

The beginning advertising student in the studio with helmet, gloves, and leg wrappings all hooked to her computer through wire connections looks like a new-tech mime artist as she appears to be picking up real, yet unseen objects, setting them on an imaginary table, and taking pictures with an imaginary camera, all within a circular railing that surrounds the student. Premack walks over to the computer monitor where he can see the image that the student sees through the helmet. She is working on a basic advertising picture assignment. On the computer screen, Premack can see that she is almost finished. Before she started the VR-3000 machine, she selected a number of props within the computer's directory, similar to the procedure for selecting clip art materials for a publication. The difference here is that the objects have three-dimensional shape and depth. The student places each selected object in a holding box where they can be accessed once she is hooked up to the virtual reality equipment. The student can also preset tables, counters, or stands for her props to rest upon, select backgrounds and foregrounds, decide upon lighting and color combinations, and even use objects that appear to be real people that act as models. What appeared to be a mime with wires attached is actually the photographer taking objects out of the box and placing them on the table she selected. The background is composed of various pastel colors selected by the student. Advanced students use much more elaborate on-location scenarios that involve complicated arrangements of computer-generated models and objects.

She moves over to one of the virtual reality light stands and changes the position of a white umbrella. Now she takes a number of pictures at slightly different angles with her virtual reality camera. When she is satisfied with her picture taking, she'll take off the VR-3000 equipment, look at the images she made on the computer monitor, select one, manipulate it, perhaps add images from other photo sessions, and make a high-quality printout. As Premack walks to the classroom, he smiles at the thought of the technology that makes these wonders possible.

He turns on the light for the classroom and sees the 11 VR-3000 players. Each student workstation contains a circular railing that the student stands within and a computer with a color monitor resting on a table next to the railing. For every station, there is a helmet, two gloves, and two leg wrappings with wire connections linking them with the computer. The separate student workstations look like the individual booths used for language instruction when he was a student. Each student's workstation is linked with the instructor's computer that is networked to the university's mainframe system and ultimately linked to other computer installations around the world.

At the front of the room sits his workstation. It is almost exactly like the students' stations except for a bigger monitor and an expanded keyboard. He turns on his computer workstation. It takes a few minutes to boot up, which gives him time to select a program for today's viewing. From a locked cabinet, he sees the titles of the VR-3000 educational programs available to him. Since this virtual reality classroom is used by all of the sequence instructors for their students, there is a wide variety of software programs on the shelves.

It was about eight years ago that he first started to hear about virtual reality. When he asked other faculty members about it, most of them had never heard of the technology. Now as he reviews the lesson programs on the shelf, he realizes how valuable the technology is as a teaching tool. The television and film students can enter a sound stage and watch how a movie is made. They can also make their own films, record and edit them, and show their work on traditional projectors so everyone can view their work. The advertising students can sit in on an agency's meetings with clients and its creative team concerning a new product's campaign. They can even give their own input to the group. The public relations students have a lesson where they work for a large company that had a product that recently was responsible for a number of deaths. The students speak to the media and try to overcome the damage to the company's reputation that the product made. Journalism students have an elaborate role-playing lesson called "Newspaper—3000." In the simulation, students can take the role of a reporter, copy editor, graphic designer, section editor, managing editor, or publisher for a medium-sized newspaper. It's a big news day with many quick decisions needed from the students for this complicated virtual reality program. And finally, visual reporting students learn how to make their own virtual reality programs for entertainment, communication, and educational purposes. Since the advent of virtual reality technology, the field of presentation graphics, as might be expected, has seen a tremendous growth with much student interest.

Premack's photojournalism students can work with journalism students on the newspaper simulation, work in the studio with the VR-3000 to create food, fashion, or editorial illustrations, or take the role of a photographer in a number of different situations and assignments. For example, there is a lesson that teaches sports photography based on Super Bowl LXXV, where a dramatic come-from-behind win gave the Dallas Cowboys football team their third Super Bowl win in a row. The recent Cuban War is represented in a lesson so that students can experience the difficulties involved with taking pictures during war conditions. There is a lesson on shooting a rock concert that most students like because they enjoy the loud music, a lesson that takes students to a remote area of Alaska to complete a picture story on Native American fishermen, and the lesson Premack selects for today's class, the Budd Dwyer press conference and suicide. Although the event happened several years ago, Premack thinks it is an excellent example of a general news assignment, a press conference that suddenly turned into a horrifying spot news assignment. It tells students that they must be prepared for any type of eventuality. And since this week the students are learning about spot news coverage, this is an excellent program choice. He takes it off the shelf, locks the cabinet, and slips the cassette into his VR-3000 player.

At the top of the hour, Premack's students come filing into the classroom and sit at the workstations. Out of the 10 in the class, 8 of the students have worked on newspapers as interning staff photographers. This class is filled with serious photojournalism students. This is Premack's favorite class because the students are professional in their command of the technology and also are caring individuals who are concerned about the people they photograph. It is also the class where he's known the students the longest because for most, this is their last photography class before graduation. Although they receive a healthy dose of ethics throughout the curriculum, in this class they are challenged more than at any time in their coursework.

As he watches the students find their seats, he thinks, "I wonder if I'll have trouble with Hancock today?" Hancock is the exception. "If I were a secret service agent protecting the President on a campaign stop at the college," Premack thinks to himself, "I would focus most of my attention on this nervous, sloppily dressed student in the back of the room." Premack wonders if Hancock will make it as a photojournalist. One of the hardest things about teaching photojournalism is to tell a student that he or she might need to think about another profession. Yet Premack admires Hancock's creativity. Although he is not good around other people, as is necessary for a journalism career, he may do well in commercial or even art imaging. He could also become a computer systems operator for a newspaper or a college. He just needs to gain a bit more confidence.

After a few general announcements and the students have settled down, Premack explains what they are about to experience. A detailed description is necessary because of the problems in the technology when it was first introduced. Some students became upset as it was too real for them. Besides, the Dwyer episode is an intense viewing experience that may easily upset the unprepared. Pennsylvania State Treasurer, R. Budd Dwyer had just been convicted of bribery. Journalists from several newspapers, news services, and television stations gathered around a small podium that sat on a table expecting to hear Dwyer announce his resignation from state government. What they heard were the long, rambling last words of a seriously troubled man. Dwyer pulled out a .357 Magnum long barrel pistol, waved back reporters, stuck the revolver in his mouth, pulled the trigger, and ended his torment before a stunned audience.

Even though his students have heard all of the instructions before, Premack finds it is to everyone's interest to go through the safety devices built into the system. Users should never forget that they are essentially watching a movie. He explains that if it gets a little too real, they can stop the lesson at any time or look the other way. They can try to prevent what is happening or use their cameras to record images of what they are witnessing. Each student's computer records images. After the lesson ends, the students can review the images on their computer monitor, pick their favorite, manipulate it, crop it, use it in a layout, print it out, and turn it in.

Finally, Premack reminds them not to go through the gray zone unless there is an emergency because that ends the program for everyone. After they all seem to understand what is coming up, he tells them to start their computers and put on the equipment. He helps a couple of students adjust the straps on their helmets. After everyone is ready, Premack asks each one to breathe deeply and calmly so that the computer can register bodily signs. This procedure takes two minutes. Premack checks his computer's monitor to make sure he can see the output from every student. When all of his students are registered, he slips on his gear and starts the lesson.

Entering the virtual reality world is always a bit disorienting at first. It takes a few moments to get used to the view inside the helmet's monitor. The visual perspective is a bit wider than normal vision. Although the user is initially astounded at how real the scene appears, after a few moments, the newness wears off and the player can see inconsistencies. As with colorized black and white movies, sometimes the edges of objects bleed into adjoining objects contributing to a slightly unrealistic effect. Since none of the objects and people is real, a player can walk through any of them, although if a user goes through a person, the program automatically makes the computer character respond with an unflattering comment. Finally, there is the gray zone noticeable on either side of the scene that reminds the student that the vivid scene is a product of computer-generated magic.

All of his students walk onto the press conference scene as if it were a set in a stage play. Dwyer is in the middle of his long, rambling speech at the front of the room behind a podium with many microphones attached to it. The room is crowded with reporters and photographers, so his students, to get any good pictures, must weave their way between the computer-generated figures. All of the students have digital cameras around their necks and shoulder bags that contain an assortment of lenses supplied by the computer program.

Premack notices Hancock in the back of the room off to himself looking a bit bored. He goes over to him and says, "Shouldn't you start taking some pictures?"

"To tell you the truth," Hancock replies, "I got a copy of this tape from my bulletin board a couple of months ago. It's really gross. Can't I do something else?"

Always a troublemaker, Premack thinks. "Just hang out here in the back and watch the others. Why don't you take pictures of the others taking pictures?"

"Okay, that's an original idea," Hancock replies sarcastically. He makes an attempt at taking pictures, but he would clearly rather be anywhere else. He is standing next to the gray zone at the right side of the room.

Premack cautions, "Don't get too close to the edge. I don't want you stopping the program, got it?"

"Yeah. Yeah."

The lesson continues with Dwyer talking about his career as a public servant. Most of the students are now close to the podium along with the computer-generated photographers and videographers. Suddenly Dwyer pulls out his gun. Even though Premack has seen this lesson several times, it is still a bit of a shock. There is some yelling and chaos among the spectators. One of his students tries to rush Dwyer and take the gun from him. Dwyer points the gun in his direction and waves him back. Premack makes a mental note to caution the student about trying that action in the real world. Suddenly there is a huge explosion as Dwyer shoots himself.

Premack happened to be watching Hancock when the shot fired. The sound of the blast so surprised him that he jumped back instinctively and fell into the gray zone. Expecting the program to end, Premack started working on his speech to chew out Hancock when it occurred to him that the program did not stop. Premack's curiosity is piqued when he realizes that something must be wrong with the software. He tells the other students to get out of the program and start editing their images. He's going into the gray zone and see what happened to Hancock.

Premack slowly walks through the gray zone. He is suddenly transformed into a light being as his body is immediately sucked into a tube of light. His body is no longer recognizable. He is a band of light traveling extremely fast through a kind of light highway. He realizes that he is moving along a fiber optic link between the school's computer and the network. He remembers that the school's network is linked with the supercomputer at Rutgers University. "Oh god, I hope I'm not going to New Jersey," he thinks to himself.

He is able to look around and see other bands of light with other light beings like himself flying through the network wires. He is aware that Hancock is in front of him on the same light-band highway. He likes this sensation of flying.

He calls out, "Hancock. Can you hear me?"

"Yea," Hancock quickly responds. "Isn't this cool? I think it's a bug in the program that lets you into the network. We're headed for the source."

Premack worries a bit about the students back in the classroom, but he's enjoying this new sensation too much to stop now.

Suddenly there's another, somewhat muffled voice, "Daddy. Daddy. Dinner's ready."

He knows the voice is not from Hancock or any of his students.

"Daddy. Dinner's ready."

It's his 15-year-old daughter, Allison.

"Okay, honey. I'll be right there," Premack answers.

He looks at Hancock and wonders if he should try to stop him. But then he thinks, "Screw Hancock. I'm hungry."

Premack touches the quit button on his keyboard and stops the program. The light highway pauses in mid-flight. A graphics display superimposes the words, "You have elected to quit. Do you want to save up to this point?" Premack presses the OK button on the keyboard. "Program saved under the previously named file: Premack3." Then the last words from the program are projected that always make him smile, "Thank you for playing the VR-3000: Photojournalism Adventure Game. Have a real day."

The screen goes blank. Premack slowly takes off his helmet, gloves, and leg wrappings and steps out of the circular railing. He sets the equipment on his desk and turns on the lamp in his office. He sits down at his chair and rubs his eyes for a few moments, turns off the computer, and walks downstairs.

His daughter is already sitting at the dinner table.

"More trouble with Hancock?" she asks with a smile.

"Yea," Premack answers with a laugh. "This time he really screwed up. He disappeared into the gray zone and I had to go in and find him. It was great. I was a flying beam of light."

Allison gives him a glass of water and says, "You know, Dad, if your school could afford VR workstations for students, they would really learn a lot from the programs."

"I know. I know. Some day during my lifetime," Premack sighs. "Pass the peas, please."

INDEX

NET WORKS

Case Studies in Web Art and Design

edited by xtine burrough

Net Works offers an inside look into the process of successfully developing thoughtful, innovative digital media. Using websites as case studies, each chapter introduces a different style of web project—from formalist play to social activism to data visualization—and then includes the artists' or entrepreneurs' reflections on the particular challenges and outcomes of developing that web project. Scholarly introductions to each section apply a theoretical frame for the projects. A companion website offers further resources for hands-on learning.

Combining practical skills for web authoring with critical perspectives on the web, *Net Works* is ideal for courses in new media design, art, communication, critical studies, media and technology, or popular digital/internet culture.

routledge.com/cw/burrough

paperback | 978-0-415-88222-4
ebook | 978-0-203-84794-7

xtine burrough
& PAUL MARTIN LESTER

VISUAL COMMUNICATION ON THE WEB

Principles and Practices

by xtine burrough and Paul Martin Lester

This book is more than the typical web design manual. *Visual Communication on the Web* integrates practice with theory, providing technical how-to alongside the theoretical, aesthetic, and historical framework you'll need to create thoughtful, functional, and beautifully designed web pages.

By working your way through this text from start to finish, you will learn how to think visually about communicating online and also how to think analytically about assembling code to display your message. By the end of this course-in-a-book, you will have created a web page with a centered container div, a Lightbox image gallery, and an external style sheet using HTML, CSS, and copy-pasted and modified code.

Includes access to Interactive eTextbook

Pack – Book & Online |
978-0-415-52148-2